A COMMENTARY ON
ECCLESIASTES

Charles Bridges, M.A.

THE BANNER OF TRUTH TRUST

THE BANNER OF TRUTH TRUST
3 Murrayfield Road, Edinburgh EH12 6EL
P.O. Box 621, Carlisle, Pennsylvania 17013, U.S.A.

*

First Published 1860
First Banner of Truth Trust edition 1961
Reprinted 1981
Reprinted 1985
Reprinted 1992
ISBN 0 85151 322 0

*

Printed in Great Britain by
Billing & Sons Ltd., Worcester

PREFACE.

THE Book of Ecclesiastes has exercised the Church of God in no common degree. Many learned men have not hesitated to number it among the most difficult Books in the Sacred Canon.* Luther doubts whether any Exposition up to his time has fully mastered it.† The Patristic Commentaries, from Jerome downwards, abound in the wildest fancies; so that, as one of the old interpreters observes, ' the trifles of their allegories it loatheth and wearieth me to set down.' ‡ Expositors of a different and later school have too often " darkened counsel by words without knowledge" (Job, xxxviii. 2) ; perplexing the reader's mind with doubtful theories, widely diverging from each other. The more difficult the book, the greater the need of Divine Teaching to open its contents. However valuable be the stores of human learning, they will not throw one ray of true light upon the word, without the heavenly influence of the Great Teacher. Separate from Him, " the light that is in us is darkness." (Matt. vi. 23.)

---

* Merceri *Comment.* fol. 1651 (Hebrew Professor at Paris). See also *Poli Synopsis, Prolegom.; Comment.* by Rev. George Holden, 8vo. 1822, *Prelim. Dissert.* ii.

† Quoted in Geier's *Comment.* 4to. Lips. 1668.

‡ Serranus on chap. iv. 12, also on iii. 15. 'A godly and learned commentary upon this excellent Book of Solomon, commonly called

The Author confesses that he has felt his measure
of difficulty as to some of the statements of this Book.
But the result of his inquiry into its Divine credentials
has been solidly satisfactory. The conclusion therefore was
natural, that a Book that ' had God for its Author,' must
have ' truth, *without any mixture of error*, for its matter.'*
Some of its maxims have indeed been too hastily supposed
to countenance Epicurean indulgence. Nay—even Voltaire and his Monarch disciple have dared to claim detached passages as favouring their sceptical philosophy.
But ' all of them'—as Mr. Scott observes—' admit of a
sound and useful interpretation, when accurately inves-
tigated, and when the general scope of the book is attended
to.'† If any difficulties still remain, as Lord Bacon remarks—' If they teach us nothing else, they will at least
teach us our own blindness.' Thus Pascal profoundly
remarks on the Scriptures — ' There is enough brightness
to illuminate the elect, and enough obscurity to humble
them. " All things work together for good" to the elect;
even the obscurities of Scripture, which these honour and
reverence on account of that Divine clearness and beauty,
which they understand.'‡ There is, however, a wide difference between what appears upon the surface, and what a

"Ecclesiastes." 12mo. 1585. Translated out of Latin by John Stock-
wood (the translator of several of Calvin's Commentaries). A mass
of the various Patristic interpretations may be seen in a Jesuit
commentary Joannis Lorini, 4to. 1606.

* Locke.

† Preface to Ecclesiastes. Witsius confirms this judgment.—
Miscell. Sacra, vol. i. chap. xviii. § 36–39. See also Holden, *Prelim.
Dissert.* ii. iii.

‡ *Thoughts*, xviii. ' No learning is sufficient to make a proud
man understand the truth of God, unless he first learn to be humble.'
—Bp. Taylor's *Sermon before the University of Dublin.*

thoughtful mind in a prayerful spirit will open from the
inner Scripture. It is most important to study the Bible
in the spirit of the Bible—to exercise a critical habit in a
spiritual atmosphere. Prayer, faith, humility, diligence, will
bring rest and satisfaction to minds exercised in the school
of God. As an able preacher remarks—' We expect to
find some difficulties in a revelation from a Being like God
to such a creature as man. We even rejoice in these
difficulties. They are the occasion of our growth in grace.
They exercise our humility. They are like the leaves and
flowers, of which the crown of faith is woven. They remind us of our own weakness and ignorance, and of Christ's
power and wisdom. They send us to Him and to the
Gospel.'*

Our last testimony on this anxious point we draw from
the highest school of instruction—the death-bed. ' We
must acknowledge'—said the late Adolph Monod—' that
in the beginning of the study of Scripture, there are many
difficulties, and much obscurity. Some labour is necessary
to dissipate them; and the mind of man is naturally slow
and idle; and he easily loses courage, and is satisfied with
reading over and over again, without penetrating further
than the surface; and he learns nothing new; and the
constant perusal of the same thing causeth weariness, as
if the word of God was not interesting; as if we could not
find some new instruction in it; as if it were not inexhaustible as God Himself. Let us ever'—he adds—' beware of thinking these difficulties insurmountable. We
must give ourselves trouble. For here, as in every part

* Canon Wordsworth's *Sermon on the Inspiration of the Old
Testament.*

of the Christian life, God will have us to be labourers with
Himself; and the knowledge of the Bible, and a relish for
the Bible, are the fruit and recompence of this humble,
sincere, and persevering study.'*

But to come more closely to the difficulties connected
with this Book—Besides the objections brought against its
principles, the peculiar construction of some of its maxims
occasionally gives rise to perplexity. Mr. Holden adverts
to the mistake of—' taking in their utmost extent expressions designed to convey a qualified and limited signifi-
cation.' He wisely remarks—' General propositions are not
always to be received in the strictest sense of the words.
And particular observations must not be stretched beyond
the intention of the writer. This results from the inherent
imperfection of language, that his expressions ought to be
interpreted with such restrictions, as are necessarily required
by common sense, and the scope of the context. If several
expressions in the Ecclesiastes, which have been condemned,
be understood in this qualified sense—a sense clearly suggested by truth and reason—they will be found in every
respect worthy of the inspired Author, from whom they
proceed.'†

But with all its difficulties, we must admit the book to
be fraught with practical interest. It teaches lessons peculiarly its own—lessons, which we are too slow to learn; and
yet, which we must thoroughly learn for our own personal
profit and happiness. They are essential, as preparatory to
our enjoyment of the Gospel. The precise place of the Book
in the Sacred Canon is somewhat remarkable. Its juxta-

---

* Adolphus Monod's *Farewell Addresses:* xv. Address.
† *Prelim. Dissert.* lxxviii. lxxix.

position with 'The Song' illustrates a fine and striking contrast between the insufficiency of the creature and the sufficiency of the Saviour. 'What a stimulus to seek after the true and full knowledge of Christ is the realized conviction of the utter vanity of all things else without Him.' *
To " drink and thirst again" is the disappointment of the world. To " drink and never thirst" is the portion of the Gospel.†

We must not however linger upon particular points. Some preliminaries yet remain to be noticed, ere we enter upon a detailed Exposition. A few words upon—

I. *The Writer of this Book.*—This we should have thought had been a matter placed beyond controversy. *The words of the Son of David—King of Jerusalem*—seem to point with absolute precision to Solomon—the only *Son of David,* who was the possessor of that royalty. (Ch. i. 1. 12.)‡
But some critics of name§— from the difference of style— the use of a few words of supposed later origin—the introduction of incidental matters not—as they think—falling within the ken of Solomon's vision—on these and other grounds they have determined the writer to belong to some

* See *A Brief Exposition of Ecclesiastes,* by Mr. John Cotton. Boston, New England, 12mo. 1654.

† See John, iv. 13, 14.

‡ Lampe also (the commentator on St. John) remarks on the description of his extraordinary wisdom (v. 13), magnificence, and luxury (Chap. ii.), which could not attach to any other man than Solomon. He adverts also to the analogy of some of his sentiments as expressed in the Book of Proverbs, *e. g.* Eccles. i. 8, with Prov. xxvii. 20, *et alia. Notæ in Eccles.* 4to. 1741.

§ Such as Grotius, Dathè, and others. Even Lampe doubts whether the *whole* was written by Solomon. But his ground is weak and inconclusive.

later era. The arguments however in favour of this hypothesis amount only to theoretical doubts or plausibilities;
while they involve a supposition utterly unworthy of Inspiration — namely — that some unknown writer has palmed
upon the Church in the Sacred Canon his own thoughts
and words under the deceptive cover of the name of *the Son
of David — King in Jerusalem.* Apart from this conjectural
hypothesis — if any weight be due to the unanimous consent
of all the Hebrew manuscripts and ancient versions — confirmed by the concurrent voice of Jewish Tradition — we
must without doubt or hesitation acknowledge the wise *Son
of David* to be *the Preacher* in this Book.

II. The date of this Treatise is a matter of much interest. ' He seemeth ' — says Bishop Reynolds — ' to have
written it in his old age, when he took a more serious view
of his past life — the honour, pleasure, wealth, and wisdom
he had so abundantly enjoyed — *the errors and miscarriages* *
he had fallen into — the large experience, and many observations he had made of things natural, moral, domestical,
sensual, Divine — the curious and critical inquiry he had
made after true happiness, and what contributions all things
under the sun could afford thereunto.' †

All internal evidence confirms this date. It could not

---

* Words far too soft to express his gross enormities.

† *Annotations on Ecclesiastes — Works*, vol. iv. They are not
found in the folio edition of his works. They originally formed a
part of *The Assembly's Annotations*, and, as Poole intimates in his
Synopsis, 'the most valuable part of the collection.' They were
edited separately by the Rev. D. Washbourne, 8vo. 1811, and were
ultimately included in Mr. Chalmers' edition of his works, 6 vols.
8vo. 1826.

have been written before his fall—that is—before that awful state of madness, which he so graphically describes. Neither could it have been penned at the time, since it evidently is a record of the past reviewed in penitence. We are thrown back therefore upon the later date with clear conviction. Add to which—he mentions his great works (the building of which employed upwards of twenty-five years of his life) (chap. ii. 4–10. 1 Kings, ix. 10)—his immense riches (Chap. ii. 8 with 1 Kings, x. 20, 25) and multiplied sources of sensual pleasure (the gathering and enjoyment of many years); his revolt from women—doubtless with the poignant remembrance of his sinful connexion with them (Chap. vii. 26–28 with 1 Kings xi. 3.) His exquisite picture also of old age (chap. xii. 1–6) bears the mark of personal identity. And altogether, 'he writeth in such sort, as if he had learned the doctrine of the vanity of earthly things by very great experience and long use.'* Assuming therefore the later date to be accurate, the circumstances remind us of his father's example—the one writing a Psalm (Ps. li.) the other a Book—as a solemn and perpetual testimony in the face of the Church of their godly repentance.†

This date is a matter of some anxiety clearly to ascertain,

* Serran.

† This was Lightfoot's judgment. 'After his great fall Solomon recovereth himself again by repentance, and writeth his Book of Ecclesiastes, as his peculiar dirge for that his folly' (*Works*, i. 76). Witsius speaks of this book 'as written in his old age, when led, under the influence of the Divine Spirit, to repent of his past life.'—*Misc. Sacra*, vol. ii. *Exercit*. vi. 1. See also Scott's Preface. The Patristic Expositions generally confirm this view. See Lorin, *Comment. Prolegom.* c. ii. The expression, *when he was old*, as applied to his turning to sin (1 Kings, xi. 4), may include a period sufficient to include both his fall and recovery.

as bearing upon the momentous point of Solomon's final salvation. If we admit, that Scripture hath pronounced no *certain* judgment upon this matter, we yet contend, that the balance of testimony and inference lies strongly upon the favourable side. His name given to him at his birth— "Beloved of the Lord" (2 Sam. xii. 24, 25)—was surely the seal and pledge of unchangeable love. The covenant made with his father concerning him before his birth included— not the temporal kingdom only—but the privilege of personal adoption and mercy (Ib. vii. 14, 15 ; 1 Chron. xxii. 10). His express designation as a type of Christ (Ib. with Heb. 1–5. Comp. also Ps. lxxii.) leads us naturally to ask—' Could an apostate represent the Saviour—the inexpressible glory of the Son of God?' The notice of "*the rest* of his acts"—his last days—speaks of his "wisdom" (1 Kings, xi. 41), as if it had returned to him—as if he had spoken wise words (might it not have been this very Book ?) *after* his fall, as he had done before it. A posthumous record also links his "way" with that of his penitent father (2 Chron. xi. 17), which surely could not have been, if he had not a fellowship with him in the way of repentance. One thing is clear—he has not written a line in this book that tends to give one particle of palliation of his sin. The whole treatise has a sad character about it—a mournful commentary—mainly a book of confession. The brighter exercises of Evangelical repentance are but dimly exhibited.

Upon the whole therefore we judge of him as a child of that covenant, which provided a rod for his backslidings (Comp. 2 Sam. vii. 14, 15, with 1 Kings, xi. 25, 26); while it secured a happy issue in the end. If his sun set in a cloud, might not this be the chastening of the child—not to be cast off?*

But we pass from this interlude—too important however to be omitted—to mark

III. *The Divine Authority of the Book.*—We admit that the writers of the New Testament have not given any express reference to it.† But we know it to have formed a part of that canon, which by special Providence has been preserved to us—authenticated by the most ancient nation in the world (Rom. iii. 2)—and yet more, attested by our Lord and his Apostles as the final appeal—"the Scripture that cannot be broken."‡ The Old Testament as a whole having received this undoubted sanction, the stamp of authority affixed to the whole Book obviously attaches to every part of it—to this Book of Ecclesiastes, as a component part of the Divine whole.

Nor have the corrupt propensities of the writer any influence in deteriorating its real authority, which depends—not upon the instrumentality employed, but upon the dignity of its great author, and the truthfulness of the testimony. There is therefore no solid ground to question, that this book—like every other part of "Scripture—is given by inspiration of God." (2 Tim. iii. 16.) Many surface objections may be produced; but all—as we have observed—are grounded upon

* Comp. Ps. lxxxix. 30–35. Henry, adverting to the total omission of this dark history in the Book of Chronicles, remarks—'Scripture silence sometimes speaks. When God pardons sin, he "casteth it behind his back, and remembereth it no more."'

† Mr. Holden gives from a German critic (Carpzov) a list of texts with more or less resemblance. But few of them carry any weight of strict parallelism or reference.

‡ Matt. xxii. 29. John, x. 35. Comp. Rom. iv. 3.

misconception, and admit of easy refutation. It may be noted here—as it has been observed generally of religion—'It presents few difficulties to the humble, many to the proud, insuperable ones to the vain.'* To believe the word, because God hath spoken, is the one and true resting-place of faith. Every other course is "going from hill to mountain, and from mountain to hill, having forgotten the resting-place." (Jer. L. 6.)

We advert lastly to

IV. *The main scope and object of the Book.*—It may be simply stated—to solve the problem, 'which from the day when Adam fell has been the great enquiry among men;'† and on which philosophy could throw no light—"Who will shew us any good?" (Ps. iv. 6.) It is to bring out into clear view the chief good—the true happiness of man, *in what it does not consist*—not in the wisdom, pleasures, honours, and riches of this world—*in what it does consist*—the enjoyment and service of God. Beggars we are, with all the riches of the Indies, without Him. He is the substitute for everything. Nothing can be a substitute for Him. The world is full of gaspers—and, alas! they gasp in vain. They only draw in air. They know not where the true substance lies—*in Him* the supreme good and satisfying portion—*in His service*—no hard and gloomy exercise—but full of liberty and joy.

We give a testimony of some interest.—'Began expounding the Book of Ecclesiastes. Never before had I so clear a sight either of its meaning or beauties. Neither did I imagine, that the several parts of it were in so exquisite a manner connected together, all tending to prove that

* *Guesses at Truth*, 1st Series, p. 367.
† Hamilton's *Royal Preacher*, Lect. ii.

grand truth, that there is no happiness out of God.'* If
we are living at the Fountain Head in communion with Him,
we shall realize this *summum bonum*, or ' true wisdom—not
including a single particle of that which is worldly and
carnal ; but that which is holy, spiritual, and undefiled, and
which in the writings of Solomon is but another word for
religion. Guided by this clue, we can easily traverse the
intricate windings and mazes, in which so many commenta-
tors upon ' The Ecclesiastes' have been bewildered.'†

The Preacher's object—as the learned Whitaker has
determined—is, ' not to allure men to the pleasures of the
world, but rather to deter them from such pleasures, and
exhorts them with a Divine eloquence to despise the world.
After having disputed through the whole book against those,
who desire to satisfy themselves with such good, he at the
close teaches them that happiness consisteth not in things of

* The Rev. John Wesley's *Journal*, Jan. 2, 1777. How melancholy is it to see the man of letters at the last crisis seeking
his happiness in Heathenism instead of Revelation! Thus Cosmo de'
Medicis writes to his friend Ficino, just before his death,—' Come to
me as quickly as possible, and bring with you Plato's Treatise on
The *Summum Bonum*, which I believe you have now translated from
the Greek into the Latin. There is nothing I so ardently desire to
know as what way of life most readily conduces to happiness.'
Referring afterwards to this time, Ficino writes to Cosmo's grandson
—the celebrated Lorenzo—in the same Pagan tone. ' When we had
thus read together (as you, who were present, well know) the treatise
of Plato, Cosmo died soon after, as if to enter on the abundant good
he had tasted in discussion.' We are thankful to add, that, in his
latter days, under the influence and preaching of the monk Savana-
rola, Ficino became a humble and devout learner in the school of
Christ, and declared in his last illness, that he derived more comfort
from a single sentence of the New Testament than from all the dog-
mas of the whole tribe of Philosophers. See Harford's *Life of
Michael Angelo*, vol. i. pp. 53, 64, 70.

† Holden, *Prelim. Dissert.* lxv.

this kind, but in true piety—and thus concludes, *Fear God, and keep his commandments; for this is the whole of man.* This is not the judgment of an Epicurean, but of an holy prophet, withdrawing foolish men from the pursuit of worthless objects, and recalling them into the true path of a pious and happy life.'*

Nor is the great object of the Book limited to any age or nation. It is not, like many of the prophetic messages, the burden of this or the other nation—a distinct message to a distinct people. The Book, with all its lessons and illustrations, is the property of the Church and of the world in every age. The Preacher—as upon a former occasion— lifts up his voice, and causes it to be heard amid the din and dissipation of a careless world—"Unto you, O men, I call; and my voice is to the sons of men." (Prov. viii. 4.) Is there not in our hearts an awakened conviction of an evil course? Then let the voice be heard once more in tender seriousness—*Moreover, by these, my son, be admonished.* (Chap. xii. 12.)

On no account therefore could we have spared this book from the canon. It has its own sphere of instruction—and that—as we have before hinted—of no common value. Does not its full development of this world's delusions excite us to search for the true rest? The water of gall, springing up from the "broken cisterns," stirs up the search for "the Fountain of living waters." May it not be, that we are permitted to taste the bitter wormwood of the earthly streams, in order that, standing by the heavenly Fountain, we may point our fellow-sinners to the world of vanity we have left, and to

---

* *Disputations on Holy Scripture*, pp. 31, 32. Parker Society's edit.

the surpassing glory and delights of the world we have newly found? At all events success is the sure issue of the persevering search. The desponding cry—"*All is vanity!*" is now changed for the joyous burst of experimental confidence —"Precious Saviour! be thou my portion. All without thee is *vanity*. All with thee—all in thee—is true substance." 'My blessed hope'—said a dying Christian—'is worth a thousand worlds.'—This is the grand discovery—the *summum bonum* indeed. How does this discovery once made and enjoyed, become the living principle of every godly grace—"perfecting holiness in the fear of God!" (2 Cor. vii. 1.)

The Writer has only to add a few words relative to his own labour. The various commentaries on this book would fill a large compass. A few only need to be mentioned, that have been more prominently useful. Bp. Reynolds' *Annotations* are richly fraught with scriptural instruction. Dr. Wardlaw's *Lectures* are a fine specimen of exposition.* Dr. Hamilton's *Royal Preacher* sparkles with brilliant imagination, perhaps sometimes with a colouring too gorgeous for the pure simplicity of Scripture. The Rev. G. Holden's *Commentary* stands foremost for the accuracy of critical exegesis. Scott's *Notes* in solid weight of instruction rarely disappoint. Henry brings out from his lively store original and profitable thought. Other commentaries less known— Ancient and Modern—Romish and Protestant—Home and Foreign—will be found to have been consulted. A few may be wanting from the list, not having come across the author's path. In the use of them sometimes a train of thought has been suggested, where exact quotation in-

---

* *Lectures on the Book of Ecclesiastes,* 2 vols. 8vo. 1821.

advertently may not have been given. Practical instruction
and Christian edification have been considered, rather than
novelty or originality. The Author has felt warranted to
expound this Old Testament treatise as " a minister of the
New Testament"—to expound' Solomon by Christ; not
forcing an unnatural interpretation, but feeling that both the
Testaments, like our two eyes, mutually assist and enlighten
each other. Or—to use another figure. The Book of Ecclesiastes — as a component part of the Revelation—is the germ
of what the Gospel more fully developes. It is the same
God—the same creature—the same duties and obligations.
We cannot therefore fully enforce and apply Ecclesiastes,
except by the aid of Gospel light.

He does not presume to have swept away all obscurities from the sky. But possibly a few rays of light
may have been cast upon the dark clouds. For instances of
failure in interpretation he would crave forbearance. For
success he would give the glory where alone it is due. He
has endeavoured to place before him the apostolical rule—
*As every man hath received the gift, even so minister the same
one to another, as good stewards of the manifold grace of God.
If any man speak, let him speak as the oracles of God ; if any
man minister, let him do it as of the ability which God giveth :
that God in all things may be glorified through Jesus Christ, to
whom be praise and dominion for ever and ever.   Amen.*
(1 Pet. iv. 10, 11.)

        Hinton Martell Rectory,
            Wimborne, Dorset.
                December 10, 1859.

EXPOSITION OF ECCLESIASTES.

CHAPTER I.

*1. The words of the Preacher, the Son of David, King in
Jerusalem.*

THESE are no common *words*. They are weighty in substance,
golden in value. But their highest stamp is, that they are,
as with the olden prophets, *words* from the mouth of God.*
Let us take them, not only as the words of Solomon, the
wisest of men, but as the *words* of "the only wise God."
Let them come to us in the full conviction of their Divine
original. Folly and weakness is our name; but, oh, let us
be as a little child before every word of the testimony, with
a supreme desire to know the mind of God, not disputing;
"not leaning to our own understanding" (Prov. iii. 5); but
patient, humble learners before our heavenly Teacher. Thus
must we "humble ourselves" (Matt. xviii. 3, 4), if we would
profit by the precious instruction. 'When a man' (such was
the dying witness of an intellectual Christian) 'comes to that
book as a child, he will find wonders in it to make him
marvel.'†

Observe Solomon in his new name and character, given
to him only in this book — *the Preacher.* This sacred office

---

* Preface, with Jer. i. 1, 2. Amos, i. 1.
† Newman Hall's *Memoir of Dr. Gordon*, p. 152.

he places in the foreground.   For was it not more honourable to be the instructor of his people* than to be *King in
Jerusalem ?*   If this was a just estimate in Solomon's time,
much more is it in our own.   The ordinance of preaching is
now more fully consecrated, as the grand instrument of
Divine grace. (1 Cor. i. 21.)   It tunes the heavenly song of
"joy over the repenting sinner." (Luke, xv. 10.)   It brings
out the purchased jewels to be eternally fixed in the media-
torial crown.   It anticipates the work of angels in "gathering together the elect of God." (Matt. xxiv. 31.)   Surely
then this office may be recognized as a far higher glory
than to have discovered a planet, or to have founded a
dynasty.

But let us see the Royal PREACHER in office, 'garnished
by God with great and glorious gifts.'†   Behold him consecrating that temple, on which he had centred his whole
heart, and his untold treasures.   With him is the "assembly
of the elders of Israel, and all the Heads of the tribes of
Israel."   No priest or Levite performs the service.   "Kneeling
down upon his brazen scaffolding," "the king turned his
face about, and blessed all the congregation of Israel."   And
when with pleading confidence he had led the solemnities of
the national worship, he dismisses the assembly with a valuable word of practical exhortation.—"Let your heart be
perfect with the Lord our God, to walk in his statutes, and
to keep his commandments as at this day."‡

The Preacher's ordinary course combined oral and written
instruction.   "He *taught* the people knowledge; and that

* The best critics render the original word, *Koheleth*, "One that
gathereth ;" collecting the people for public instruction — *the
Preacher.*— See SCOTT.   Holden strongly defends the feminine ter-
mination.— *Prelim. Dissert.* pp. xxxviii.-xlvii.   See also Poli *Synopsis*, and Rosenmuller's *Scholia*.

† Serran.

‡ 1 Kings, viii. 1 ; xiv. 55–61, with 2 Chron. vi. 13.

which was *written* was upright, even words of truth,"
(chap. xii. 9, 10.) His oral teaching was wondrously
diversified in every track of science. ' He was the en-
cyclopædia of that early age.' (1 Kings, iv. 30–33.) From
all nations around, and from all ranks, they flocked to hear
his wisdom. (Ib. 34.) Our Lord reads us a lesson of conviction from one of these illustrious strangers : " The queen
of the south shall rise up in the judgment with this generation, and shall condemn it : for she came from the uttermost parts of the earth to hear the wisdom of Solomon,
and, behold, a greater than Solomon is here." (Ib. x.
Matt. xii. 42.)

At his last period of life *the Preacher* laboured with
unwearied devotedness, to repair the dishonour to God from
his evil example. " He *still* taught the people knowledge, and
sought to find out acceptable words." (chap. xii. 9, 10.)
Perhaps this office, as with restored Peter in after days,
was the seal of his restoration. " When thou art converted, strengthen thy brethren. Feed my sheep." (Luke,
xxii. 32 ; John, xxi. 15–17.)

But however his vast stores of wisdom may have fitted
him for his work, the school of experience furnished a far
higher qualification. His main subject is the utter vanity
of earthly show, and the substantial happiness of the enjoyment and service of God ; and who could touch these
points with such sensibility and demonstration, as he, who had
so grossly " committed the two evils — having forsaken the
fountain of living waters, and hewn out to himself cisterns,
broken cisterns, that could hold no water ? "* (Jer. ii.
13.) Most poignantly would he witness to the " evil and
bitterness" (Ib. 19,) of this way of folly. (Jer. ii. 13, 19.)

---

* Hamilton's *Royal Preacher*, Lect. ii. 'He pierced everything
to the very ground.'— Hooker, b. v. 2.

The Preacher's parentage also added weight to his in-structions — *the Son of David!* How much did he owe to his godly and affectionate counsel ! * Indeed he stands out as a bright illustration of his own confidence, that the " trained child," though for a while — perhaps a long while — he may be a wanderer from the path, yet, when *he is old*—in his last days — he shall not depart from it." (Prov. xxii. 6.) Let God be honoured in the practical exercise of faith, and his promise will be made good in his own most fitting time—" I will be a God to thee, and to thy seed after thee."†

We have also before us the Preacher's dignity—King in Jerusalem. His royal influence must indeed have been shaken by the gross display of idolatrous lust. . On the other hand, the special credentials of his birth (2 Sam. vii. 12–14), the seal of Divine love upon him (Ib. xii. 24, 25 ; Neh. xiii. 26), and his rich endowments (1 Kings, iii. 5–12) could not be forgotten.

In looking backward we find, that the sacred office has been filled from all ranks of life, from the *King in Jerusalem* to the herdman of Tekoa (Amos, i. 1), and the fishermen of Galilee. (Matt. iv. 18–22.) But in all this diversity of mini-stration, " the treasure has been in earthen vessels, that the excellency of the power may be of God." (2 Cor. iv. 7.)

---

* 1 Kings, ii. 2–4. 1 Chron. xxviii. 9. Prov. iv. 3–13.

† Gen. xvii. 7. ' Though descent from wicked parents ought to be no ground of prejudice against their godly children, yet descent from godly parents is a comfortable advantage to godly children, as clearing up their right to such promises as are made to the seed of the upright. Ps. xxxvii. 26 ; cxii. 2.'—Nisbet *On Ecclesiastes*, 4to. 1694.

2. *Vanity of vanities, saith the Preacher, vanity of vanities,*
all is vanity.

This verse appears to have been intended to be the com-
pendium of the whole treatise.   The subject opens upon us
abruptly; and no wonder ; *The Preacher's* heart is so filled with
it.   He longs to make a forcible impression.   His text is ' the
whole world, with all the pleasures, and profits, and honours,
and endeavours, and business, and events that are under the
sun.'*   He brings out his subject with a vast variety of
illustration, and then closes with emphatically repeating his
judgment.   He seems as if he could not give full expression
to his convictions.   It is not only vain, but *vanity* † itself.   He
redoubles his asseveration to shew the certainty of it, and that
all is unmixed *vanity* in its highest degree—*vanity of vanities.*‡
Nor does this belong only to a part.   Everything severally, all
things collectively— all is one expanse—one vast heap of
numberless perishing vanities.   ' I affirm again and again,
that there is nothing in this world, but what is the vainest
vanity.' §   All is therefore utterly inefficient for the great
end of man's true happiness.   It only enlarges his desires in
the endeavour to gratify them.   But it leaves behind ' an
aching void,' a blank, that it cannot fill up.‖

* Bp. Sanderson's *Sermon on Eccles.* vii. 1.
† Chap. xii. 8.   ' The original word means a thing insufficient
and worthless, that soon vanishes away, like a vapour or a bubble.'—
Taylor's *Hebrew Concordance.*   ' It shows that man cannot find in
the world that which he aims at.'—Dathii *Notæ in Eccles.* 8vo.
Halæ, 1721.   ' It made a show of contentment, but performed
nothing of that which it seemed to promise.'— Bp. Patrick.
‡ A superlative form of speech, to set forth the highest vanity,
like "Song of Songs," &c.   Cant. i. 1.
§ Bezæ *Periphrasis,* 12mo. 1589.
‖ Cowper.   The picture of Lord Chesterfield, given by himself,
furnishes the most striking commentary on this statement—' I have

So *saith the Preacher*—repeating his office, to give weight
to his decision.   Nor is it the judgment of a soured mind—
of one, who was leaving the world, only because the world
was leaving him.   The book bears evidence, that his mind
was in full and clear vigour.   He had lived the life all over.
He loathed himself for his dear-bought experience of it, and
was now " come to himself," and seeking a better portion in
his Father's house. (Luke, xv. 13–20.)

Yet *the Preacher's* verdict casts no reflection on the works
of God, which at their original formation their Maker had
pronounced to be " very good."*   He speaks of them here—
not as God made, but as sin has marred, them.   Things
intrinsically excellent are perverted by their abuse.   " The

run the silly rounds of business and pleasure, and have done with
them all.   I have enjoyed all the pleasures of the world, and consequently know their futility, and I do not regret their loss.   I ap-
praise them at their real value, which is in truth very low ; whereas
they that have not experienced always overrate them.   They only
see their gay outside, and are dazzled with the glare.   I have been
behind the scenes ; I have seen all the coarse pulleys and dirty ropes,
which exhibit and move the gaudy machine ; and I have seen and
smelt the tallow-candles which illuminate the whole decoration, to
the astonishment and admiration of an ignorant audience.   When I
reflect back upon what I have seen, what I have heard, and what I
have done, I can hardly persuade myself that all that frivolous
hurry, and bustle, and pleasure of the world, had any reality.   But
I look upon all that has passed as one of those romantic dreams
which opium commonly occasions, and I by no means desire to
repeat the nauseous dose for the sake of the fugitive dream.   Shall
I tell you, that I bear this melancholy situation with that meri-
torious constancy and resignation which most people boast of ?
No ; for I really cannot help it.   I bear it, because I must bear it,
whether I will or no.   I think of nothing but killing Time the best
I can, now that he is become mine enemy.   It is my resolution to
sleep in the carriage during the remainder of the journey.'— See Bp.
Horne's interesting Sermon on ' Joshua's Choice,' and compare the
fine contrast, Isa. lxv. 14.

   * Gen. i. 31.   Comp. chap. iii. 11 ; Ps. xix. 1 ; cxi. 2, 3.

creature is" now "made subject to vanity." (Rom. viii. 20.)

Repeatedly does Solomon remind us that the blessings of the creature, when used for the glory of God, are lawful in themselves, and become the source of rich and legitimate enjoyment.* But here lies the evil. Man buries his heart in their vanity. He makes them his chief good — his happiness and rest. But "vanity" is the stamp on "man" even "in his best estate."† It pervades—as we have said— every class. The rich, the learned, the ambitious, build their Babels upon the cheat of the great deceiver.—Nay—the poor have 'their little Babylon of straw.'‡ Everywhere it is one picture. To give a deeper impression of it, the wise man puts it forth in a vehement exclamation, as if overwhelmed with his own perception of it, and wondering at the delusion of seeking happiness from a mere vapour. So deeply has the love of vanity struck its roots into the heart, that the delusion cannot be too strongly exposed.

But have we no balancing reality ? Are we to fret under the desponding inquiry—"Who will shew us any good?" (Ps. iv. 6.) 'May I have Christ with me in the world'— prayed the heavenly Martyn—'not substituting imagination in the place of faith, but seeing outward things as they really are, and thus obtaining a radical conviction of their vanity.'§ Here we mark the hero of faith, his "victory overcoming the world." (1 John, v. 4.) Here is the grand thing—that which alone is important. Earthly things look grand, till the trial has proved their vanity; heavenly things look mean,

* Chap. ii. 24-26; iii. 12, 13; ix. 7-9. Comp. 1 Tim. vi. 17; iv. 3, 4.

† Ps. xxxix. 5, 6. 'Behold then, O Lord'— prays the pious Bishop Horne—'the vanity of man; and be so merciful unto him, as to open his eyes, that he may behold it himself.'

‡ Young's *Night Thoughts.*   § See his Life.

till the trial has developed their glory.　Calculate both worlds
—each in its relative value.　' In " looking at the things that
are not seen and eternal," how is the brightness of " the
things that are seen and temporal" eclipsed ! ' *　And yet
never can we look off from this " seen and temporal" sphere,
till we look beyond it.　*Then* truly the sight of the brighter
world will make this world a wilderness !

> ' O world ! thou art too small ;
> 　We seek another higher,
> 　　Whither Christ guides us ever nigher,
> 　Where God is all in all.' †

3. *What profit hath a man of all his labour which he hath done under the sun ?*

The mass of mankind revolt from *the Preacher's* judgment.
He therefore throws down the challenge.　*What profit ?*
General propositions must often admit of limitations.　Labour,
physical and moral, brings its own harvest. (Prov. xiv. 23.)
Nay, there is a dignity in manual labour.　Hath not the example of the Son of God ‡ blotted out all the stain of meanness, and made it a work worthy of the greatest of men ? §
But as regards the chief good, what can all our resources
effect ?　Apart from God, the world is poor indeed.　Disappointment brings weariness.　Success gives no permanent
satisfaction.

> ' The world's all title-page, without contents.' §

Cast up its account.　Nothing but cyphers remain.　The
theory is falsified by experience.　Its comforts are withering.

---

* See 2 Cor. iv. 18.
† Tersteegen in *Lyra Germanica*, 17th Sunday after Trinity.
‡ See Mark, vi. 3.— Scott.
§ Young's *Night Thoughts*.

They stop on this side the grave. All is dark beyond. As one said, who had built for himself a splendid elysium, ' I have no comfort in all this, because I meet death in every walk.' To expect, therefore, from the world that which is not in it, is surely to " spend labour for that which satisfieth not." (Isa. lv. 2). Yea, as a punishment for this perversity —" Behold, is it not of the Lord of Hosts that the people shall *labour* in the very fire, and the people shall weary themselves for very vanity?" (Hab. ii. 13.) In fact, men are so willing to be deceived, that they take up with the very shadow of *profit*. For what appears to be substance is more accurately described as an unreal thing, having no being at all.* The appetite indeed for wisdom, riches, honour, and sensual indulgence, may be indefinitely enlarged. But supposing the possession of this world's all—" *What shall it profit a man*, if he shall gain the whole world, and lose his own soul?" (Matt. xvi. 26.) The man of the world may be orthodox in his creed and moral in his practice. But he has stumbled at the very threshold. He has placed the world before God—the body before the soul—time before eternity.†

What, then, will it be at the last, when the account of all our *labour* must be rendered up? when the man of pleasure and the servant of sin shall stand before God? Will not the question then flash upon the conscience—" What fruit had ye then in those things, whereof ye are now ashamed?" ' There is none of you'—saith Bp. Taylor—' that ever entered this house of pleasure but he left the skirts of his garment in the hands of shame, and had his name rolled in the chambers of death. What fruit had ye then? This is the question.' ‡ And where will the answer be given, but in

---

* See Prov. xxiii. 5.
† See Luke, xii. 15–20.
‡ *Sermons on Apples of Sodom.* Part I.

darkness and despair? "The end of those things is death."
(Rom. vi. 21.) Such is the fruitless *labour under the sun.*
Let man spend his pains on a world (as Henry somewhat
quaintly contrasts) '*above the sun,* that needs not the sun, for
the glory of God is its light, where there is work without
labour, and with great profit.'* "They are before the throne
of God, and serve him day and night in his temple." † *The
pleasures of this service never wear out.*

4. *One generation passeth away, and another generation cometh;
but the earth abideth for ever.* 5. *The sun also ariseth, and
the sun goeth down, and hasteth to his place where he arose.*
6. *The wind goeth toward the south, and turneth about unto
the north; it whirleth about continually, and the wind
returneth again according to his circuits.* 7. *All the rivers
run into the sea, yet the sea is not full; unto the place from
whence the rivers come, thither they return again.*

The changeableness of man, as contrasted with the per-
manency of his abode, furnishes another proof of utter *vanity.*

---

* In loco.

† Rev. vii. 15. Comp. xxii. 3. Robert Burns, the poet of nature,
while a young man, writes to his father, ' I am quite transported at
the thought, that ere long—perhaps very soon—I shall bid adieu to
all the pains, and uneasiness, and disquietudes of this weary life;
for I assure you I am heartily tired of it. It is for this reason I am
more pleased with the last three verses of the seventh chapter of
the Revelation, than with any ten times as many in the whole
Bible; and would not exchange the noble enthusiasm with which
they inspire me for all that this world has to offer me.' See his
Life. Yet all this was only the religion of sentiment. It brought
neither holiness nor peace. Burns, with all his emotion, was the
wretched slave of lust. How sad to admire, without the taste to
enjoy! The picture is glowing. The scenery is lovely. But is the
holiness of God the element of the atmosphere? Is it the heaven
of imagination that we love? Or is it the heaven where Christ is
the Sun—the centre—the everlasting joy? See Rev. xxi. 23.

Man and *his labour* are swept away, as if they had never been. '*The earth* is a stage — persons passing and vanishing before our eyes.'* It is continually shifting its inhabitants. *One generation passeth away* to make room for another. Fathers are going; children are coming after. None stayeth. The house *abideth*, but the tenants are continually changing. Could they remain to enjoy it, there might be some solid, because some permanent, *profit*. But eternity and unchangeableness are the necessary grounds of happiness.† The ultimate destiny of *the earth* is, that it, "and the works that are therein, shall be burned up." (2 Pet. iii. 10, 11.) Yet a substratum for the "new earth," which "we, according to his promise, look for" (Ib. v. 13), may be reserved. At all events, as compared with man's passing away, *it abideth ever*, till its end in connexion with the purpose of God be eternally accomplished. So long as there shall remain "a seed to serve him," and "one generation to praise his works to another" (Ps. xxii. 30 ; cxlv. 4), so long it *abideth*.

See how everything presents the same picture. *The sun*, after so many thousand courses, *ariseth and goeth down* . . *hasting to his place* (Ps. xix. 4–6; civ. 19–22). *The wind* is always shifting, *returning again according to his circuits*. (Ps. cxxxv. 7 ; Jer. x. 13.) The currents of *the rivers run into the sea*, which *yet is not full*, but returns them in clouds and vapours to water the earth. (Ps. civ. 8, 9.)‡ All this

---

* Beza.

† 'Solomon reasons that a man's happiness cannot be upon this earth, because it must be some abiding thing that must make him happy—abiding, to wit, in his enjoyment. Now, though *the earth abideth*, yet, because man abides not on the earth to possess it, therefore his rest and happiness cannot be here.' Leighton on 1 Pet. i. 3, 4.

‡ See Bp. Horne's beautiful note. 'The whole passage seems only intended to express, *in a popular manner*, the stated revolutions of the visible creation.' Holden *in loco*.

seems a weary go-round—constant movement combined with constant sameness. So many emblems of man's restless state! Should they not rouse us to "work while it is day" (John ix. 4)—filling up our own little sphere "of service according to the will of God in our generation" (Acts, xiii. 36) —looking to "fall asleep in Jesus, resting from our labours, and our works following us?" (Rev. xiv. 13.)

8. *All things are full of labour; man cannot utter it: the eye is not satisfied with seeing, nor the ear filled with hearing.*

Every step of advance shews more clearly the "weary land." *Labour*, not rest, is our portion. (Chap. ii. 11, 22.) "Man riseth up early, and late taketh rest, and eateth the bread of carefulness."* *All things*, even the most cheerful exercises, *are full of labour.* What therefore brings toil, brings only additional proof that *all is vanity.* Indeed, in so many ways is this weariness felt, that *man cannot utter it.* In all the inconceivable variety, we are as far from rest, as *the sun, the wind, the rivers,* in their respective spheres. As the Christian philosopher profoundly remarks—'Our own will, although it should obtain its largest wish, would always keep us in uneasiness.'† Men seek, and they find; and yet they toil again, no nearer the prize than at the beginning. Nay, even the delights enjoyed through the medium of the senses cloy. *Seeing* and *hearing* bring no permanent *satisfaction.* (Chap. iv. 8; v. 10, 11. Comp. Prov. xxvii. 20; xxx. 15, 16.) They would fain describe, if they could, the bitterness and extent of their disappointment. Men cry for more and more of the world. But when it comes, it does not satisfy. Do they ever dream of rest? 'Whence arise distractions of heart, thoughts for to-morrow, rovings and inquisitions of the soul after infinite varieties of earthly things, swarms of lusts,

* Ps. cxxvii. 2, Prayer-book Version.   † Pascal.

sparkles of endless thoughts, those secret flowings, and ebbs, and tempests, and estuations of that sea of corruption in the heart of man—but because it can never find anything on which to rest, or that hath room enough to entertain so ample and so endless a guest ?'*

Never, surely, can there be *satisfaction to the eye,* till it be singly fixed upon the one object—*to the ear,* till it listens to those breathings of love, which welcome the "heavy-laden labourer" to the only true rest. (Matt. xi. 28.) Is it not the real apprehension of the Saviour, that gives life, energy, and joy to our religion ? The object is full of fresh and sweet variety. To "the new creature" it is a new existence ; "all things become new." The appetite is fully *satisfied* even with present gratification. "He that cometh to me shall never hunger ; and he that believeth on me shall never thirst." (John, vi. 35. Comp. iv. 13, 14.) Eternity opens with the bright anticipation of perfect enjoyment. The heavenly Shepherd shall be our Feeder. The living fountain of waters shall be an eternally satisfying delight. (Rev. vii. 16, 17.)

9. *The thing that hath been, it is that which shall be ; and that which is done, is that which shall be done : and there is no new thing under the sun.* 10. *Is there anything whereof it may be said, See, this is new ? it hath been already of old time, which was before us.*

The Preacher extends his view on all sides. He includes all ages to the very end of time. *The thing that hath been and hath been done,* he assures us, *is that which shall be.* —Nothing new. This, indeed, must be a qualified statement. Amid endlessly diversified changes and modifications some things, doubtless, there are, *which have not been already of old time.* But the main features of the universe are the same.

* Bp. Reynolds *on the Vanity of the Creature,* sec. 5.

Things animate and inanimate remain as they were from the beginning. (2 Pet. iii. 4.) "The works were finished from the foundation of the world." (Heb. iv. 3.) The same causes produce the same effects. The laws of the heavenly bodies, the courses of the seasons (Gen. viii. 22 ; Ps. lxxiv. 16, 17 ; Jer. v. 24), the arrangements relative to the animal world, ' the chemistry of the creation,' the chemical properties of natural bodies and objects—have never changed. *There is no new thing under the sun.* Nay, indeed, we may throw out the challenge—*Is there anything of which it may be said, See, it is new ?* Man's active intellect, assisted by the experience of former ages, is indeed always at work. But the most that he can boast of is little more than an enlarged discovery of the properties of matter, and a more accurate application of what has been from the beginning. And may we not class the vast discoveries, mechanical and scientific—the power of steam and electricity—as developments of natural principles— therefore *nothing new ?* ' For novelty,' said the great Bacon, ' no man that wadeth in learning or contemplation thoroughly, but will find that printed on his heart—nothing new upon the earth.' * Solomon had just before beautifully described the process of evaporation—the waters of the sea forming clouds, which empty themselves upon the earth, and fill the rivers, which again carry them into the sea. (vv. 6, 7.) But here is *no new* creation of waters ; only the successive reproduction of the clouds, vapours, and rivers. In the wondrous economy of nature there is, therefore, *no new thing under the sun.* Nay, even many discoveries, that appear to be *new,* have been shewn to be the unknown work of bygone ages. The art of printing was known in China some centuries before it was proclaimed in Europe as a *new* invention.

The history of the Church furnishes abundant evidence

* *Advancement of Learning,* b. I. viii.   Markby's Ed. 12mo. 1856.

of our point. All ecclesiastical revolutions, and the ever-varying phases of doctrine, are only ' the same scene over and over again.'* We sound the warning. Beware of being dazzled by the glare of new things—new philosophy—a new show of truth. Faithful men value the old truths, ask for the good old way, " the footsteps of the flock."† " The present truth," *the truth then taught,* was the truth in which the Apostle exhorted his people to " be established." (2 Pet. i. 12–15.) ' A new truth—in the sense of something neither expressed nor virtually asserted before—not implied (involved) in anything already known — cannot properly be looked for in religion. A full and final revelation having been made, no discovery, properly so called, of any high importance is to be expected.' ‡

Look again at man in all his pleasures, pursuits, and changes of life. His intellect may be gratified, and his appetite for novelty supplied, in the multiplied new openings of science. But no *new* springs of vital happiness are opened to him. ·He is as far as ever from true rest. Our disappointed forefathers in bygone days never found it. We shall find the world as they did. And so we shall leave it to our children—a world of vexation, a shadow, and a bubble.

But what is the end of all this restlessness? Is it not (as Augustine finely describes it)§ our gracious Father

---

* Scott. Thus Bp. Sanderson — ' He that shall impartially look upon former and the present times, shall find that of Solomon exactly true — *There is no new thing under the sun.* The things we see done are but the same things that have been done, only acted over again by new persons, and with a few new circumstances. It was in the Apostles' times, and in the Churches of Galatia, even as it is with us in these days.' Sermon on Gal. v. 22, 23.

† Jer. vi. 16. Cant. i. 8.

‡ *Detached Thoughts from Abp. Whately's Writings.* 1854. 12mo. p. 74.

§ *Confess.* B. iv. c. 4.

'pressing upon the backs of his fugitive children,' to bring them home to himself? Thus does he make them feel the love and wisdom of his own will, that they should enter into no rest but his?

11. *There is no remembrance of former things; neither shall there be any remembrance of things that are to come, with those that shall come after.*

This, like the last, is a general, rather than an universal, truth. But the fact that 'there is more oblivion than *remembrance*,'* shews another feature of this world's vanity. Not only the things themselves, but *the remembrance of the former things* passeth away. Time blots out a multitude of events, as if they had never been. Men, as well as events, have passed away, so that the remark forces itself upon us, 'How few—how easily to be counted up—are the cardinal names in the history of the human mind!'† How little is the *remembrance* of the great empire of Nimrod, of the early beginnings of Rome, or the first dynasty of France! The traditionary records are most imperfect, only (as an old expositor stamps them) 'rugged and rusty guesses at these matters.'‡ Much that used to form a part of ancient history is now cast out of *remembrance*. 'The river Lethe runneth as well above ground as below.'§ Thus the idols and heroes of the world—the mighty and illustrious—with all their titles and grandeur—like a pageant of the world—pass by, and are forgotten. A miserable fool, indeed, is he, who has no better stay and portion than this shadowy *remembrance*.

Those that shall come after will be covered with the same veil of death and oblivion. The objects now so vividly before

* Lorin *in loco*.   † *Guesses at Truth*, 2d Series, p. 11.
‡ Serran.   § Bacon's *Essays*, lviii.

us, and engrossing our highest interest—to the next generation will gradually pass away in the haze of distance. Nor
need this be a sadness to us. For—save where God has been
the supreme object, the retrospect is a blank—yea—a blot
in our existence. And as to our happiness—none of this
life's changes have altered the character of this world to us.
Is it not still—Christian—a world of "vanity and vexation
of spirit?"

Now contrast with this oblivion *of former things* the great
miracle of Providence—the preservation of the Bible—God's
own Book—and therefore under his special cover. Here is
indeed the *remembrance of former things*—free from the injury
of time—free from the mists of uncertainty—still full and
clear, as from the beginning. What do we owe to the Divine
Keeper for this precious transcript of himself—his will—his
love!

Contrast, again, this want of *remembrance* with the recollection, that with God nothing is blotted out—nothing forgotten. All the history of every child of man, from the
beginning to the end of the world—all that he has done, said,
thought, and felt—every moment—all is ever-present to his
eye in perfect order and accuracy—not one atom missing
from the whole—not one particle of confusion—the end
seen from the beginning without a cloud. "Such knowledge"—the Psalmist reverently acknowledges—"is too
wonderful for me; it is high; I cannot attain unto it."
(Ps. cxxxix. 1–6.)

12. *I the Preacher was king over Israel in Jerusalem.*

The Preacher hitherto had only given a general view of
this world's vanity. He now confirms it from his own history. His royal dignity gave him every advantage of obser-

vation.   He was *King* also—not of a barbarous and ignorant people—but *of Israel*—the only people on the face of the earth, who professed the true knowledge of God, and the right standard of principle. (Deut. iv. 7, 8.)   He was *in Jerusalem*—the Mother Church in Israel—'the city which God had fixed as the habitation of his glory.'*

Who does not know his sadly instructive history?   His day opened as "a morning without clouds."   His meridian was brightness "above his fellows."   But the shadows of evening how dark!   Instead of the fruitfulness of a long course of devotedness, all was sorrow and shame, with only a few last rays of the setting sun to brighten the thick cloud. But how could Solomon thus fall?   Could he, who so highly exalted wisdom, degrade himself into the lowest folly?   Could he, who was so conscious of the snares of sin, and warned so wisely—so earnestly†—could he fall, so as to become a proverb of Apostacy?   He who had tasted such gracious manifestations of the Saviour's love,‡ leave the Beloved of his soul for abominable idols?   Only those who have been taught by experience, no less than by Scripture, the total corruption of the heart, can solve the mystery.   But to such the lesson is most valuable.   The moment that utter weakness loses its hold, and forgets the need of *habitual* dependence —this is the moment of a certain fall.   The most exalted Christian attainments—the longest standing in the Church —the most extensive usefulness in the world—the richest store of spiritual gifts—all furnish no security against the crisis.   The most experienced is exposed, no less than the weakest babe in the family.   Oh! what need is there to "watch unto prayer" (1 Pet. iv. 7), and to walk closely with God!

* Lampe.   † See his Book of Proverbs.
                ‡ See Song of Solomon.

13. *And I gave my heart to seek and search out by wisdom,
concerning all things that are done under heaven: this sore
travail hath God given to the sons of men, to be exercised
therewith.*

The wise man throws himself with intense energy into
his hazardous inquiry! *He gave his heart to seek and
search out.* All his extraordinary treasures of *wisdom*
were employed to know — Why is man — the noblest of
God's creatures — placed in the world to be *exercised with
sore travail,** during his short continuance? Why his unsatisfied desires — his weariness of life — his strivings and
toilings—his unsuccessful search after happiness, even while
all the sources of earthly gratification are spread at his feet?

The Preacher himself subsequently explained the problem
—" God hath made man upright, but they have sought
out many inventions." (Chap. vii. 29.) Man by his fall
alienated himself from the only source of life and rest.
Fallen man of himself cannot recover one atom of his
former perfection. *God hath given him this travail* as the
chastening for his apostacy. All is dark with him, till he
shall see that all is vanity, and himself the chiefest of all
vanities. This is the Lord's training — the discipline of his
school — the ordinary method of his Sovereign grace. Oh!
sinner—thou must know the depth of thy ruin—the bank-
ruptcy of thy nature. Thou must learn to trample upon the
petty objects of the world—to set in full view its meanness
—its vanity—its nothingness. Thus the Lord will bring
thee to thy home, wearied with the unsuccessful efforts to
seek in thyself or in the world what is only to be found in
him. But once brought home—oh! the contrast of present

* Solomon's frequent use of the term is a strong evidence of
the fact. See the Son of Sirach's testimony to the same point.
Ecclus. xl. 1.

repose with the *sore travail*—what Lord Bacon beautifully calls 'sacred and inspired Divinity—the Sabbath and port of all men's labours and peregrinations.'* All the creatures can never be to me in his stead. I have found in him a portion —soul-satisfying and eternal. (Ps. lxxiii. 25, 26.) Trials follow me—sometimes enough to stagger the strongest faith. But "I know whom I have believed." (2 Tim. i. 12.) I know him to be an unfailing confidence for time and for eternity. He has engaged to take charge of all, and I bid my soul "return únto her rest" (Ps. cxvi. 7), upon the engagements of an unchangeable, covenant-keeping God.

14. *I have seen all the works that are done under the sun; and, behold, all is vanity and vexation of spirit.*

Solomon's research extended to *all the works done under the sun.* All this he *had seen* with his mind's eye. He had earnestly heeded, and clearly understood it. He had before given his judgment in part—*all is vanity.* A more full investigation brings in a more complete verdict—*all is vexation of spirit.* Disappointment possesses us in trifles, as well as in matters of moment. The intensity of interest in the pursuit of a shadow—the precious time wasted never to be recalled—frets the spirit. The golden opportunity of feeding our faith upon the promises of God, and of nourishing our graces in the pastures of the Good Shepherd—all is stolen from us by the over-eager pursuit of comparatively unworthy objects. *Behold!* is not this *vexation of spirit?* He would have us not pass it by heedlessly.

Whence, but in one quarter, can we extract the balm for the vexed spirit? 'Labour ever'—writes good Bishop Reynolds—'to get Christ into thy ship. He will check every

---

* *Advancement of Learning*, Book II. xxiv. See also vi. 1.

tempest, and calm every *vexation* that grows upon thee.   If
I have Christ with me, there can no estate come, which can
be cumbersome unto me.   Have I a load of misery and
infirmity, inward, outward, in mind, body, name, or estate ?
This takes away the *vexation* of all, when I consider it all
comes from Christ, and it all runs into Christ.   It all comes
from Him, who is the distributor of his Father's gifts, and it
all runs into Him, who is the partaker of his members'
sorrows.' *

15. *That which is crooked cannot be made straight ; and
that which is wanting cannot be numbered.*

The wise man directs our attention to two points—the
things that are, and the countless multitude of things that
are *wanting*.   The world in its present constitution from the
fall—is full of *crookedness* and defect.   Yet a reverential
enquiry will shew many apparent irregularities to be component parts of a system, which "God hath made beautiful
in his time." (Chap. iii. 11.)

But let us look at this aphorism more minutely.   *Physi-
cally*, it lies upon the surface.   We have no power to alter
our stature, or to change one hair of our heads. (Matt. v. 36 ;
vi. 27.)   *Intellectually*, man's wisdom can never discover
— much less remove—the causes of his restless misery.
Spiritually, every faculty of man is under the perversity of
the fall, and we have no more power to *make straight its
crookedness*, than to restore the whole work of God to its
original "uprightness."   *Providentially*, how often do the
Divine appointments appear *crooked* to man's eyes !   Nay,
there is ' a *crook* in his lot' which he cannot alter or amend
—something opposed to his own will, which he labours in

* *Vanity of the Creature*, sect. lxiii.

vain to *make straight* to his own wishes. With all our struggling, crosses will be crosses still. (Chap. vii. 13.) We must leave them, where God has placed them. And if we gather wisdom from their discipline, they will ultimately become the springs of our happiness, and the crown of our glory.

But man " in the fulness of his sufficiency is in straits." (Job, xx. 22.) He is a creature of so many wants. *That which is wanting cannot be numbered.* One little *crookedness* is enough to wither his largest sources of satisfaction. Ahab, with all the wealth of his kingdom, for want of a little plot of ground, lays himself down on his bed in *vexation.* (1 Kings, xxi. 4.) Haman, with the monarch's favour—the adoration of the people—immense riches and honours, had a *crook, that could not be made straight.* " All this availed nothing," so long as the bended knee of one poor Jew was *wanting.* (Esth. v. 11–13.)

' Nothing but the cross of Christ'—observes a spiritual writer—' makes other crosses *straight.*'* But where man's own will is his law, " woe unto him that striveth with his Maker." (Isa. xlv. 9.) That will, which is thus "enmity against God" (Rom. viii. 7), must be the enemy to our own happiness. Never can we be happy, till we be " clay in the hands of the potter" (Jer. xviii. 6) ; till there be no resisting material throughout the whole conscious range of our spiritual perceptions. "Should it be according to *thy* mind?" (Job. xxxiv. 33)—was once asked. Might not this be to thy ruin ? From the many wills spring all the miseries of earth. The one will forms the happiness of heaven. Let thy God, then, mould thy will, and he will frame thy happiness. Be thankful that it should be thwarted, even when it pleads most vehemently for indulgence. And shrink not from that

---

* *Ecclesiastes.* By G. W. Mylne, 12mo. 1856.

process — painful though it be — that moulds it into conformity with the will of Omnipotent love.

16. *I communed with mine own heart, saying, Lo, I am come
to great estate, and have gotten more wisdom than all they
that have been before me in Jerusalem : yea, my heart had
great experience of wisdom and knowledge.* 17. *And I
gave my heart to know wisdom, and to know madness and
folly : I perceived that this also is vexation of spirit.* 18.
*For in much wisdom is much grief : and he that increaseth
knowledge increaseth sorrow.*

Wisdom was Solomon's first experiment in the pursuit of
rest. — The object seemed to promise good result. *He communed with his heart;* and brought to the investigation all
the advantage of *great estate,* large *wisdom and experience.*
But here he lost his path. He sought to know *wisdom* as
the *rest of man* — thus putting the gift in the place of the
Giver.   His range of inquiry reached to the opposite quarter
— *to know madness and folly,* as if the knowledge of con-
traries would clear his mind. But truly the cost of this
knowledge was frightful. — It was — as with our first parents
— the speculative knowledge of good, and the experimental
knowledge of evil — 'the pride and wantonness of knowledge,
because it looketh after high things that are above us, and
after hidden things, that are denied us.'* So far from
increasing his happiness, it only added a deeper stamp to his
decision. — *This also is vanity and vexation of spirit.* This
path of wandering could only issue in the sober certainty of
grief and sorrow, increasing at every step. The true rest of
man could never be found there. The soul that has wan-
dered from God will search heaven and earth in vain for rest.

* Bp. Reynolds *On the Passions and Faculties,* ch. xxxvii.

Yet we are no patrons of ignorance. Far be it from us to deny the highly valuable pleasures of *wisdom and knowledge*. But if we attempt their pursuit, as Solomon seems to have done, by making an idol of our gifts—putting God out of his Supremacy—we can only expect to add our testimony to their disappointment. The more we know, the more we shall be discomposed by the consciousness of ignorance. 'The covetousness of the understanding'*—the disappointing results of favourite theories—the cloud that hangs over the brightest path of enquiry—all this places us further from happiness than the fool. Admitting, therefore, the high value of mere intellectual pleasures, their unsatisfying results are *grief and sorrow.*†

What a contrast is the substance and reality of the Gospel! "The way of life is above to the wise" (Prov. xv. 24)—higher than the highest pinnacle of this world's glory.—On the other hand, who can read the gloomy pathway into eternity of one of the most amiable of philsophers without sorrowful conviction? We might point to Sir

---

* Dr. South's Sermon on the Text.

† 'Whosoever gets much *wisdom*, shall be sure to get much *sorrow* to boot ; since the more he knows, the more cause of *grief* shall he find ; for both he shall see more that he cannot know, and in that which he doth know he shall perceive so much vanity, that shall pierce and humble his soul.'—Bp. HALL. 'If the proper happiness of man consisteth in *knowledge*, considered as a treasure, men who are possessed of the largest share would have an ill time of it ; as they would be infinitely more sensible of their poverty in this respect. Thus he who *increaseth knowledge* would eminently *increase sorrow*. Men of deep research and curious enquiry should just be put in mind not to mistake what they are doing. If their discoveries serve the cause of virtue and religion in the way of proof, motive to practice, or assistance in it ; or if they tend to render life less unhappy, and promote its satisfactions, then they are most usefully employed. But bringing things to light alone and of itself is no manner of use any otherwise than as an entertainment or diversion.'—Bp. Butler's *Sermon upon the Ignorance of Man.*

Humphry Davy as one of the most accomplished men of
his day. His science was the medium of the most important usefulness. He had his full cup of worldly honour
and respect. And yet one of the later entries in his journal
tells us — 'Very miserable.' The remedy for his misery he
did not seek from some new and untried path of science.
'I envy' — said he — 'no quality of mind or intellect in
others — not genius, power, wit, or fancy. But if I could
choose that which would be most delightful, and I believe,
most useful to me, I should prefer a firm religious belief to
every other blessing; for it makes life a discipline of goodness, creates new hopes, when all earthly hopes vanish, and
throws over the decay, the destruction of existence, the most
gorgeous of all lights; calling up the most delightful visions,
where the sensual and the sceptic view only gloom, decay,
and annihilation.'*

Hard indeed is it for the philosopher to " receive the kingdom of God" — in the only way in which it can be received
— "as a little child." (Mark, x. 15.) Here will he find the
only remedy for his *grief and sorrow*. Intelligence in all the
branches of natural science gives no help to a right understanding of the Gospel. It is a science of itself — peculiar to
itself, and therefore only to be rightly understood through its
own organ — *Divine Teaching*. Barren indeed is mere theoretical knowledge. Correct views without practical influence
are only the surface of knowledge — the lifeless mass. It is not
knowledge in itself — but knowledge under Divine Teaching —
that works the main end. He is the wise man — and happy in
his wisdom, who is thus " wise unto salvation." If Solomon
with his mighty grasp of intellect could find no rest in earthly
wisdom, who else can expect it? Let the glowing stimulus
be given to the pursuit of 'that heavenly and never-perishing

* *The Last Days of a Philosopher*, quoted by Hamilton,
Lecture v.

wisdom, which pours through the mind with singular
delight, and, as a kind of honey, affects all its legitimate
exercises with its own sweetness.'* This wisdom stands out
in striking contrast to every "vain show." It is "life
eternal" (John, xvii. 3),—the source—not of *grief and sorrow*
—but of everlasting joy: 'To be wise without Christ is plain
folly.'† Alas! for that *knowledge* that shews the vanity, not
the rest. A mercy indeed is it to be turned away from the
empty shadow, and to lay hold of the solid substance.
Here is unwavering repose. All is pure and heavenly. All
is freely offered. Once having tasted the blessing—can we
ever weary in the wondering delight?

"With thee is the fountain of life, in thy light shall we
see light." (Ps. xxxvi. 9.)

CHAPTER II.

1. *I said in mine heart, Go to now; I will prove thee with
mirth, therefore enjoy pleasure: and, behold, this also is
vanity. 2. I said of laughter, It is mad: and of mirth,
What doeth it?*

SOLOMON was disappointed in the thorny path of *wisdom and
knowledge*. *Grief and sorrow*—not happiness and rest—
were the harvest of the soil. 'God had never sown man's
happiness here. How then shall we there reap it?'‡ Yet
not disheartened by the failure, he will try a new path.
The man of *wisdom* turns himself into a man of *pleasure*.
Laughter and mirth promise a brighter sky. In a fever of

---

* Thos. Cartwright *On Ecclesiastes*, 4to. 1604.
† Serran.   ‡ Cotton.

excitement he urges on *his heart*, as if it were too sluggish for the plunge. *' Go to now, I will prove thee with mirth. Enjoy thy pleasure.   Take thy fill of it.'*

Contrast his godly father, stirring up *his heart*—every exercise and faculty of his soul—to godly *mirth*—" wakening up his glory—psaltery and harp"—to sing the high praises of his God. (Ps. lvii. 7–11; ciii. 1, 2.)   This was indeed to *enjoy pleasure*, such as his son in the idle *mirth* of vanity could never know.   A great downward step indeed was it from the ways of God, or even from the pleasures of enlarged intellect, to the froth of an empty mind—to the brutal pleasures of sense!   A fearful experiment!   One pleasure might bring a thousand woes.

Surely he must have been at this time a wanderer.   For had he not commended to others the " pleasantness and peace of wisdom's ways?" (Prov. iii. 13–18.)   And now was he looking to sensual mirth as the only substantial good?   This wisest of men was here in a very strange atmosphere, surrounded by those ' choice spirits, as they counted and called themselves, who fancied the secret of happiness to lie in banishing all reflection, in *laughing* at preciseness and melancholy, and drowning care in merriment and revelry.'*   Must we not again give judgment?—*Behold, this is also vanity!*   For " in the midst of *laughter* the heart is sorrowful, and the end of *that mirth* is heaviness." (Prov. xiv. 13.   Comp. Isa. l. 11.) *' Laughter'*—as Bp. Hall reminds us—' is only an argument of a *mad* distemper of the mind.   *Mirth* is a vain and unprofitable passion, not fit for a wise man's entertainment.'†   We

---

* Wardlaw *in loco*. See also Scott, and specially Henry's note in his own style.

† *Hard Places*. See Mr. Wilberforce's interesting record of his early conviction of religion—' Often, while in the full enjoyment of all that this world could bestow, my conscience told me, that in the true sense of the word I was not a Christian.   I *laughed*.   I sang.

ask, therefore, of all the masters of mirth the emphatic question—'*What doeth it?* What is it all worth? Where is to be found one atom of satisfactory result? What a deceitful lie it proves at the last!' The crumbs of the Gospel are infinitely richer than the dainties of the world. But this is man's common delusion—to suppose that happiness is the creature of circumstances. If, therefore, he is disappointed in one course, he will seek it in another. Little does the self-deluded victim, know that he carries the principle of his misery in his own bosom. Far, indeed, is he from his object. What he wishes is one thing. What he really needs is another.

Now take the scene as it lies before us in its widest extent, comprising "*all that is in the world*" in its three divisions—"the lust of the flesh, the lust of the eye, and the pride of life" (1 John, ii. 16). And what are all its crowded assemblies—its luxurious pleasures—all the outward show of person, dress, and equipage—the time and care spent on their preparation—the anxiety attending them—the weariness and frequent disappointment following them? Must we not give our verdict—*This also is vanity?*

Not that this forms the whole, or even the chief part of the evil. The citadel is in the heart. The main power—the strength of the principle—lies deep within. It is the apostacy of the heart from God—the cleaving of the heart to the things of time and sense. Ah! Christian professor, —this may consist with a very sober exterior, or even with total indifference to outward show. But look well to it. See whether in this more quiet atmosphere there be not the same revolt from Him, who claims thy first love—who must

I was apparently gay and happy. But the thought would steal across me—'What *madness* is all this! to continue easy in a state, in which a sudden call out of the world would consign me to ever-lasting misery, and that when eternal happiness is within my grasp!"—*Life,* i. 88.

be sought as Everything to thee—as thine only satisfying rest. When wilt thou ever regret this thy choice? Nor is this evil confined to the wealthy in the community. The coarser *mirth* and loud gatherings of the people are no less depraved. Sober, enlightened reason could not endure the degraded level. Every successive change in this world of pleasure brings up the question afresh—*What doeth it?* Unalloyed happiness—the object of pursuit—was still beyond grasp.

Yet the Christian is not to be an anchorite. He must guard against 'a stern chubbishness' *—a cold forbidding gloom. He must shew 'that elasticity of mind and buoyancy of spirit, that even temper and sunshine disposition, that cheers the man himself, and all that know him.'† This glow *in a Christian atmosphere* is the token of a good conscience. Thus let the world see happiness to be a felt reality—an expectation abundantly fulfilled—a principle heightening and enlarging to all eternity. We need not go to the world for happiness. Its resources have their end. Here is a principle, that has all the elements of true joy in itself—" a well of water springing up into everlasting life." (John, iv. 14.) Every fascinated child of pleasure is an object of compassion. Bright without—but how dark and hollow within! It is a light tread, but it is the path of death. The exterior may " be blameless." But there is a revolt from holy and humbling truth—a stirring up of the native enmity with fearful intensity.‡ True joy has its own character. It is—as the heathen philosopher teaches—'a serious thing.'§ It centres in truth. It is the natural ebullition of redeemed souls, singing (Ps. cxxvi. 1, 2) on their way Zionward, and tuning their hearts for the everlasting song. (Isa. xxxv. 10.) Here we can answer the question—*What doeth it?* Let the trial prove.

---

* Serran.   † Mylne.   ‡ See Philip. iii. 6.

§ Seneca, quoted by Bp. Reynolds.   See *Treatise on the Passions and Faculties of the Soul*, chap. xix.

"I sat under his shadow with great delight, and his fruit was sweet to my taste." (Cant. ii. 3.)

3. *I sought in mine heart to give myself unto wine, yet acquainting mine heart with wisdom; and to lay hold on folly, till I might see what was that good thing for the sons of men, which they should do under the heaven all the days of their life.*

Solomon here records a third most extraordinary experiment, to discover the object of his search — Where shall it be found? *Wisdom* saith, "It is not in me." Pleasure, with the same impressive emphasis, saith, "It is not in me."* If neither hath it singly, let them both be tried together — the intellectual with the sensual pleasure — the grosser with the more refined. His purpose was to *give himself to wine, yet acquainting his heart with wisdom.* Was not this venturing on the brink of the precipice — a wilful indulgence of "the lust of the flesh?" But if we are not seeking heavenly pleasures, we shall soon be hankering after those that are shadowy and delusive. While they last, indeed, they are nothing for the great ends of soothing sorrow, satisfying want, quieting conscience. And when they have passed away —they are—as Bp. Taylor solemnly warns us—'nowhere but in God's Book, deposited in the conscience, and sealed up against the day of dreadful account.' † To see the man of God here! Turn we back again to the glorious day, when he stood with outstretched hands as the chief minister of his people in his own consecrated temple. Had it been now demolished—not one stone left upon another—the calamity would have been as nothing when compared with the present darkness and desolation of the spiritual temple.

* See Job, xxviii. 14.
† *Sermons on The Apples of Sodom.*

(Comp. 1 Kings, viii. 22, with xi. 1–8.) How desperate is
the wickedness of the heart of man — even of regenerate
man! The sparks of unmortified corruption — long kept
under — not wholly extinct—may burst out into a flame, even
after apparent maturity of godliness. Surely to gray hairs
must we "work out our salvation with fear and trembling"
(Philip. ii. 12); adoring the mercy and forbearance of God,
that follows his backsliding child even in his foulest course,
and brings him back.

We cannot suppose that Solomon sympathized in taste
with the carousals of *wine.* Indeed he declares that he did
it 'not viciously, but to make an experiment.'* But could
he forget the danger, lest true godliness should flow out,
and waste away in the experiment? Every indulgence
would tend to fix the heart to a most ruinous choice. That
wisdom, with which his heart was acquainted, could not give
a right balance in such a mass of defilement. Much less
could he expect to *find* here *that good thing for the sons of
men,* while he was "making provision for the flesh, to fulfil
the lusts thereof." (Rom. xiii. 14.)

Elsewhere he directs a moderate use of *wine.* (Chap.
ix. 9. Prov. xxxi. 6, 7. Comp. Ps. civ. 15.) But though
his *wisdom* might have in some degree kept him master of
his pleasures, and restrained him from foul excess (which is
not numbered among his sins); yet to *give himself to wine*
was transgressing the bounds of godly liberty. Could he
hope to maintain communion with God, in the merriment
of the convivial board? Was it not quickening those
members of the earth, "which we are bound to mortify?"
(Col. iii. 5.) How could he fix his own bounds of restraint?
"Wine is a mocker." (Prov. xx. 1.) Who under the power

* Bp. Reynolds. Henry seems to admit this excuse—'He went
over into the enemies' country, not as a deserter, but a spy, to discover the nakedness of the land.'

of this cheat could venture to say—"Thus far will I go, and no further?" There is indeed a great subtilty of delusion in the effort *to lay hold on folly,* as an experiment for the purpose of exposure. Self-discipline and self-distrust are the laws of self-preservation. The real *good* of which we are in search, is to be found in a higher and holier clime. Of one ray of reconciliation and love will we not say— "Thou hast put gladness in my heart, more than in the time that their *wine* increased?" (Ps. iv. 6, 7.)

These pleasures must surely have "taken away the" wise man's "heart,"* when he attempted to link them with holy communion with his God. The purity of a godly taste can only be maintained in a close and heavenly walk. When the heart is right, this will be the life, which our soul loves, and in which alone we shall desire to live.—'To read, to think, to love, to hope, to pray—these are the things that make men happy.'†

4. *I made me great works; I builded me houses; I planted me vineyards :* 5. *I made me gardens and orchards; and I planted trees in them of all kinds of fruit :* 6. *I made me pools of water, to water therewith the wood that bringeth forth trees :* 7. *I got me servants and maidens, and had servants born in my house; also I had great possessions of great and small cattle above all that were in Jerusalem before me :* 8. *I gathered me also silver and gold, and the peculiar treasure of kings and of the provinces : I gat me men singers and women singers, and the delights of the sons of men, as musical instruments, and that of all sorts.* 9. *So I was great, and increased more than all that were before me in Jerusalem : also my wisdom remained with*

* See Hos. iv. 11.

† Ruskin's *Modern Painters,* vol. iii. 310.

me. 10. *And whatsoever mine eyes desired I kept not from them; I withheld not my heart from any joy ; for my heart rejoiced in all my labour : and this was my portion of all my labour.* 11. *Then I looked on all the works that my hands had wrought, and on the labour that I had laboured to do : and, behold, all was vanity and vexation of spirit, and there was no profit under the sun.*

Perhaps the whole course of this world's experience does not furnish a more vivid picture of the unsatisfactory nature of earthly greatness. No element of rest or pleasure seems to be wanting. And yet the result is barren indeed. It is the converse of the Christian. He seems to be "possessing all things;" yet in reality it is—"having nothing." (Comp. 2 Cor. vi. 10.) God employed Solomon not only to shew the picture, but to shew it—as we have before hinted—from his own experience. He therefore poured in upon him the full confluence of earthly happiness, that he might see, and prove, and tell its utter insufficiency for rest. Here is therefore, 'not only that general map of the world, that all things are vanity and vexation of spirit, but many other more particular cards.'* The many broken cisterns that he had tried—the wormwood that he had tasted from so many streams of earthly enjoyment—all set forth in detail a vivid picture fraught with instruction.

Solomon's metropolis must have been the wonder of the world. *He made himself great works. His houses,* from their description, must have been wonderful buildings, both as to art and magnificence†—framed, probably, like the buildings

---

* Lord Bacon's *Advancement of Learning*, B. II. xxiii. 41.

† 1 Kings, vii. 1–13 ; ix. 15–17, 19. The splendid remains of art, which are still found in the countries under his rule, have been ascribed to him. But the Grecian style of architecture seems to point to a much later date. 'The house that he built was one of

of Babylon, for state or for pleasure. (Dan. iv. 28-30.)   His
vineyards, orchards, and gardens, were filled with trees (Cant.
viii. 11 ; vi. 2 ; iv. 13), pools of water, with some mechanical
contrivance for conveying it. (Comp. 2 Kings, xviii. 17 ; xx.
20.)   His retinue of *servants,* no less than his house, commanded the Queen of Sheba's highest admiration. (1 Kings,
x. 5-8.)   His extensive *herds and flocks* (Ib. iv. 23, 26, 28)
were beyond what had heretofore been known.   Immense
treasures of silver and gold—all that was rare and precious
—flowed in from all quarters. (Ib. ix. 26-28 ; x. 10, 14,
15, 25, 27, 28.)   Vocal and instrumental music ministered
to his indulgence. (Comp. 2 Sam. xix. 35 ; 2 Chron. xxxv.
25.)   His intellectual *wisdom remained with him* (alas ! his
spiritual wisdom had departed), to give the full scope to
his comprehensive mind.   Added to this — he had the most
free and unabated enjoyment of his resources.   There was
little of outward tumult to disturb. (1 Kings, iv. 25.) — All
therefore that royal treasures could procure, largeness of
heart desire, vast wisdom contrive—this *was the portion of
his labour — the rejoicing of his heart.*

And yet, when he *looked back on all his works which he
had wrought, and the labour which he had laboured,* it seemed
only as the chasing of shadows.   The pleasure faded with
the novelty.   The appetite was palled without satisfaction.
The sad vacuity still remained—a wearisome *vexation,* as if
'he had been abundantly filled with the wind,' * or "feeding
upon ashes." (Isa. xliv. 20.)   Here, then, is the man, who
drank the fullest cup of earth's best joy—who ' set nature
on the rack to confess its uttermost strength for the delight-

the sights that overwhelmed the Queen of Sheba with astonishment.'
(Ib. x. 4.)   Mr. Fergusson ably contends for the analogy of Solomon's
houses to the Assyrian palaces.—*Nineveh and Persepolis Restored,*
Chapter on Jerusalem, pp. 225, &c.   See also Layard's *Nineveh and
Babylon,* pp. 642-650.

* Beza *in loco.*

ing and satisfying of man.'* What the result is, hear from
his own mouth—*vanity and vexation.* 'To so small a purpose is it'—as Lord Bacon remarks—'to have an erected
face towards heaven, and a perpetual grovelling spirit upon
earth, eating dust, as doth the serpent.'† Is not, then, the
lowest condition in godliness far happier and far safer than
the highest ground of earthly prosperity? And yet so strong
is the spell of delusion, that Solomon's experiment continues
to be tried with the same unvarying result—*There is no
profit under the sun.* 'The man wakes from his dream, and
finds that he possesses not an atom of the rich possessions he
had dreamed of.'‡ Take the lesson from one of this world's
brightest favourites: 'I shall never'—wrote Sir Walter Scott
at the last—'see the threescore and ten, and shall be summed
up at a discount. No help for it, and no matter either.'§
In so dark a cloud set one of the finest suns of human intellect!

Unrestrained desire was the source of this vanity and vexa-
tion. He would *keep back from his eyes nothing that they desired.*
How little was this in the spirit of his father's prayer—
" Turn away mine eyes from beholding vanity!"‖ Wisdom's

---

* Leighton's Sermon on Ps. cxix. 96.
† *Advancement of Learning,* ut supra.   ‡ Lorin.
§ Lockhart's *Life,* vol. ix. pp. 61, 62. 'We cannot wonder at
this dark passage, if the judgment given by one of our first writers
be correct in any degree. 'Nothing is more notable or sorrowful in
Scott's mind, than his incapacity of steady belief in anything. . . . .
He is educated a Presbyterian, and remains one, because he thinks
it is the most sensible thing he can do, if he is to live in Edinburgh.
But he thinks Romanism more picturesque, and profaneness more
gentlemanly—does not see that anything affects human life, but love,
courage, and destiny. Throughout all his work there is no evidence
of any purpose, but to wile away the hour. All his thoughts were,
in their outcome and end, less than nothing and vanity.'—Ruskin's
Modern Painters, vol. iii. pp. 270–272.

‖ Ps. cxix. 37. See the patriarch's wise resolve, Job, xxxi. 1.
Comp. Augustine's humbling and instructive exercises—'Suffer not

voice warns not to cast one hankering look toward the wilderness. Its unholy breath fades the freshness and purity of our
enjoyment. It is in the spiritual world that we realize things
in their true colour. 'The empire of the whole world' — said
the noble Luther— ' is but a crust to be thrown to a dog.'*
The highest honour in science forced from Henry Martyn the
confession at the moment of success —' I have grasped a
shadow!' †

Mistake not, then, the glare of this world's glory for
solid happiness. God would have us *rejoice in our labour* —
enjoy our earthly blessings, but not rest in them—" Rejoice,
as though we rejoiced not." ‡   A momentary pleasure is all
that can be looked for. Let earth be the cistern only, not
the fountain.   Let its best blessings be loved after him — for
him — as the sunbeam of his love. Let nothing of earth be
our rest — God never intended so poor a portion for his redeemed ones. Our rest is built upon unchangeable promises.
Meanwhile the real joy is, when God is the centre, and the
Saviour (as one of the German Reformers beautifully expresses it) is to us ' the treasure and the key of all the good
things of God.' §   What were the pleasures of Solomon's
earthly Paradise, compared with the unspeakable delight of
" eating of the tree of life, which is in the midst of the Paradise of God!" (Rev. ii. 7.)

12. *And I turned myself to behold wisdom, and madness, and
    folly: for what can the man do that cometh after the King?
    even that which hath been already done.* 13. *Then I saw
    that wisdom excelleth folly, as far as light excelleth dark-*

these to hold possession of my soul. Let my God rather be Lord of
it, who made all these. Very good they be indeed ; yet is he very
good, not they.'— *Confess.* Book x. c. 34.

* Quoted by Cecil.   † *Life*, Part 1.
‡ See 1 Cor. vii. 29–31.   § Brentius *in loco.* 12mo. 1528.

ness. 14. *The wise man's eyes are in his head; but the fool walketh in darkness: and I myself perceived also that one event happeneth to them all.* 15. *Then said I in my heart, As it happeneth to the fool, so it happeneth even to me; and why was I then more wise? Then I said in my heart, that this also is vanity.*

Solomon had tried *wisdom and folly* — both separately and together — as independent sources of happiness. He had pronounced judgment upon them as *vanity and vexation.* But might he not have passed over some matters of weight in the decision? A second review might discover some error. He *turns himself,* therefore, as he had done before (chap. i. 17), to behold the two things, and compare together his contrary experiments of *wisdom and folly.* But here is no retractation — no modifying of his judgment. Though it was only the judgment of one man; yet *who could come after the King* — with such a vast mind and treasure? The trial would only be *what had been already done.* The search of happiness in anything beside God must be disappointment.

Yet though *wisdom,* as a source of rest, bears the stamp of *vanity,* we must not underrate its relative value. It is the gift of God, opening to us channels of rich pleasure and important usefulness to our fellow-creatures. It *excelleth folly, as far as light excelleth darkness. The wise man's eyes are in his head* — looking as from a watch-tower — ready for instant use — discovering distant or unexpected trial. Thus when the trial comes — 'Do not I know who hath appointed it? Shall not I commune with him about it? Cannot he who sent it, stay me under it?' Here, Christian, is your straight, clear, onward course. If sometimes "faint," always "pursuing" (Judg. viii. 4), going through darkness and light — storm and sunshine — one object in view — knowing that there is no progress without unlimited confidence, and that nothing can be the way of duty, that is contrary to any other known duty.

Now turn our eyes *to the fool**—*walking in darkness* (be it remembered—*responsible darkness*). It is as if his eyes—instead of being *in his head*—were at his back. He blunders on as if he were blind, or in the dark; his steps going backward, running in his own folly. ' He wants the lantern of God's Word and Spirit to direct him into a right path.'† Whatever be his earthly wisdom, an angel would say of such a man—" There goes a poor blind creature, groping his way to hell." ‡

But a melancholy sight it is—to see natural light break-ing in upon the mind, without one ray of spiritual light dawning upon the heart! the want of reality—of Divine impression—laborious trifling in the letter of Scripture—knowing nothing of His teaching, whom Augustine beauti-fully designates as the ' inner master of the inner man—teaching in the school of the breast.' ‖

But wide as is the difference between the *wise man and the fool,* on some points they are one. Solomon himself was on the same level with his meanest pauper. Both were sub-ject to the same vicissitudes of Providence.¶ The same last event laid them low together. ' *Why was I then more wise?* What is the use of my wisdom, if at the last it brings me to no higher level than *the fool?*' Here surely *the wise man* becomes *the fool*—disputing the ways of God—looking for some elevation above his fellow-creatures. Such is the depth of selfishness and depravity yet to be purged out! Only another picture! *This is also vanity.* O my God! how

---

* See the same contrast, c. x. 2.

† *A Familiar Commentarie on Ecclesiastes,* by Thomas Grainger, 4to. 1621.

‡ Cecil's *Original Thoughts,* p. 205.

‖ See his *Confessions,* B. IX. c. 9.   ¶ See Chap. ix. 2.

does every view within bring fresh matter for self-loathing in thy sight! Where is the natural heart, without some niche to the chosen idol? Is the renewed heart gaining ground in the struggle—the hard and fierce struggle—with its deadly influence?

16. *For there is no remembrance of the wise more than of the fool for ever; seeing that which now is in the days to come shall all be forgotten. And how dieth the wise man? as the fool.* 17. *Therefore I hated life; because the work that is wrought under the sun is grievous unto me: for all is vanity and vexation of spirit.*

We have been before reminded how fleeting is the *remembrance* of names mighty in their generation.* The great actors, that fixed the eyes of their fellow-men, and kept the world awake—where are they? 'Time is a depth, that swallows up all things.'† The man of science hoped to secure—though not his body—yet his name from decay. But to the mass there is often *no remembrance of the wise more than the fool.* Every new generation raises up a new race of rivals for renown. But after a short-lived day, that which *now is, in the days to come shall all be forgotten.* Few, comparatively, survive the wreck of time. Such a phantom of life is posthumous fame.‡ Soon comes the levelling stroke—*How dieth the wise man? As the fool.* The grave

---

* See Chap. i. 11.   † Grainger.

‡ 'Posthumous reputation!' said the venerable Scott on his death-bed (who had as strong a claim to it as most of his fellow-men), 'the veriest bubble, with which the devil ever deluded a wretched mortal! But *posthumous usefulness*, in that there is indeed something. That was what Moses desired, and Joshua, and David, and the Prophets—the Apostles also—and most of all, our Lord Jesus Christ.'

is the "long home" (chap. xii. 4) for both till the resurrection morn.

But take another contrast of the two classes—how different the issue! For the one is secured "everlasting
remembrance;" the other is doomed to degraded oblivion.
(Ps. cxii. 6. Prov. x. 7.)—Does the *one die as the other?*
Darkness and light are not more different. Hear the wise
man's history of them both. "The wicked is driven away in
his wickedness: but the righteous hath hope in his death."
(Prov. xiv. 32.) 'The one is dead, even while he is alive.
The other lives even in death.'*

Yet this equalizing level was a source of deep exercise to
the Preacher. Estranged as he now was from God, fretfulness stirred up—if not an hatred†— yet a disgust and weariness of life. All was now become a *grievous* vanity. To die
and to be forgotten *as the fool*—to the man of wisdom—this
seems living to no purpose. He would almost as soon be
blotted out of life, as be disappointed of his airy vision—an
enduring name. When self is thus the centre of happiness
—the great end of life—what a treasure of vanity do we lay
in store for ourselves! Would it not have been better for
Solomon—instead of being weary of his life, ' rather to have
been weary of his sin in seeking happiness in earthly things?' ‡
Again—the contrast forces itself upon us—Solomon once
consecrating his high wisdom to the glory of God—now alien-
ating it from the great object, and all his life *vanity and
vexation of spirit!*

This *disrelish of life* belongs both to the ungodly and the

* Bp. Reynolds.

† The word used here and in the next verse means—not only
to *hate* in the literal sense of the term, but to have little regard for
—to be indifferent to. (Gen. xxix. 30, 31.) TAYLOR's *Hebrew Concordance.* Geier translates it — ' I have loved less. I have not cared
for—I have not made of great account.'

‡ Cotton.

godly, though on very different grounds.* '*I hate life*'—
wrote Voltaire to his friend—'and yet I am afraid to die.'
Can we wonder? The infidel's bosom, so full of disappointed
ambition—tormenting conscience—a dark eternity! Hell
seemed to have begun on earth. Thus it is with the mass of
the world—burdened with present evils—no sunbeam in the
prospect—either not believing the life beyond—or with no
hope of attaining it.† And even in minds cast in a better
mould, the revolt still remains in fretfulness and impatience.‡
Nothing can set things right, or keep them so, but the clear
confidence that God's will is our happiness, and that all is
ordered in the school of discipline, so as to "work together
for our good." (Rom. viii. 28.) 'Thou bruisest me, O Lord'
—said the dying Calvin, in a moment of intense suffering—
'but it amply sufficeth me, that it is thy hand.'§ 'My
affliction'—said another saint at the same crisis—'is but
the smiting of his merciful hand, and therefore it is an ointment savouring of heaven.' ‖

This tædium of life in a Christian habit is in a heavenly
mould. It is the weariness of the man of God in the conflict.
Happy though he be, "he groans, being burdened"—a

---

* Lavater, *in Ecclesiasten.* Tigurini, 12mo. 1584.

† See also Lord Chesterfield's Letter, pp. 4, 5. F. Perthes gives an
affecting account of a visit to his friend Niebuhr (see his *Life and
Letters,* i. 350) shortly before his death. 'The purer his heart—the
deeper his sensibilities—the more he feels the want of some firm
support for his soul. He fights with uncertainty, and quarrels with
life. He said to me, *I am weary of life;* only the children bind
me to it. He repeatedly expressed the bitterest contempt for mankind. And, in short, the spiritual condition of this remarkable man
cuts me to the heart, and his outpourings alternately elevated and
horrified me.'—*Memoirs of Frederick Perthes,* ii. 123.

‡ *Job,* iii. 1. *Elijah,* 1 Kings, xix. 4. *Jeremiah,* xx. 14, 15.
Jonah, iv. 3.

§ Scott's Contin. of Milner; *Life of Calvin,* p. 474.

‖ *Life of Rev. J. Macdonald,* Missionary at Calcutta.

tempting enemy, a corrupt heart—a disappointing world—
all quicken the "desire to depart, and to be with Christ, which
is very far better." (Philip. i. 23, Gr.) Oh! let not the cry
be dormant or feeble—' Come, Lord Jesus, come quickly.'
(Rev. xxii. 20.)

18. *Yea, I hated all my labour which I had taken under the
sun: because I should leave it unto the man that shall be
after me.*   19. *And who knoweth whether he shall be a wise
man or a fool? yet shall he have rule over all my labour
wherein I have laboured, and wherein I have shewed myself wise under the sun.   This is also vanity.*   20. *Therefore I went about to cause my heart to despair of all the
labour which I took under the sun.*   21. *For there is a man
whose labour is in wisdom, and in knowledge, and in equity;
yet to a man that hath not laboured therein shall he leave
it for his portion.   This also is vanity and a great evil.*
22. *For what hath man of all his labour, and of the vexation of his heart, wherein he hath laboured under the sun?*
23. *For all his days are sorrows, and his travail grief;
yea, his heart taketh not rest in the night.   This is also
vanity.*

This passage presents another aspect of *vanity*, and to the
wise man a *great grief*.   All his *great works* of wisdom and
labour, which had ministered to him a temporary satisfaction,
after a while became to him objects of disgust.   They must
be left, and to whom he could not tell.   David had no such
anxieties.   His heart had not been set upon his treasures,
and therefore it was no sacrifice to him to part with them.
Besides, he well knew the consecrated use to which his wise son
would apply them. (1 Chron. xxviii. 11–21; xxix. 1–22.) But
Solomon probably had his forebodings of *the man who should
come after him*.   And the history of the son fully justified

the anxious question—*Who knoweth whether he shall be a wise man or a fool?* (Ps. xlix. 10. Comp. xxxix. 6.) So deeply did this trial touch the Preacher, that he again adverts to it. Must he—after a life of *labour in wisdom, knowledge, and equity*—must he after all become a drudge to his successor, of whom he knows nothing with any certainty? What advantage hath he of all his labour?* He heaps up his words one upon another (*labour, sorrow, grief, travail*), to describe more emphatically the painfulness of his exercise.

And yet this *great evil* may have been overruled for Solomon's good. His heart had clung to the world, and it required sharp discipline to break it away. 'Often had he bored and sunk into the earth for some rich mine of satisfaction.'† But repeated failures *caused his heart to despair.* And might not this restlessness of earthly rest have been his Father's restoring discipline? This is the canker on the supreme pursuit of this world's portion. We may *possess* the creature; but never shall we enjoy it, till God is on the throne above it. (Ps. lxxiii. 25.) There will be no cleaving to God, till the vanity of all, in comparison with him, has been experimentally acknowledged. O my God! may I feel the vanity of everything, that turns away my heart from thee! We must have an holdfast somewhere; and we sought it in the creature, because we knew not where else to look for it. But when we have once gained an everlasting footing on an unchangeable covenant—better promises—higher privileges—richer prospects, fix our hearts, and " give us peace: not as the world giveth." (John, xiv. 27.)

The special trial, however, to which Solomon here alludes, presses heavily upon many a Christian heart. The fruits of our labour—*in wisdom and knowledge*—or in providential gifts—will they descend from us into worthy or unworthy hands? *to a wise man or a fool?* will they be devoted to the

---

* See Chap. i. 3; iii. 9.   † Henry.

Church, or be desecrated to the world ? Shall we be able to perpetuate a good name in godly, well-doing children, and to commit our trust into their hands with peaceful confidence ? How does this anxious exercise urge upon us the obligation of training our children for God ! Hence a lively glow to our last act of parental faith. If there be a cloud upon our setting sun, behind that cloud will be "a sun that goeth down no more"—the display of eternal love and faithfulness.

If this be a sore "trial of faith" to the Christian, what is the threatened chastisement to the ungodly ! (v. 26. Deut. xxviii. 30–33.) Without a refuge—without covenant promises—without sustaining support ! All his labour barren ! All his days—not sorrowful only, but actual *sorrow*—the very mass of *sorrow and grief*—a mind racked with care. Even *night* brings no rest. 'See what fools they are, that make themselves drudges to the world, and do not make God their rest'*—*all is vanity*. Who will not listen to the pleading voice of the Saviour—contrasting this field of fruitless disappointment with his own offer of solid peace and satisfaction ? " Wherefore spend ye your money for that which is not bread, and your labour for that which satisfieth not ? Hearken diligently unto me, and eat ye that which is good, and let your soul delight itself in fatness." (Isa. lv. 2.) Welcome every sinner, that feels his need of this precious remedy !

24. *There is nothing better for a man, than that he should eat and drink, and that he should make his soul enjoy good in his labour. This also I saw, that it was from the hand of God. 25. For who can eat, or who else can hasten hereunto, more than I ? 26. For God giveth to a*

* Henry.

man that is good in his sight wisdom, and knowledge, and joy : but to the sinner he giveth travail, to gather and to heap up, that he may give to him that is good before God. This also is vanity and vexation of spirit.

The surface view of this passage might seem to savour of the rule—"Let us eat and drink, for to-morrow we die." (1 Cor. xv. 32. Comp. Luke, xii. 19.)   But did Solomon really mean, that *there was nothing better for a man*—for a sinner—with an immortal soul—with an eternal stake at issue—*nothing better for him* than sensual indulgence ?   Far from it !   The case before us determines and limits his true meaning.   Solomon is not here 'speaking of the Supreme good, but of that greatest good, which may be had from earthly things.'*   A man is brooding over his disappointments.   Let him take a brighter, and a more thankful view and enjoyment of his mercies. (1 Tim. vi. 17. Comp. iv. 3–5 ; Deut. xvi. 11.)   Let him give diligence to prove his character—*good before God;* and then, in the confidence of the Divine favour, let him rejoice in his temporal blessings.   This pleasure of *eating and drinking* is totally distinct from the mere animal appetite.   It recognizes the Christian principle—"Whether ye *eat or drink*—do all to the glory of God." †   "The world"—with all its legitimate

* Desvoeux's *Dissertation on Ecclesiastes,* p. 22.
† 1 Cor. x. 31. 'This,' as Geier remarks, 'is Christian—not Epicurean doctrine.' Pascal's asceticism belonged to a very different school, to a religion of superstition and self-righteousness. His sister—Mrs. Perier—informs us, 'that he was on a continual war against his senses, and constantly denied them everything that they could find pleasure in. When necessity forced him to do anything, from which he might have received some delight, he used a wonderful art to withdraw his mind from it, lest he should take any share of pleasure.'—*Life of M. Pascal,* p. 26. Amsterdam, 1711. Much more in accordance with the Gospel was the spirit and experience

enjoyments—is the Christian's portion. (1 Cor. iii. 22.)—
None beside have right to them.   And he only with this
reserve—"using the world, as not abusing it." (Ib. vii. 31.)
—making its pleasures subordinate—not primary.   For ill
does it become us to give our first joy to an earthly feast, with
the bright prospect before us—"of eating and drinking with
our Lord in his kingdom." (Luke, xxii. 28–30.)

We might ask also—Whence this present enjoyment?
Is it not reached out to us *from the hand of God*—that most
loving Father, whose blessing puts love into all our outward
mercies ?   Can we think anything ill, that comes from this
source ?   Here we receive—not only the good things themselves, but the power to make a right use of them. *The
Preacher* himself could speak with a deep-toned experience.
—*For who can eat, or who haste hereunto, more than he?*
'What power could others have to enjoy them, when he
could not ?'*   And yet in the path of wandering how
barren—yea—how poisonous was the sum total !   "The
pleasant plants were planted, and set with strange slips;
and the harvest was a heap in the day of grief and of
desperate sorrow." (Isa. xvii. 11.)

This seems to be the Divine dispensation.   Good and
evil are portioned out according to character.   Where the
stamp—*Good in his sight*—is broadly marked, gifts and
grace flow out abundantly.   *Wisdom and knowledge* brighten
the path heavenward.   *Joy* gladdens the heart.   Common
mercies are sealed with covenant love.   Two words suffice to
describe the man of God's present happiness—"Godliness

---

of an eminent Christian—'I can truly say, that while I become daily
more convinced of the empty and unsubstantial nature of all earthly
possessions and enjoyments, I find all the innocent pleasures and
accommodation of life doubled and trebled to me.'—*Correspondence
of Rev. J. T. Nottidge.*   Seeleys.

* Bp. Reynolds.

with contentment." (1 Tim. vi. 6.) 'This only makes him master of the utmost comfort worldly things can afford.' *
Here is the substance of "the promise of the life that now is," and the earnest "of that which is to come." (1 Tim. iv. 8.) In this school of Divine instruction (Philip. iv. 11, 12, Gr.) the man of God is disciplined for heaven.

No such brightness beams upon *the sinner's* lot. Prudent and prosperous he may be. *But God giveth to him travail* as his portion—*to gather and heap up*—not to enjoy. The unfaithful steward is cast out. His privileges are transferred, for better improvement, *to him that is good before God.*†
Yes—he is the man accepted and honoured. To all beside the burden of the song is still the same—*This also is vanity and vexation of spirit.* "But to him that soweth right-eousness shall be a sure reward." ‡ (Prov. xi. 18.)

* Pemble's Works, folio, 1568. Solomon's *Retractation and Re-pentance. The Book of Ecclesiastes Explained.*

† Comp. Luke, xix. 20–26, with Esth. viii. 2; Prov. xiii. 22; xxviii. 8. 'It is the end of God's predestination, that all things befalling the wicked should redound to the glory of God's mercy towards the elect.'—Cotton. Perhaps, however, this is rather the exercise of his sovereignty, than his rule of universal government.

‡ Mr. Venn remarks in a letter to a friend—'On Sunday I preached with comfort and liberty on a text (shame be it to me !) I never spoke from before. It is one of those texts, which hath great complaints against Gospel ministers for neglecting it. You will find it in Eccles. ii. 26.' —*Life and Correspondence*—a precious biography. Many excellent ministers, though here falling under Mr. Venn's censure, stand clear before their Master in not shunning to declare all the counsel of God from other scriptures equally important. We give Mr. Venn's judgment, only as illustrating the various degrees of force and interest, with which the Spirit applies the Divine testimony.

CHAPTER III.

1. To everything there is a season, and a time to every purpose under the heaven.

Solomon is still pursuing his argument. Everything around us is in a perpetual change. What vanity, therefore, is it to seek solid happiness in so shifting a scene! As well might we find rest on the tossing ocean, as in a fluctuating world. There is no stable centre. It is "the wheel of nature." (Jam. iii. 6.) Sometimes one spoke is uppermost —sometimes the opposite. But all is constant motion.

And yet all these fluctuations are under absolute control. It is not a world of chance, or of fate. All events—even the most apparently casual—all those voluntary actions, that seem to be in our own power, with all their remotest contingencies—are overruled. *To everything there is a season* —a fixed time*—a predetermined purpose, on which—and not on man's care, thought, or effort—everything depends. Of this purpose we know nothing. But "known unto God are all his works from the beginning of the world." (Acts, xv. 18.) His eye has been upon everything, great and small, from all eternity. All is his unchangeable will. 'If God' —as Charnock writes—'could change his purpose, he would change his nature.' †

The perversity of sin has indeed disturbed the order of God's providence. But the work progresses. "The wheel in the middle of the wheel" (Ezek. i. 15–21) moves forward, and performs the appointed work. Caprice, short-sighted ignorance, and fickleness of purpose, distinguish the works of man. But here everything is worthy of God. "He hath

---

* See the word Ezra, x. 14 ; Esth. ix. 27, 31.
† *Discourse of the Immutability of God.*

abounded towards us in all wisdom and prudence." (Eph. i. 8.) It is 'the wise, and regular, and orderly administration of One, who sees the end from the beginning, and to whom there is no unanticipated contingency; and whose omniscient eye, in the midst of what appears to us inextricable confusion, has a thorough and intuitive perception of the endlessly diversified relations and tendencies of all events, and all their circumstances, discerning throughout the whole the perfection of harmony.'*

There is, then, *a season* for every work of God, and it comes in its *season.* Every work has its part to fulfil, and it does fulfil it. There was *a season* for Israel's deliverance from Egypt, and for the return from Babylon. Nothing could either force on, or keep back, the time. "*On the self-same day,*" the deliverance was at once developed and consummated. (Exod. xii. 41. Ezra, i. 1.) To have looked for it at any other time—whether sooner or later—would only have brought disappointment. There was "the fulness of time," the appointed *season*—the fittest time—for the Saviour's advent. (Gal. iv. 4.) An earlier period would have hindered many important *purposes,* or at least clouded their full development. The delay demonstrated the utter weakness of all other remedies. What could reason do with all her intellectual energy (1 Cor. i. 21), or the law with all its heavenly sanctions? (Rom. viii. 3.) Successive disappointments prepare the welcome to the one—alone—efficient remedy.

Rightly to time things is the property of wisdom. And here indeed "the Lord is a God of judgment," not only willing, but "waiting" the time, "that he may be gracious, and have mercy. Blessed"—truly "blessed are all they that wait for him." (Isa. xxx. 18.) Child of God! Remember it

* Wardlaw.

is thy Father's will, which hath appointed the *season,* and determined the *purpose.* All the wheels of Providence subserve the *purposes* of grace. Every dispensation is most fitly chosen, and issued under the commission to do for thee nothing but good. (Rom. viii. 28.) It is the will of the Omnipotent God of wisdom and love. His will is always the best reason, and without it there could be no reason at all. If thy "times are in his hands" (Ps. xxxi. 15), in what better hands could they be?

> Our times are in Thy hand ;
> O God, we wish them there ;
> Our life, our friends, our souls, we leave
> Entirely to Thy care.
>
> Our times are in Thy hand ;
> Why should we doubt or fear ?
> A Father's hand will never cause
> His child a needless tear.

Here is thy best happiness in a world of vanity and sorrow. The grace for the present moment is inexhaustible and always ready, and (so writes an excellent Christian) 'as exactly and exquisitely suited to your case and mine every instant, as if it had been appointed and contrived only for that single case, and that single moment.'*

2. *A time to be born, and a time to die; a time to plant, and a time to pluck up that which is planted.*

Solomon has laid down his general proposition. His illustrations he draws partly from the government of God, and partly as the result of man's own thought and purpose. Yet the most contingent are under the same law of controul as the most determinate.† He begins with the life of man—

* Nottidge's *Correspondence,* p. 65.
† See 1 Kings xxii. 24, with Isa. x. 5-7. Comp. Acts, iv. 27, 28.

his *time* of coming into the world, and his *time* of going out. Neither is in his own purpose or will. If it be the course of nature, it is the appointment of God. And could we see with the eyes of God, we should find these points to be the fittest *times* that Infinite Wisdom could ordain, connected with our present responsibilities and our hopes for eternity.

A time to be born! What a moment! A wondrous miracle is wrought! An heir of immortality brought into being, "fearfully and wonderfully made!" "The Spirit of the Lord hath made me, and the breath of the Almighty hath given me life." (Job, xxxiii. 4.) Can I forbear the question— ' Why was I born?' Shall I have cause to curse, or to bless, the day of my birth?—to say with Voltaire—'I wish I had never been born'—or with dying Halyburton—'Blessed be God that *ever I was born?*' Am I "working out" the great end of my birth with holy fear and diligence? (Philip. ii. 12.) What am I doing for God—for my soul—for my fellow-creatures? Let me remember that 'a capacity to do good, not only gives a title to it, but also makes the doing of it a duty.'* 'Let us then love life, and feel the value of it, that we may fill it with Christ.'† Oh! think of life—rising in the morning as one consecrated to God—making the world's work the Lord's work, because doing it to him, and feeling the littleness of everything that is not done for him. The men that we want are lively, warm, real men — men who have a daily contact with a personal living Saviour—men, whose religion is the element in which they breathe, the principle by which they work—men, who think of life, as the seed-time for eternity. What if we should come to the last stage—

---

* 'A sentence'—says Cotton Mather—'letters of gold were too mean to set out the preservers of it.'—*Essays to do Good.*

† Adolph. Monod's *Farewell Addresses,* II.

without even having learned how to live! with the great end
of life yet unaccomplished!

This stirring exhortation reminds us of another appointment—

A time to die. How came this time? Immortality was
our original being. (Gen. i. 26.) "By one man sin entered
into the world, and death by sin." (Rom. v. 12.) Ever
since "it is appointed unto men once to die." (Gen. iii. 19;
Heb. ix. 27.) None can evade the law. Voltaire could
not purchase a reprieve with half his fortune. Our "days
are determined; the number of our months is with God; he
hath appointed our bounds, that we cannot pass." (Job,
xiv. 5, 6.) The sentence of death may be revoked, but *the
time* predetermined is unchanged. (Isa. xxxviii. 1–5.) *The
time to die* can never be premature. God's time must be
right and best. God's work must be done; and man is immortal, till it be done.

If "our steps are ordered by the Lord" (Ps. xxxvii. 23),
much more is the last step of all—the step out of one world
into another—out of time into eternity. But if that step
were taken to-night, would it be a cheerful or a forced leaving
of all? Oh! to realize our solemn concern with this great
moment! Death the gate of heaven or of hell!—O my
soul!—of which to thee? "Man giveth up the ghost—
and"—awful question!—"where is he?" (Job, xiv. 10.)
We may leave all the circumstances of death to the Lord—
whether we shall die in pain or in peace. But our safety—
our readiness is everything. This readiness for death is the
energy of life. Then comes the sunbeam upon the valley—
'Is this dying?'—said one—'How have I dreaded as an
enemy this smiling friend!'* 'O world! produce a good

---

* Dr. Goodwin.

like this'—we may boldly say; and then it shall have our best affections. 'Till then—may we be only for the Lord!' *
The time to die! what is it but the "entrance *into* the Kingdom?" (2 Pet. i. 11.) There may be indeed a special *purpose.* It is the father caring for his delicate child—sending his messenger to bring him home, ere the threatening tempest rage. Thus is he "taken away from the evil to come. He enters into peace." His Father "rests in his love, and joys over him with singing." (Isa. lvii. 1, 2; Zeph. iii. 17.)

But not only the two great points, but every atom of life has its relative importance. *To everything there is a season and a purpose.* Within the boundary of life there is therefore *a time to plant, and a time to pluck up that which is planted.* *Planting* had been to Solomon a matter of primary interest. (Chap. ii. 4, 5.) But how soon might the season come to undo his own work, and *to pluck up that which was planted!* Often is a garden or estate laid out with *plantations*—whether for present pleasure or future advantage. Yet change of mind or of taste—withering winds—over-luxuriant growth—pecuniary necessity or profit—may induce the owner to *pluck up.* † Thus does the most ordinary course of life exhibit a changing world—therefore no centre of rest.

3. *A time to kill, and a time to heal; a time to break down, and a time to build up.*

The time to die is the immediate appointment of God. *The time to kill* is the act of man under permissive Provi-

---

* *Venn's Life.*

† Some excellent expositors give a figurative application, *e. g.* Jer. xviii. 7–9. But all the other instances are literal. This—as Lord Bacon says—'has more of the eagle.' But the other seems more natural as a part and parcel of common life.

dence.* The same Providence gives the *healing* blessing.
In both cases God claims his own prerogative — 'I kill, and
I make alive ; I wound, and I heal.'† Hezekiah's case displays the exercise of both these branches of prerogative. For
while the Disposer of life declared his purpose to *kill,* he
shewed, after the manner of men, his repenting mercy to *heal.*
(Isa. xxxviii ; also 2 Kings, v. 7.) Nor was there any fatalism
here. For when a word would have been enough, the healing means were appointed. (Ib. v. 21, with Matt. viii. 8.)
Thus the uncertainty of life shews that man's true earthly rest
is only to be found in practical dependence upon his God.

The same changeableness belongs to our estates as to our
persons. Solomon had been much occupied in *building up.*
(1 Kings, ix. 15–19.) But many of his buildings — even
the walls of Jerusalem — were destined to be *broken down.*
(2 Kings, xxv. 4–10.) Of only one *building* is our confidence
secure — the "house not made with hands, eternal in the
heavens." (2 Cor. v. 1.) To have an interest here — as
our home and our rest — this is brightness unclouded — unchangeable.

4. *A time to weep, and a time to laugh ; a time to mourn,*
and a time to dance.

These two instances are evidently a repetition with increasing emphasis. The *mourning* is the most poignant
weeping.‡ The *dancing* expresses not only the *laughter* of
the lips, but the exuberant excitement of the whole man.
These are God's *times.* Beware of changing them. It is a
fearful provocation to respond "joy and gladness" when
"the Lord God of Hosts calls to *weeping and mourning.*"
(Isa. xxii. 12–14.)

---

* See Exod. xxi. 13.
† Deut. xxxii. 39. Comp. 1 Sam. ii. 6 ; Hos. vi. 1.
‡ The word used, Zech. xii. 10–12.

Who has not found the *time to weep and mourn?* "Man is born to trouble, as the sparks fly upward." (Job, v. 7; xiv. 1.) And yet lesson after lesson is needed to make us know the world to be a vale of tears. We look around to the right or the left to avoid this or that trouble. Is not this looking out for some bye-path from the road, where we shall meet neither with promises, comfort, nor guidance? Be content with thine appointed lot. The tears of the child of God have more of the element of happiness than the *laughter* of the ungodly. The darkest side of the Canaan road is brighter than the light of a thousand worlds. Yet we may look for a change of seasons in God's best and fittest time. "Thou hast turned *my mourning into dancing*"*—was the experience of the man of God. Into Job's bosom was poured a portion "double for all his sorrows."† The mouths "of the returning captives" were filled with *laughter*, and their tongue with singing. (Ps. cxxvi. 1, 2.)

Let God's afflicted ones mark the wisdom and grace of these appointments. He giveth both these *times* in their season. Yea—he maketh the one to spring out of the other. "Joy" is the harvest of the seed-time of tears. "I will make them rejoice"—so runs the promise—"*from their sorrow.*" (Ib. vv. 5, 6; Jer. xxxi. 13.) The sorrow may not "for the present" seem (Heb. xii. 11) acceptable to us. But let it be accepted by us. As time rolls on, the special ends of Divine love in the sorrow will be displayed in

* Ps. xxx. 6–11. Nothing can be more foreign than the perverted application of *a time to dance* to worldly amusements. Scripture restricts it to the exercise of religious worship (Exod. xv. 20. 2 Sam. vi. 14–16. Ps. cl. 4), or to some occasion of universal joy. (Judg. xi. 34; xxi. 21.) But the exercise in companies was confined to maidens. It was performed in open day, and never supposed the promiscuous assemblage of both sexes, for the express purpose of worldly dissipation or frivolous amusement.

† Job, xlii. 10. Comp. Isa. xl. 2, lxi. 7; Zech. ix. 12.

beauteous arrangement. And that which in the beginning
was accepted in dutiful acquiescence, will afterwards become
acceptable as matter for adoring praise. The child of God
will acknowledge — ' It may be a dark dispensation. But I
know it is a wise one. It brings God to me, and I am
happy.'

But far from us be that anomaly in religion — the gloomy
religionist. Truly is he a stumbling-block to the world, and a
discouragement to the saint. He who lives, as if he was afraid
of being happy — as if he doubted his right to be so — as if
God grudged him his happiness. With perverse ingenuity he
believes the Gospel to be true for others, not for himself.
He lives in an atmosphere of his own creation — dark indeed
— but from himself. ' Look up, and be cheerful; honour
God and His Gospel' — was the wise counsel given to one of
this class. Take the balances of the sanctuary. Compare
the moment of the night-*weeping* with the eternity of the
morning joy. (Ps. xxx. 5. 2 Cor. iv. 17.) The vicissitudes of
weeping and joy will soon be overwhelmed in one unmingled
eternity of joy. This is the only world where sickness, sorrow, and death can enter. And the world of health and joy
and life — without sin — without change — without tears (Rev.
xxi. 4) — is near at hand. Oh! let it be in constant view —
and Him with it, who, ' when he had overcome the sharpness
of death, opened this kingdom to all believers.'*

5. *A time to cast away stones, and a time to gather stones
    together; a time to embrace, and a time to refrain from
    embracing.*

The natural reference would be to *casting away of stones*,
when they were useless, or perhaps an hindrance to the soil —

---

* *Te Deum.*

gathering them, when they were used for some profitable purpose. Such use was often made of them in olden times. They were the memorials of the covenant between Jacob and Laban. (Gen. xxxi. 44–51.) They were the remembrance of God's miracle in the passage of Jordan. (Josh. iv. 1–9.) Shortly after they were the broad beacon of rebuke in Achan's sin. (Ib. vii. 26.) In later days—they were the trophy of the victory over Absalom. (2 Sam. xviii. 17.) In every such case there was a Divine *purpose,* and a suitable *season.*

Passing into the social sphere, the exercise of the affections affords instances of change—sometimes indulgence ; sometimes restraint. (1 Cor. vii. 3–5.) The *embrace* of parental love would naturally be warm. (Prov. xxiii. 24.) Yet it might be wisely *refrained* towards a refractory child. (Ib. xvii. 25.) The Lord's voice may sometimes command restraint in the most hallowed earthly affections. (Joel, ii. 16.) So that from various causes, in the indulgence of caprice (2 Sam. xiii. 14)—or even in the atmosphere of love, there may be much uncertainty, and therefore no ground for rest.

6. *A time to get, and a time to lose ; a time to keep, and a time to cast away.*

To instance other rapid changes—Look around us. We see men with their whole heart in their business. Industry is successful. Money flows in. Here is the *time to get* (Prov. x. 4, 5), and—for a while at least—*a time to keep.* But the Providence of God has fixed *a time to lose.* We look again—The tide has turned. Speculation, or untoward circumstances, have given " wings to riches, and they have flown away." (Ib. xxiii. 5.) Many a fortune, *gotten* by the toil of years, and *kept* with care, has been lost in a day. Many an estate, *gotten* by inheritance, has been *cast away* by reckless extravagance. Such is the uncertainty of

a worldly portion ! How shadowy—how delusive—utterly
without rest !

There are *times* also, when we may be called to *cast
away* what we may have *kept*. A shipwreck (Jonah, i. 5;
Acts, xxvii. 38)—may demand the sacrifice. The cross of
the Gospel may require it. (Matt. xiii. 44–46; Luke, xiv. 33.)
The early Christians were called to a sharp exercise of their
confidence, " taking joyfully the spoiling of their goods;
knowing in themselves, that they had in heaven a better and
an enduring substance." (Heb. x. 34.) But sacrifices for
Christ bring no repentance. (Philip. iii. 7–9.) The grand
object swallows up all the cost, as not to be counted of.
Abundant compensation is secured for both worlds, " in this
life"—though with "much tribulation"—"an hundred
fold, and in the world to come everlasting life." (Mark, x.
29, 30.) Here then is a treasure, which there is *a time to
get*—blessed be God—there is no *time to lose*. "The good
part," once " chosen, shall never be taken away." (Luke,
x. 42.) All the malice and power of hell is stirred to rob
us of it. But a double security holds it fast. It is " reserved in heaven for us." We are ' kept on earth for it.' *
The security is no less firm for the heirs, than for the inheritance. Whatever, therefore, else we may *lose*, let Christ
be our heart's treasure, and we are safe for eternity.

7. *A time to rend, and a time to sew ; a time to keep
silence, and a time to speak.*

The reference to the garment is obvious. The *rending*
was the sign of intense grief.† The *sewing*, therefore, was

---

* Leighton on 1 Pet. i. 4, 5.

† *Reuben*, Gen. xxxvii. 29 ; *his Father*, 34 ; *David*, 2 Sam. i. 11 ;
iii. 31 ; xiii. 31. *Job*, i. 20. *His friends*, ii. 12. *Caiaphas*, Matt.
xxvi. 65. It was prescribed as a mark of godly sorrow, though too
often unconnected with it. Comp. 1 Kings, xxi. 27; Joel, ii. 13, 14.

probably the preparing of the garment for some joyful occasion. Here then we have again the time to *weep, and the time to laugh.* An emphatic repetition! With all its trials we love the world too much for our soul's prosperity. We need stroke upon stroke to separate the heart from its deadly influence. Yet let us not think evil of the ways of God on account of this discipline. All is sealed with that word of rest—"*Appointed*—unto affliction"—praised be God—"not appointed unto wrath." (1 Thess. iii. 3 ; v. 10.) Must we not bless God for the special love of the *rending time?* Many a dark remembrance has it blotted out. (Heb. xii. 11, with Rom. v. 3–5.) The recollection of God's hand in the trial—the good he designs from it—the confidence of support under it—the certainty of being carried through it—all this, realized by faith, will bring brightness and peace. ' Shall I '—said a chastened child of the family—' think much to be crossed, who deserve to be cursed ?'*

But let us once more advert to the change of seasons—the joyous as well as the sad. There are those—as one of our finest writers remarks †—'who dwell on the duty of self-denial, but they exhibit not the duty of delight.' But, as he had just before beautifully observed—' it is not possible for a Christian man to walk across so much as a rood of the natural earth, with mind unagitated and rightly poised, without receiving strength and hope from some stone, flower, leaf, or sound, nor without a sense of a dew falling upon him out of the sky.'

The next contrast is of enlarged and important application. The well-disciplined man of God will be a man of opportunities, carefully marking and improving them, as they pass before him. The tongue is the most responsible mem-

* *Memoir of Mrs. Savage*, one of the godly daughters of Philip Henry.
† Ruskin's *Modern Painters*, Part III, s. i. chap. xv.

ber—for evil or for good. 'The wise man observes, that there
is a "time to speak, and a time to keep silence." One meets
with people in the world, who seem never to have made the
last of these observations. And yet these great talkers do
not at all speak from their having anything to say (as every
sentence shows), but only from their inclination to be talking.
Their conversation is merely an exercise of the tongue: no
other human faculty has any share in it.'*

Many *times of silence* may be profitably remembered.
When *to speak* would be "casting pearls before swine"
(Matt. vii. 6. Comp. Ps. xxxix. 2)—revolting, not convincing
—"the prudent will keep silence in that time, for it is an
evil time." (Amos, v. 13. Comp. Mic. vii. 5, 6.) We
must often use the same restraint in the treatment of "a
fool;" lest by unguarded indulgence of his folly, we "also be
like unto him." (Prov. xxvi. 4.) The dealings also of our
loving Father with our souls solemnly call for a *time of
silence*. We "hold our peace" under his frown. (Lev. x. 3.)
We "become dumb, and open not our mouth, because he
did it." (Ps. xxxix. 9.) We learn to "be still" under the
assurance of his mysterious sovereignty. (Ps. xlvi. 10.) We
"sit alone, and keep *silence*, because we have borne the yoke
upon us." (Lam. iii. 28.)

A time of sorrow also must be mentioned as a time of
restraint. Precious words are often wasted at this season.

---

* Bp. Butler's *Sermon on the Tongue*. Abp. Whately draws the
same picture in his own style. He makes the distinction (which he
thinks Bacon overlooked) 'between those who speak, *because they
wish to say something*, and those who speak, *because they have something to say*—between those who are aiming to display their own
knowledge and ability, and those who speak from fulness of matter,
and are thinking only of the matter, and not of themselves, and of the
opinion that will be formed of them.'—*Notes on Bacon's Essays*, xxxii.
The son of Sirach often spoke words of wisdom, though not of
inspiration. See Ecclus. xx. 5-7.

The time of silence is more soothing.* We had better restrain our words, till the waters have somewhat assuaged. A voluble comforter adds to the trouble he professes to heal. He is rather a sore than a balm. Great wisdom is required to know when, as well as what, to *speak*.

The wise improvement of *the time to speak* brings a diversified and fruitful blessing. The fool is restrained. (Prov. xxvi. 5.) The afflicted is comforted. (1 Thess. iv. 18 ; v. 14.) Christian rebuke is rightly and lovingly administered.† The ignorant is instructed. (Prov. x. 21. Isa. l. 4.) Succour is given in the time of extremity. (Esth. vii. 4. Prov. xxxi. 8, 9.) Christian intercourse is improved. (Mal. iii. 16.) Sound knowledge is "dispersed" in our respective spheres. (Prov. xv. 7.) But, oh! to have the word ready for *the time!* (Ib. v. 23, M.R. Comp. also c. xxv. 11) —the heart, as in the praises of "the king, inditing a good matter"—the "tongue the pen of a ready writer" (Ps. xlv. 1, 2)—the heart pouring out "the good treasure" in abundant and suitable application. (Matt. xii. 34.)

Oh, Christian, ever think of your responsibility! The tongue is an important talent for Christ and his Church. Let it not be kept too much for your own private use. Yet value the discipline of it. A talent for conversation will be of little use, except as combined with a talent for silence. Flowing humility, kindness, and wisdom give beauty to the social accomplishment. But considering how weighty the influence of the "little member"—both in restraint and constraint—upward let the heart be lifted for guidance. Hence it must come. For "the answer of the tongue"—no less than "the preparation of the heart—is from the Lord." (Prov. xvi. 1.)

* Lam. ii. 10. See Job, ii. 12, 13. Prov. xxv. 20.
† Prov. xxvii. 5, 6. 1 Sam. xxv. 24. Esth. iv. 13, 14.

8. *A time to love and a time to hate; a time of war and a time of peace.*

The first clause probably refers to the individual feelings; the latter to public movements. ' At one time, men meet with kindness, which excites their *love;* at another, with injuries, which tempt them to resentment and *hatred.* Then nations experience seasons, when they must wage war, as well as opportunities for the renewal of peace; nor can individuals on all occasions shun dispute and contention.' * *Love* is emphatically called "the bond of perfectness"—the very bond of peace and of all virtues.† *A time to love* is, therefore, the appointed time and sphere for the exercise of love in the natural flow of sympathy, or gratitude, or the impulse of a natural affection. *Hatred,* under the most aggravated personal provocations, is forbidden. (Matt. v. 43, 44.) It can only therefore be admissible in our relation to God, which constrains us to count his enemies to be ours. Their abhorrence from our standard naturally stirs up opposition of feeling.‡ ' The master wheel, or first mover in all the regular motions of love, is the love of God grounded on the right knowledge of him.' § This principle vehemently excites the passion of *hatred.* Each energizes the opposite—"*I hate* vain thoughts; but thy law do I *love.* Therefore I *esteem* all thy precepts concerning all things to be *right,* and I *hate* every false way." (Ps. cxix. 113, 128.)

The same principles find the full sphere for their exercise in the wider field. There is *a time of war,* whether arising from men's ungoverned passions (Jam. iv. 1), or the just reparation of injury (Gen. xiv. 14–17), or some legitimate occa-

* Scott.

† Col. iii. 14. Collect for Quinquagesima Sunday.

‡ Comp. Ps. cxxxix. 21, 22, and Bp. Horne's excellent note. See also Rev. ii. 2.

§ Bp. Reynolds, *On the Passions,* chap. x.

sion of self-defence. (2 Sam. x. 3–6.)   All this is not chance. It is the providence or permissive controul of the Great Ruler of the universe.*   *War* is his chastisement ;† *peace* his returning blessing.   It is his prerogative to "make *wars* to cease unto the ends of the earth" (Ps. xlvi. 9), to "scatter the people that delight in war" (Ib. lxviii. 30) ; and, when the sword has done its appointed work, to " make *peace* in the borders of his people." (Ib. cxlvii. 14.)   "When he giveth quietness, who then can cause trouble ? and when he hideth his face, who then can behold him ? *whether it be done against a nation, or against a man only.*" (Job, xxxiv. 29.)

And what are the lessons we learn from this picture of change ? — Man's impotence and inconstancy — the certainty of disappointment in expecting stable happiness from such an unstable world.   All is with God.   The order is in his own mind.   The issue will be to his own glory.   Yet many of the wheels of his Providence are very mysterious. Nay — even " they were so high, that they were dreadful." (Ezek. i. 18.)   But in whose hands are the wheels, with all their motions ?   Look — not on the wheels — but on the Great Worker, His wisdom and love.   The voice speaks peace. " Be still, and know that I am God." (Ps. xlvi. 10.)

But a pondering mind is greatly needed to mark the loving display of the dispensations of God. (Ps. cvii. 43.)   The endless vicissitudes belonging to them throw great light upon the path Divinely appointed for us from eternity, as that most suited to our individual work.   Hence we learn that lesson of happiness, which, if St. Paul had not declared his attainment of it (Philip. iv. 11), we should have thought would have been the labour of a life.

'In fine, thus Solomon, by an induction of divers particulars, and those very various, and each by way of antithesis,

---

* Judg. ix. 23, 56, 57 ; 1 Kings, v. 4 ; xi. 11–14; 2 Kings, xxiv. 2.
† See Ezek. xiv. 17–21.

with his contrary joined to him—some natural actions, some
civil, some domestical, some vicious, some virtuous, some
serious and solemn, others light and ludicrous, some wise,
some passionate—by all these he assureth us, that there is a
holy and wise work of God in pre-defining, ordering, limiting,
tempering, disposing of all these and the like affairs of men,
and so qualifying in the life of a man one contrary with another,
and balancing prosperity and adversity by each other—that in
every condition a good man may find cause of praising God,
and of trusting in him, and of exercising this tranquillity and
contentment of mind even in contrary conditions, because the
holy hand of God is in the one as well as in the other.'*   Yet
the diversified changes in all this work of special Providence
greatly exercise faith and patience.   If the sun shines to-day,
the darkening cloud may come to-morrow.   One thing only
remains unchangeable—" the glorious Gospel of the blessed
God"—God's love to his people—Christ's work perfected for
them, and in them.   Not a shadow of change is found here.
All is a rock firm for eternity.   As regards the contrast
between earth and heaven, ' there are many of the things for
which there is *a time* on earth, for which there is no time
there.   To those who are *born* into that better country, there
is no *time to die.*   Those that are *planted* in God's house on
high shall never be *plucked* up.   There, there is nothing to
hurt nor to destroy; but perpetual health, and lasting as
eternity.   There the walls of strong salvation shall never be
broken down.   There, there is no *time to weep,* for " sorrow
and sighing are " for ever " fled away "—no *time to mourn;*
for when they have left this vale of tears, " the days of their
mourning are ended."   There, it is all *a time of peace,* and
all *a time of love.*   There, monuments are never defaced nor
overthrown.   For those who are " pillars in the temple " above,
with the new name written on them, "shall go out no more."

* Bp. Reynolds.

There, in the sanctity of the all-superseding relationship, there will be no severance; but those friends of earth, who have been joined again in the bonds of angel-hood, will never need give the parting embrace; for they shall be ever with one another, and ever with the Lord.'* Meanwhile " have faith in God." Calmly and joyfully wait his best time, in the assurance, that in his own mind, and in the dispensations of his love—*to everything there is a season, and a time for every purpose under the sun.*

9. *What profit hath he that worketh in that wherein he la-boureth?*   10. *I have seen the travail, which God hath given to the sons of men to be exercised in it.*

The question is again repeated†—*What profit* can man's *labour* bring out for his true happiness? We may thank God for a thousand disappointments, if only we have learned the valuable lesson, not to look for indulgence, where he intends discipline. He may permit some apparently casual event to sweep away the result of years. After all it is only a broken cistern. ' All man's best *labours* here only increase his heap of vanities.'‡ The soul is impoverished. Nothing is added to its comforts. The Lord alone offers the substance.§

Looking then to him—anxious soul—stretch your expectation to the uttermost. The world has left you dissatisfied, restless, and unhappy. Now let God's remedy be fairly tried. If this does not fill up the void, ease the disquietude, and sustain the heart in the conflict—let it be cast

* Hamilton, Lect. viii. Conclusion.

† See chap. i. 3 ; ii. 22, 23. Comp. v. 16.

‡ Anonymous *Exposition of Ecclesiastes.* London, 1680. Reprinted at Brighton, 1839.

§ Comp Prov. viii. 21. Isa. lv. 2.

away.   The testimonies to its efficacy are undoubted.   ' It is
all that is valuable'—said the dying Scott.   'You may think
that it does little for me now.   *But it is All.*   I have found
more in Christ, than I ever expected to want.'*   Another
witness we have in the last exercise of the venerated Simeon
—'I am in a dear Father's hand.   All is secure.   I see
nothing but faithfulness—and immutability—and truth.   I
have not a doubt or a fear, but the sweetest peace.'†   ' Firm
in hope'—was the last breath of the revered Bishop of Calcutta.‡   So fully does the precious remedy unfold its entire
satisfaction and triumph in the moment of nature's extremity!

Then as to the present state of trial.   Solomon had *seen*
all the changes of life, and marked the Divine reason for
them.   They were not the fruit of blind confusion, but the
chastening *travail,* which *God hath given to the sons of
men to be exercised in it.*   Never was it his purpose, that
earth should be his children's home.   The consecrated pathway
therefore to the "rest that remaineth to" them is appointed
" through much tribulation"§—Praised be God! through
a wilderness—not through an Eden.   If we do not find our
happiness in his dispensations, where shall we look for it?
' I love'—said the saintly Fletcher to Mr. Venn—' the rod

* *Life*, pp. 556, 549.   † *Life*, pp. 807, 808.
‡ Preface to Bishop of Winchester's valuable Funeral Sermon.
§ Heb. iv. 9 with 1 Thess. iii. 3. Rev. vii. 14.

    ' God to the sons of men this world hath given,
    Not for a place of rest, but exercise ;
    To try their patience, and submission learn
    To his disposal, who hath all things rank'd
    In beauteous order, though to us confus'd
    Their motions seem, because the wondrous plan
    Is hid from human eyes.'—

Choheleth; or, The Royal Preacher.   A literal paraphrase of the Book
of Ecclesiastes with considerable spirit, by an unknown author, 1768
—with the strong imprimatur of Mr. Wesley, Dr. A. Clarke, and
Professor Lee.

of my heavenly Father. How gentle are the strokes I feel! How heavy those I deserve!'* Christian confidence is the present fruit of this *travail* in the school of discipline. And all will end at last in the unclouded brightness of the eternal consummation.

11. *He hath made everything beautiful in his season; also he hath set the world in their heart, so that no man can find out the work that God maketh from the beginning to the end.*

This was the judgment of God of his created works— "very good." (Gen. i. 31.) Each was marked by its own peculiar *beauty*. The minutest insect to the eye of Christian intelligence displays a *beauty*, as if the whole Divine mind had been centered in its formation. The seasons of the universe—" seed-time and harvest—and cold and heat— and summer and winter—and day and night (Ib. viii. 22)— all bear the same marks"—*beautiful in his season*. But the more direct reference here is to those endless vicissitudes of life, which have just been detailed. ' Works of Providence, as works of creation, may begin in a chaos, and seem " without form and void" (Gen. i. 2); but they end in admirable order and *beauty*.'† Everything is suited to its appointed use and service — perfect in all its parts—not only good, and without confusion; but *beautiful*—if not in itself—yet *in his season* — all circumstances considered — most orderly, and every way befitting. Nay—even evil, though in itself most revolting, yet by a wise exercise of Omnipotence, is overruled for good, and exhibits the *beauty* of the Divine workmanship. The histories of Joseph and Esther illustrate this *beauteous*

* Venn's *Life and Correspondence.*
† Bp. Reynolds. Gen. i. 2.

harmony—the combination of circumstances fitting in their proper places—all in due connection and dependence.

Also the world—not this vain world of pleasure—but the Universe—the Book of nature — the whole course and changes of human affairs—this *he hath set in the heart of man*—as the object of his intense interest and delight.   He has put *into his heart* a vast desire to study, and great power to comprehend it in all its order and beauty—except that* the field is so wide—the capacity so limited—life so short—our knowledge of the past so imperfect, and of the future so clouded, that *no man can find out the work that God maketh from the beginning to the end.*   Indeed much of his work is begun in one age, and finished in another.   The development therefore is necessarily imperfect.   Many things seem to lie in a confused heap.   But when one part is compared with another—when all is put together, and God's work viewed as a whole—all is beauty and order.†   The elaborate work in the loom is often only seen piece by piece.   The wise mixture of the colours, as the work advances, tends to form the elegance of the piece.   The full beauty of the work *from the beginning to the end* is only known to the Great Director, who sees the end from the beginning.   We can neither unravel the thread of his counsels, nor grasp the infinite perfection of his work.   Thoughtful study and reverential praise are our most profitable exercise.   "O the depth!"‡

* A friend has directed attention to this translation of Gesenius (Gibbs's edition).   Lord Bacon gives it—' Yet cannot man,' &c.

† 'We have seen the part only—not the whole.'   Locke, quoted by Rosenmuller, who very justly adds—' No sentiment is more powerful to check the unwarrantable complaint relative to our condition.'—Scholia *in loco.*

‡ Rom. xi. 33.   The writers in *Poli Synopsis* remark upon this as a most difficult verse.   Dr. Chalmers writes—' This is one of the most remarkable verses in the Bible, with a preciousness of meaning

12. *I know that there is no good in them, but for a man to rejoice, and to do good in his life.*   13. *And also that every man should eat and drink, and enjoy the good of all his labour, it is the gift of God.*

This statement is often in substance repeated.* The repetition shews its importance. God would have us observe it. He encourages us to trust him. And how does he return our trust by the overflowing fulfilment of promised grace beyond prayer and expectation ! Have we him with us ? Then surely joy should be our element. Endeavour to enjoy him in everything—everything in him. Look at our temporal mercies only. When can we find time to count them ? Yet if we do not bring them before our mind, how can we ever be thankful for the receipt of them ? But never let the enjoyment of the present swallow up the recollection of, and gratitude for, past mercies. Of the future we know nothing. It is evidently therefore the path of wisdom to make the best use of the present—not perplexing ourselves with that which

in it, and great profundity.'—*Daily Scripture Readings.* Lord Bacon thus expounds it (*Advancement of Learning*, B. I. section iii.) 'Solomon declares—not obscurely—that God hath framed the mind of man as a mirror or glass, capable of the image of the universal world, and joyful to receive the impression thereof, as the eye joyeth to receive light ; and not only delighted in beholding the variety of things and vicissitude of times, but raised also to find out and discern the ordinances and decrees, which throughout all those changes are infallibly observed. And although he doth insinuate, that the supreme or summary law of nature (which he calleth the work which God made from the beginning to the end) is not possible to be found out by man ; yet that doth not derogate from the capacity of the mind, but may be referred to the impediments, as of shortness of life, ill conjunction of labours, ill tradition of knowledge, ever from hand to hand, and many other inconveniences, whereunto the condition of man is subject.'

* See v. 22 ; ii. 24 ; v. 18–20.

we cannot alter, but improving the fittest opportunities for practical usefulness, and cheerfully bearing the natural changes which belong to a changing world.

A cheerful expectation of the best hath a fountain of joy with him ;
Ask for good, and have it ; for thy friend would see thee happy.*

This thankful godliness is a bright portion in a cold, disappointing world—a true enjoyment—a real good—not to be found ' in the creatures, but from *the gift of God* to do good with them, or to enjoy the good of them.'†

This addition is here made to the former statement. The man not only *rejoices*, but he *does good all his days*. And what an increase is it to our own happiness, that our God and Saviour should have indulged us with the privilege of thus promoting his glory! We might have been secluded in a monastery, conflicting with our own corruptions, or occupied with the selfish contemplation of our own happiness; and never have had our hearts enlarged with the joyous privilege of *doing good*. Whereas now he has made us not only the recipients, but the almoners, of grace ; not only "enriched" with all blessings in our own souls, but "unto all bountifulness" (2 Cor. ix. 11), to supply the wants of others. Thus the happiness of every member of the body is increased by contributing to the welfare of the body. We are blessed with our father Abraham, that we may be made "a blessing." (Comp. Gen. xii. 3, with Gal. iii. 9.) Is it not a privilege to feel, that as the servants of God, we have no work to do *merely* on our own account ? We are chosen of God, that, by doing his work, we may be a blessing to man. To enjoy our own blessings is the stimulus to communicate them. Never can we ourselves "eat the fat, and drink the sweet" (1 Tim. vi. 17, 18), and forget to "send portions to them for

* Tupper's *Proverbial Philosophy.*
† Cotton.

CHAP. III. 14, 15.

whom nothing is prepared." (Neh. viii. 10–12.)   'It is
human nature to live to self—Divine grace to live to the
Lord—the highest luxury of enjoyment to serve him through
our fellow-creatures.'* In the act of *doing good*, we *enjoy
the fruit of our labour*.

If therefore—as our Lord assures us—"it is more
blessed to give than to receive" (Acts, xx. 35)—how can a
selfish man be happy?   Yet it is not for us to cast away the
gifts of God.   Let us rather stand upon a higher level, and
acknowledge the responsibility of being stewards for him.†
If this be *the gift of God*—'that we may have this *good*'—
as a pious expositor instructs us—'ask it of him.' ‡   The
man of prayer will receive largely.   Nay—what is there
that he is not warranted to expect?

14. *I know that, whatsoever God doeth, it shall be for ever:
nothing can be put to it, nor anything taken from it: and
God doeth it, that men should fear before him.   15. That
which hath been is now; and that which is to be hath
already been; and God requireth that which is past.*

'Often has the vanity of the works of man been declared.
It follows to describe the character of the works and counsel

---

* MS. Note of Rev. Dr. Marsh to the author.
† Luke, xix. 13. 'The goods of this world are not at all a trifling
concern to Christians, considered *as* Christians.   Whether, indeed,
we ourselves shall have enjoyed a large or a small share of them,
will be of no importance to us an hundred years hence.   But it will
be of the greatest importance, whether we shall have employed the
faculties and opportunities granted to us in the increase and diffusion
of those blessings among others.'— Abp. Whately's Notes on *Bacon's
Essays*, xxxiv.   Saurin mentions in one of his sermons an epitaph on
the tomb of a charitable Christian—'He exported his fortune before
him into heaven by his charities.   He is now gone thither to enjoy
it.'— See Luke, xvi. 9.
‡ Geier.

of God.' *   And here observe the striking view of his unchangeableness.   His works pass away, when their use is
finished. But his eternal counsel—the working of his counsel—*What he doeth, it shall be for ever*—not to be altered
or set aside by man's will or power.   The counsel of the
Lord endureth for ever ; the thoughts of his heart to all
generations. (Ps. xxxiii. 11. Comp. Prov. xix. 21; xxi. 30.)
Amid outward changes and seeming confusion all things
are carried out unchangeably.   His decrees are like the
" chariots coming out between mountains of brass" (Zech.
vi. 1)—firm and immovable.   The sentence comes from
his own mouth—" My counsel shall stand, and I will do
all my pleasure." (Isa. xlvi. 10.) Truly "he is of one
mind, and who can turn him?" (Job, xxiii. 13.) Of this
glorious unchangeableness—' that little thereof we darkly
apprehend we admire; the rest with religious ignorance we
humbly and meekly adore.' †

Thus sings the man of God of the perfection of his
works—" He is a Rock ; his work is perfect." (Deut.
xxxii. 4.)   *Nothing can be put to it, nor anything taken from
it*.   There is nothing defective—nothing redundant.   How
splendidly does his Providence display every attribute of
his name!—"All his ways"—so the song continues—
" are judgment. A God of truth, and without iniquity—
just and right is he." Turn we from the brightness of
his Providence to a yet higher display. Can we forbear
extending our view to his work of all works—his crown-
ing work—his master-piece of Divine workmanship? " It
is finished"—was the triumphant cry. One word was
enough. ‡   *For ever*—was the stamp of perfection—*Nothing
can be added to it, nor anything taken from it.*

* Lavater.   † Hooker, b. v. e. ii. 5.
‡ See John, xix. 30. Gr.

The prophet finely contrasts this immutable salvation with the fading nature of earthly things. "The moth shall eat them up like a garment. But my righteousness"— saith Jehovah—"shall be *for ever*, and my salvation from generation to generation." (Isa. li. 6.) Here there is the ground of godly *fear*, and reverential worship—"Great and marvellous are thy works, Lord God Almighty; just and true are thy ways, thou King of saints. *Who shall not fear* thee, O Lord, and glorify thy name?" (Rev. xv. 3, 4.)

And yet in the midst of all external changes there is substantial uniformity. *That which hath been is now, and that which is to be hath already been.* The work of God is the same in every age. The scene seems to be acting over again. *God requireth that which is past.* He calls it back before him as the precedent for his present and future dispensations.

Solomon had before shewn this uniformity in nature. (Chap. i. 9, 10.) In Providence the same laws of government are in force, as from the beginning. There are few events, but what may find their counterpart from the annals of the *past*. The children of God are exercised in the same trials; and the same proofs of sustaining and delivering grace are vouchsafed to them, as to Noah, Abraham, and the saints of old.* Some indeed of them are so scantily versed in their Bibles, that they "think it strange concerning the fiery trial which is to try them, as though some strange thing had happened unto them" (1 Pet. iv. 12)— as though none had ever wrestled through, as they have been called to do. But a deeper searching of the Sacred Records will shew, that "the same afflictions are accomplished in our brethren which have been in the world." "There hath no temptation taken you"—the apostle reminds us—

* See 2 Pet. ii. 4–9.

"but such as is common to man." (1 Pet. v. 9; 1 Cor. x. 13.) If then we cannot alter the dispensations of God, let us set ourselves down to the more profitable work of altering our own judgment of them. A murmuring spirit subdued to quietness will be much to the honour of God. We shall soon pronounce our verdict—that "all the paths of the Lord are mercy and truth" (Ps. xxv. 10)—all as they ought to be—all as we could wish them to have been, when we shall look back upon them in the clear light of eternity.

16. *And, moreover, I saw under the sun the place of judgment, that wickedness was there; and the place of righteousness, that iniquity was there.* 17. *I said in mine heart, God shall judge the righteous and the wicked: for there is a time there for every purpose and for every work.*

A thoughtful mind is often exercised on the apparent inequalities of the Divine Government. Solomon's observant eye could not overlook that, which has been a stumbling-block to men of reason, who only dispute about what they see, and therefore are ready to find fault with the appointments far beyond their wisdom. May we not hope that Solomon found rest in his difficulties where his father had found it (Ps. lxxiii. 16, 17)—in the sanctuary of God? This injustice is seen in the best governments. 'The guardian of the innocent often becomes the hangman of the innocent.'* This evil has also sometimes been found where we should have little expected it. Samuel was directed to rebuke it in Eli; yet it afterward appeared in his own house. (1 Sam. iii. 13; viii. 3–5.) Power, if it be not the instrument of promoting godliness, only makes its possessor a wolf or a tiger to his fellow-creatures. So dangerous is

* Serran.

worldly elevation! The pinnacle is a hazardous position. Our corrupt nature can bear but little raising. There is one ever ready to help us to climb. But let it be our desire to be kept upon lowly ground. We cannot know what is in our heart, till the stirring power of temptation has brought it before our eyes.

It is also a great aggravation of *wickedness,* when it stands in the very place of *judgment and righteousness.** How clearly does this disorder prove, that "all the foundations of the earth are out of course!" (Ps. lxxxii. 1–5.) Yet all will soon be set right. God will judge over again these unrighteous judgments, *judging both the righteous and the wicked* with unerring righteousness. (Acts, xvii. 31.)

But why does he delay his work? *There is a time for every purpose, and for every work.* "Shall not the Judge of all the earth do right? Shall not God avenge his own elect speedily?" (Gen. xviii. 25; Luke, xviii. 7, 8.) There is not a breath of "the loud cry under the altar—How long?" but it brings the pledge of a speedy decision. (Rev. vi. 9, 10.) Before us "we look" for the joyous hope, "according to his promise, of the new heavens, and the new earth, wherein dwelleth righteousness." (2 Pet. iii. 13.) Wait then the light of eternity. Hold fast the Christian confidence with unshaking grasp. "At evening time it shall be light." (Zech. xiv. 7.) All will furnish matter *on both sides* for the everlasting Alleluia. (Rev. xix. 1–6.)

18. *I said in mine heart concerning the estate of the sons of men, that God might manifest them, and that they might see that they themselves are beasts.* 19. *For that which befalleth the sons of men befalleth beasts; even one thing befalleth them: as the one dieth, so dieth the other; yea,*

---

* Ezek. viii. 6, 17. Matt. xxvi. 59. Acts, xxiii. 3.

they have all one breath: so that man hath no pre-eminence above a beast: for all is vanity. 20. All go unto one place: all are of the dust, and all turn to dust again.

This confusion before the wise man's eyes pressed heavily upon his heart. He could not forget the sad retrospect, when he had degraded himself from the dignity of a son of God, to walk before men like *a beast.* He now had before him, not only the mighty oppression just alluded to—but the mass of mankind, *the sons of men,** in the same bestial state. How could he restrain *the saying of his heart concerning their estate, that they might see that they themselves were beasts?* For indeed they will never know their honour, until they have known their shame. Yet this they will never see, until God *shall manifest unto them* their real state. So degraded is man, that he cannot understand his own degradation. Yet when we see men of vast capacity—of the mightiest grasp of mind in earthly things—living as if they had no souls —seeking happiness in sensual pleasures—never looking beyond the grave—never calculating soberly the Infinite stake of eternity—rather determined to perish in rebel stubbornness, than willing to return to God—does not man here sink his immortal nature to the very lowest "brutishness?" The testimony of God is true to the very letter—"Man that is in honour, and understandeth not, is like the beasts that perish." (Ps. xlix. 20; also 14.) This is his spiritual level. As to animal life—*all go unto one place; all are of the dust, and all turn to dust again.* (Gen. ii. 7; iii. 19.) In the mere outward respect—both breathe, and live, and die alike. *Man hath no pre-eminence above a beast: for all is vanity.*†

---

* Chap. viii. 11; ix. 3; Prov. viii. 4.

† Though the animal part lies more upon Solomon's surface, yet the spiritual level must have been before his mind. This—not the other—required a distinct and *Divine manifestation* to set it before

Let us take the death-bed confession of one of the world's grandest heroes. ' I die'—said Buonaparte—' before my time; and my body will be given back to the earth, to become the food of worms. Such is the fate which so soon awaits the great Napoleon.' Then catching a view of the sublime contrast, he exclaimed—' What an abyss between my deep wretchedness, and Christ's eternal kingdom, proclaimed, loved, adored, and spreading through the world !'

21. *Who knoweth the spirit of a man that goeth upward, and the spirit of the beast that goeth downward to the earth?*

Though there be no animal *pre-eminence of man above the beast*, yet vast indeed is the difference as to their *spirits*. The one *goeth upward* to "the Father of spirits," " returning to the God that gave it." (Chap. xii. 7, with Heb. xii. 9.) The other *goeth downward to the earth*. It dies with the body, and perishes for ever. ' The soul of a beast is at death like a candle blown out; and there is an end of it; whereas the soul of a man is then like a candle taken out of a dark lantern, which leaves the lantern useless indeed, but doth itself shine brighter.' *

We must not pass by this clear proof of the immortality of the soul. *The spirit* even of the wicked *goeth upward*. It appears in the presence of the Great " Judge of all"—who, though "filling heaven and earth with his presence, hath prepared his throne in the heavens." (Jer. xxiii. 24; Ps. ciii. 19.) Here is our lively hope—not like the feeble twinkling rays in the dark heathen cloud. Not "life" only, but "immortality is brought to light by the Gospel." (2 Tim. i. 10.)

the sons of men. 'An useful doctrine'—says a pious Romanist—'the necessary remembrance of this our abject condition, connected with our original sin.'—Lorin *in loco*.

* Henry.

But *who knoweth ?* * How few realize the confidence! All beyond the grave rests on Divine Revelation. Yet unspeakable is the mercy, when in this clear light we can see our *"spirits"* — not *going downward* to perish, but "made perfect" (Heb. xii. 23) in the presence of God for ever.

'Take then into your estimate of happiness' — as an admirable expositor exhorts — 'the whole extent of your existence. Let your enquiry be — how an eternity of existence may be to you an eternity of enjoyment. Jesus is revealed as the Son of God — the Divine Redeemer — the Hope of sinners. Believe in Him. Live to Him. Thus shall you possess true honour and true felicity. When your mortal part shall descend to the dust, your *spirit,* commended into the hands of God your Saviour, shall rise to the perfection of purity and bliss.' †

22. *Wherefore I perceive that there is nothing better, than that a man should rejoice in his own works; for that is his portion: for who shall bring him to see what shall be after him ?*

Solomon is returning to his former statement. There is a godly as well as an infidel (1 Cor. xv. 32) enjoyment of "things present." Let the Christian look for it in following the will of God. Here are *his own works* — not done in his own strength, or for his own glory and reward. And here also *is his portion.* Here he "remembers his God, and his God meets him with his acceptance." (Isa. lxiv. 5.) Here we have our "rejoicing — with trembling" indeed; yet with "the testimony of our conscience." (2 Cor. i. 12. Gal. vi. 4, 5.) Godliness is a bright atmosphere of Christian joy to the whole-hearted Christian.

---

* Not expressing uncertainty. See Ps. xc. 11. Prov. xxxi. 10.
† Wardlaw.

And if our present *portion* be so precious, what will it be, when we shall grasp "the prize of our high calling of God in Christ Jesus?"

Meanwhile the future is uncertain. None can *bring us to see what shall be afterward.* But the simple reliance for the day sweeps away the tossing cares for to-morrow. (Matt. vi. 34.) Soon will eternal rest swallow up present anxieties. Thus sings our Christian poet:—

> Set free from present sorrow,
>   We cheerfully can say—
> E'en let th' unknown to-morrow
>   Bring with it what it may.
> It can bring with it nothing,
>   But He will bear us through:
> Who gives the lilies clothing,
>   Will clothe his people too.
>   *Olney Hymns,* iii. 48.

CHAPTER IV.

1. *So I returned, and considered all the oppression that was done under the sun; and, behold, the tears of such as were oppressed, and they had no comforter; and on the side of their oppressors there was power; but they had no comforter.* 2. *Wherefore I praised them which are already dead more than the living which are yet alive.* 3. *Yea, better is he than they both, which hath not yet been, who hath not seen the evil work that is done under the sun.*

A SINFUL world is a world of selfishness. Men—instead of feeling themselves to be members of one great body— each bound to each other in mutual helpfulness— live only to "seek their own" (Eph. iv. 16, with Phil. ii. 21) at whatever cost to their fellow-creatures. Solomon had already taken one view of this sad spectacle. He had seen with his father "the vilest men exalted—the throne of iniquity framing mischief by a law." (Chap. iii. 16, 17, with Ps. xii. 8; xciv. 20, 21.) He now *returns and considers.* He takes a wider survey. He sees *oppression* in every corner—not only in the courts of justice—but in every sphere—not only for the sake of godliness—but *all the oppression that was done under the sun.** *Behold!*—he cries—*the tears of such as be oppressed.* The *power also on the side of the oppressor* darkens the picture. It is like Israel in "the iron furnace"—dragging along a heavy chain of life in a wearisome existence. (Exod. ii. 23, 24. Deut. iv. 20.) Twice does he allude to the deep and poignant aggravation—*no comforter*—no one to afford relief to soul or body. The tyranny of the oppressor here reaches his summit of cruelty. This keen trial has often been the lot of the Lord's suffering people. "I looked on my right hand"—said a true child of tribulation—"but there was no man that would know me; refuge failed me; no man cared for my soul." (Ps. cxlii. 4. Comp. 2 Tim. iv. 16.) Nay, was not this beaten track consecrated by the footsteps of the Son of God? "Reproach hath broken my heart; I am full of heaviness; I looked for some to take pity, but there was none, and for *Comforter ;* but I found *none.*" (Ps. lxix. 20.)

Sympathy with sorrow is indeed a precious privilege. "Remember them that be in bonds" (under *oppression*) "as

* 'There is not a word in our language, which expresses more detestable wickedness than *oppression ;* yet the nature of this vice cannot be so exactly stated, nor the bounds of it so determinately marked, as to say in all instances, where rigid right and justice end, and *oppression* begins. In these cases there is great latitude left for every one to determine from, and consequently to deceive himself.' —Bp. Butler's *Sermon on Self-deceit.*

being bound with them." (Heb. xiii. 3.)   If we cannot tread
in the footsteps of a Howard, might not much more be done ?
Might not there be a more active, self-denying alleviation
of suffering ?   Might not prayer and effort be in more lively
exercise to bring the sufferers to an interest in the endearing
sympathy of "The Man of sorrows"—so tenderly—even in
his glorified state "touched with the feeling" of his people's
sorrow ?   And yet how very little do we realize the sorrow of
others ; either because they are at a distance from us, or because
we have ourselves no intelligent and experimental acquaint-
ance with the particular pages of the history of sorrow !

As to the sorrow here expressed, Mr. Cecil mentions that
he often 'had a sleepless night from having seen an instance
of cruelty in the day.' *   Our tender-hearted poet thus gives
vent to his indignant grief :—

> Oh for a lodge in some vast wilderness,
> Some boundless contiguity of shade,
> Where rumour of oppression and deceit,
> Of unsuccessful or successful war,
> Might never reach me more !   My ear is pain'd,
> My heart is sick, with ev'ry day's report
> Of wrong and outrage with which earth is fill'd.
> *Task*, Book iv.

So keen were Solomon's sensibilities, that, looking at the
comparison merely in the light of temporal evil, he considered
death, or even non-existence, preferable, as a refuge from this
suffering lot.   The patriarch, in his crushing sorrow, looked
to the grave as his hope of rest.   "There"—said holy Job
—"the wicked cease from troubling, and there the weary be
at rest.   There the prisoners rest together ; they hear not
the voice of *the oppressor*." (Job, iii. 17, 18.)

Look onward to the great end.   *Behold the tears of*

* *Memoirs* by Mrs. Cecil.

such as were oppressed—then to be "wiped away"—when "the rebuke" of the *oppressor* "shall be taken away from off all the earth." (Isa. xxv. 8.) Meanwhile let us be careful to cherish our sensibilities—not in barren sentimentalism, but in practical exercise. Our Great Pattern not only gave his tears, but his blood, for the misery of man. Not only did he weep for sorrow as the fruit of sin, but he "laid down his life" for it. (1 John, iii. 16.)

4. *Again, I consider all travail, and every right work, and that for this a man is envied of his neighbour. This is also vanity and vexation of spirit.*

How vividly Solomon draws the picture of selfishness in all its features! *A man* pursues a *right work.* Yet *his neighbour envies* his rectitude. His own character suffers by comparison with him. Hence the revolt. Thus, whichever side of the world we look, it presents the same face of *vanity* —the same result—*vexation of spirit.* 'A man that hath no virtue in himself'— observes our great English philosopher—'ever envieth virtue in others; for men's minds will either feed upon their own good, or upon other's evil. And who wanteth the one will prey upon the other; and whoso is out of hope to attain to another's virtue, will seek to come at even hand by depressing another's fortune.'* This is the "evil eye,"† offended with the clear shining light. The better *the work*, the more is the man hated by those who have no heart to imitate him.‡ Thus even godliness becomes a source of evil. If our godliness "condemn the world,"

---

* Lord Bacon's *Essays*, ix: † See Mark, vii. 22.

‡ Gen. iv. 8 with 1 John, iii. 11, 12. Also Daniel, vi. 4, 5. This last example (as Abp. Whately seems to admit) contradicts Lord Bacon's observation—that 'persons of eminent virtue, when they are advanced, are less envied.'

we must expect to be hated by the world. Unbending integrity was the only charge brought against Aristides. And in an infinitely higher perfection of example, the only explanation of unprovoked and murderous cruelty, was—that, irritated by his popularity, "they had delivered him for *envy*." (Mark, xv. 10.) This is truly a fiendish passion—hating good for goodness sake. It is like "the star Wormwood,' poisoning the fountains around. (Rev. viii. 10, 11.) It works often under a subtle but plausible cover. God's work must be done. But we must be the doers of it. The thought is intolerable, that another and more honourable than ourselves should have the praise. We must throw something into the balance to depreciate his fair name, and to preserve the glory of our dearest idol—self. 'How contrary a state' —as Bp. Taylor beautifully observes—'to the felicities and actions of heaven, where every star increases the light of the other, and the multitude of guests at the supper of the Lamb makes the eternal meal more festival!'*

Hard indeed is it to work with singleness for our Master's name—'labouring'—as Dr. Arnold nobly expressed it on his death-bed—'to do God's will; yet not anxious that it should be done by me, rather than by others.'† Good old Fuller's prayers are much to the point—'Dispossess me, Lord, of this bad spirit, and turn my *envy* into holy emulation. Let me labour to exceed those in pains, who excel me in parts. Let me feed, and foster, and nourish, and cherish the graces in others, honouring their persons, praising their parts, and glorifying thy name, who hath given such gifts unto them.'‡

* *Holy Living*, chap. iv. sect. 8.

† Stanley's *Life*, ii. 322. 'Be content that thy brother should be employed, and thou laid by as unprofitable; his sentence approved, thine rejected; he be preferred, and thou fixed in a low employment.'—Bp. Taylor, *Holy Living*, chap. ii. sect. 4.

‡ *Good Thoughts in Bad Times.*

The true power of the Gospel can alone root out this hateful principle. If there be a living union with Christ, will not his honour be our joy, by whomsoever it be advanced? If there be a true communion with the body, the prosperity of one member will be the joy of the whole. (1 Cor. xii. 26. Eph. iv. 16.) 'One finger envieth not another, that weareth a gold ring, as taking it for an ornament of the whole hand—yea, of the whole body.'*

Ah! Christian—have not you often detected this lust in yourself—yea—even after the Lord has had mercy upon you? Then surely sorrow and shame will be your lot. And many a quickening desire will be stirred up for the world, where it shall never be known more. For "into that place shall not in anywise enter anything that defileth." (Rev. xxi. 27.)

5. *The fool foldeth his hands together, and eateth his own flesh. 6. Better is an handful with quietness, than both the hands full with travail and vexation of spirit.*

Another picture of vanity! The wise man looks from one scene to another—*oppression*—*envy*—now idleness. What a vast fertility of excuses does the great enemy suggest! In the business of daily life how many stumbling-blocks does he put in the way! The sluggard—wasting his precious time and opportunity—mistaking idleness for *quietness*—heaping misery upon himself—bears the stamp of *a fool*. And well does he deserve his name. He *folds his hands together* (Prov. vi. 9, 10; xxiv. 30–33) with heartless indifference, as if he would rather. *eat his* very *flesh* from his bones, than put forth any troublesome exertion. And yet an excuse was ready at hand. Above him he saw the tyranny of *the oppressor*. Many on his own level grudged their

* Cotton.

neighbour his happiness. And therefore for himself he deems a little with ease to be far better than much with toil and trouble. Nothing is to be gained without *travail*. And yet the fruit of successful *travail* becomes the object of *envy*. Far *better therefore he thinks an handful with quietness, than both hands filled* with the heavy tax of *vexation of spirit.**

The fool thus 'does nothing, because others do ill.'† And certainly no one has so little enjoyment of life, as he who is doing nothing in life. As Dr. Barrow asks, when rebuking his idle gentleman—'What title can he have to happiness? What capacity thereof? What reward can he claim? What comfort can he feel? To what temptations he is exposed! What guilt will he incur!'‡ Idleness indeed places a man out of God's order. It should therefore have no place in God's fair creation.§ Work is at once the substance and the privilege of our service. A thousand witnesses will rise up against the sluggard's excuse—"There is a lion without; I shall be slain in the streets." (Prov. xxii. 13.)

In our general calling and our daily course—'the strictest imprisonment is far more tolerable, than being under restraint by a lazy humour from profitable employment. This enchaineth a man hand and foot with more than iron fetters. This is beyond any imprisonment. It is the very entomb-

---

* Bps. Hall, Patrick, and Reynolds; Cartwright, Beza, Lorin, and Scott, mark this judgment, as the sluggard's false cover for his sloth. Dr. Wardlaw inclines to the same opinion. The wise man elsewhere gives the true and just application of this *better* portion.—Prov. xv. 16, 17; xvii. 1.

† Bp. Patrick. And yet—as Bp. Sanderson observes—'He is as desiring and craving as the most covetous wretch, that never ceaseth toiling and moiling to get more, if he might but have it, and not sweat for it.'—Sermon on Phil. iv. 11. In another part of the sermon he speaks of him as 'content to let the world wag as it will, without any care what shall become of him and his another day.'

‡ Sermon on *Industry as a Gentleman*.

§ See Gen. ii. 15.

ment of a man, quite in effect sequestering him from the world, or debarring him from any valuable concerns therein.'*

But this *folding of the hands together*—what a deadly hindrance is it in the ways of God! A life of ease can never be a life of happiness, or the pathway to heaven.†
Trifling indulgences greatly enervate the soul. 'A despicable indulgence in lying in bed'—writes the heavenly Martyn in his early course—'gave me such a view of the softness of my character, that I resolved upon my knees to live a life of more self-denial. The tone and vigour of my mind rose rapidly. All those duties, from which I usually shrink, seemed recreations.' Taking a higher standard of example, what say we to the quickening example of Him, who, after a Sabbath of ceaseless labour, "in the morning rising up a great while before day, went out, and departed into a solitary place, and there prayed?" (Mark, i. 35.) To cultivate habits of self-denial—to mind our work more than our pleasure, is of incalculable moment. Blessed, indeed, is the toil in such a service for such a Master! The crown and the kingdom brighten all. In the most fainting discouragement the effort to take one forward step—or even to resist one backward step—when made under the sense of the infinite preciousness of the favour of God, and the constraining love of Christ—will never be made in vain. Power will be given and felt to cut the way through every difficulty, and to live in all the high enjoyment of our privileged service.

7. *Then I returned, and I saw vanity under the sun.* 8. *There is one alone, and there is not a second; yea—he hath neither child nor brother; yet is there no end of his labour;*

---

* Barrow's Sermon on *Industry in General.*
† See Matt. xvi. 24. 2 Tim. ii. 3.

neither is his eye satisfied with riches; neither saith he—
' For whom do I labour, and bereave my soul of good?'
This is also vanity; yea, it is a sore travail.

Solomon's mind was in constant exercise. We find him
returning from one side to another, only to fasten upon some
new illustration of this world's *vanity.* The slothful *fool*
sits with his *folded hands*—preferring *quietness* at any cost.
Contrasted with him, we have the covetous fool—full of
active energy. He has chosen money for his God. *The*
miser—how well does he deserve his name! the *wretched*
slave of Mammon, grown old as a toiling, scraping, griping
drudge! He cannot plead in excuse the necessary claims
of a large family. *He is alone, and there is not a second;*
yea—he hath neither child nor brother. Yet so long as
he can add one farthing to his hoard, he cannot bear the
thought of giving up. *There is no end of his labour. Labour*
indeed it is, without rest or satisfaction, however he may
heap up his treasure. *His eye is not satisfied with riches.*
Still he craves for more. The less need, the more raking.
' He hath enough for his back, his calling, the decency of his
state and condition; but he hath not enough for *his eye.*' *
All is sacrificed—even to the *bereaving his soul of* common
good. And *for whom* all this *labour?* " He heapeth up
riches, and knoweth not who shall gather them." (Ps. xxxix.
6.) Illustrations from real life are not wanting. The Great
Marlborough—scraping together a fortune of a million and
half—would walk through the rain at night to save six-
pence ! *bereaving himself of good*—for whom ? for a family,
whom he had always regarded as his enemies.†

But it is not only the miser. Here also is the man that

---

* Bp. Reynolds. Comp. Prov. xxvii. 20 ; Hab. ii. 5–9.

† See *Mirage of Life,* an interesting volume published by Religious Tract Society.

spends his money upon himself, and upon his own selfish
gratifications, forgetting its true use and responsibility.
When once we acknowledge the bond—" Ye are not your
own" (1 Cor. vi. 19)—readily shall we add—Neither is
our silver or our gold our own, but God's; worthless—
worse than worthless; as a selfish possession; an acceptable gift, when consecrated to the service of God and his
Church.

The man of covetousness would keep his money within
his last grasp.   No other satisfaction can he realize.   But *all
this is vanity, and a sore travail.*   Never has he soberly calculated profit and loss.   Comfort, peace, usefulness, and—
what is infinitely more important—the interests of the immortal soul—all is sacrificed to this mean and sordid lust.
A perishing sinner—his shadowy portion snatched from
him; and his state for eternity irremediable misery—such is
the picture !   His call is sudden in the midst of all his purposes of aggrandizement.   He has " received his good
things."   All is now infinite and unchangeable ruin.   " So
is he" —adds our Divine Instructor—" that layeth up treasure for himself, and is not rich towards God." (Luke, xii.
18–21 ; xvi. 25.)   'Envy thou not the fool's paradise here,
that has hell at the end of it.' *   Now mark the contrast—
The child of God in poverty, yet in possession of the Gospel
treasure.   " As having nothing, and yet possessing all
things" (2 Cor. vi. 10)—enriched and honoured, for both
worlds—partaker with his Lord of the kingdom.   Reader
—be sure that this is thy joy—thy portion—first in thine
eye and in thy heart.

9. *Two are better than one, because they have a good reward
    for their labour.*   10. *For if they fall, the one will lift up*

* Anonym. *Exposition of Ecclesiastes.*

his fellow; but woe to him, who is alone when he falleth;
for he hath not another to help him. 11. *Again, if two*
lie together, then they have heat; but how can man be
warm alone? 12. *And if one prevail against him, two*
shall withstand him; and a threefold cord is not quickly
broken.

We have seen the misery of solitary selfishness. 'The
man is so absorbed in covetousness, that he sacrificeth all
his interest with his fellow-creatures.' * Contrast with this
dark picture the pleasures and advantages of social bonds.
Bacon quotes from Aristotle, that 'whosoever delighteth in
solitude is either a wild beast or a god'—that is (as Abp.
Whately explains it)—'to man—such as man is—friend-
ship is indispensable to happiness; and that one, who has
no need, and feels no need òf it, must be either much above
human nature, or much below it.' † In a variety of instances we shall readily admit Solomon's judgment—*Two*
are better than one—'more happy jointly, than either of
them could be separately. The pleasure and advantage of
holy love will be an abundant recompense for all the work
and labour of love.' ‡ *They have a good reward for their*
labour. For have they not richer enjoyment of the common
good in the mutual effort to promote it?

Many instances in common life illustrate this aphorism.
In a casual *fall* ready help is a Providential mercy. *Woe to*
him that is alone when he falleth. Solitude may be death.
(Gen. iv. 8. 2 Sam. xiv. 6.) As *if two lie together,* heat is
communicated. (1 Kings, i. 2.) In cases of assault, *one might*
prevail, when by additional strength we might successfully
withstand him (2 Sam. x. 11. Jer. xli. 13, 14); like *a cord,*
which, when untwisted, is weak; but when bound together
threefold (like the fabled bundle of rods) *is not quickly broken.*

* Dathè.   † *Notes on Bacon,* Essay xxvii.   ‡ Henry.

We forget however the deep and weighty substance of
Scripture, if we confine these illustrations to their literal
application.   The most sober principle of interpretation will
admit a reference to all that glowing contact of united hearts,
where each has a part and responsibility in helping and com-
forting the other.   To begin at the beginning—with that
ordinance, where God declared his own mind—"It is not
good for man to be alone." (Gen. ii. 18. Comp. Ps. lxviii. 6.)
If it was "not good" in Paradise, much less is it in a wilderness world.   What claim, then, has a monastic or a celibate
life to higher perfection ?   When *two* are brought together
by the Lord's Providence (Gen. ii. 22) — and specially when
each is fitted to each other by his grace—"dwelling together
as heirs of the grace of life" (1 Pet. iii. 7), in abiding union
of hearts—having one faith—one hope—one aim—who
can doubt the fact—*Two are better than one?*   Love sweetens
toil, soothes the sting of trouble, and gives a Christian zest
of enjoyment to every course of daily life.   The mutual exercises of sympathy give energy to prayer, and furnish large
materials for confidence and praise.

Our Lord himself, who "knew what was in man," ordered
his Church upon this wise determination.   When he "sent
forth" his first ministers, "as sheep or lambs in the midst of
wolves"—weak and unprotected—"two and two" was the
arrangement. (Matt. x. 16. Luke, x. 1–3.)   Was not this
upon the forethought, that *if they* should *fall, the one should
help up his fellow?*   The Primitive Church — so far as circumstances permitted—acted under Divine direction upon
this rule of mutual helpfulness.*

We need scarcely remark, how clearly the principle of
membership is here involved.   The live coal left *alone* soon

* Acts, xiii. 2 ; xv. 35–40.   An old expositor observes on this
text—that 'in the body all instruments of action are made by pairs ;
e. g. hands—feet—eyes—ears—legs.'—Cotton.

loses its vital heat. But heap the coals around it, and we have a genial atmosphere. The most lively professor left *alone* is in danger of waxing cold in selfishness. But the precious 'communion of saints' warms the Christian from the very centre. All is sound, when "the members of the body" (to use the Apostle's favourite illustration) "have the same care one for another." (1 Cor. xii. 25.) Thus "from the" Divine "Head, the whole body, fitly joined together, and compacted by that which every joint supplieth, according to the effectual working in the measure of every part, maketh increase of the body to the edifying of itself in love." (Eph. iv. 15, 16.)

This principle also rebukes the religious solitaire—that isolated being, who belongs to no Church, because no Church is perfect enough for him. 'Take a ladder'—was Constantine's advice to such a one—'and climb up to heaven by thyself.' Surely it is better to belong to an imperfect (not heretical) Church, than to none; better to "continue steadfastly in the Apostles' doctrine and fellowship, and in breaking of bread, and in prayers" (Acts, ii. 42) ; not only "first giving up our own selves to the Lord," but "unto" the whole body of the Church "by the will of God." (2 Cor. viii. 5.) There can be no real membership with the body, except by the communication of mutual helpfulness "according to the measure of every part." (Eph. iv. 16, *ut supra*.) The solitaire just described is in continual danger *when he falleth, for he hath not another to help him*. The soldier faulters *alone;* but, in fellowship with his comrades, he advances with confidence.

All the kindly offices of friendship—especially when cemented in the Christian bond—apply to this point. The united prayer of "any two, who shall agree touching anything they shall ask," is sealed with acceptance. (Matt. xviii. 19.) Mutual faithfulness (Gal. ii. 11–14; vi. 1), consideration,

inspection, and godly provocation (Heb. x. 24)—all enter
into the sphere of Christian responsibility, and minister to
the glory of our common Lord. Each of us has something
to impart, to prevent discouragement—to receive, to teach
us humility. The receiver is united to the giver by gratitude
—the giver to the receiver by tender compassion.

In this sympathizing union of kindred spirits, " ointment
and perfume rejoice the heart; so doth the sweetness of a
man's friend by hearty counsel. Iron sharpeneth iron; so
a man sharpeneth the countenance of his friend." (Prov.
xxvii. 9, 17.) The inferior may be the helper. The great
Apostle acknowledged instrumental support through his own
son in the faith. (2 Cor. vii. 6. Tit. i. 4.) Jonathan, no
less than David, " strengthened " his brother's " hands in
God." (1 Sam. xxiii. 16.) Here the *two were better than
one;* when each was employed in *lifting up his fellow.* Lord
Bacon quotes the old proverb —'A friend is another himself '— and then beautifully adds—' No receipt openeth the
heart but a true friend, to whom you may impart griefs, joys,
fears, hopes, suspicions, counsels, and whatsoever lieth upon
the heart to oppress it.' *

Oh! let us ponder well the deep responsibility of our
social obligations. Are we discharging them as unto the
Lord—for the honour of his name, and for the edifying and
increase of his Church? Did we but pray for each other as
we ought, what a brotherhood would the family of man be!
The time is short. Opportunities are passing away. Happy
those, who have been fellow-helpers upon earth! They shall
rejoice before their gracious Lord with joy unspeakable—
uninterrupted—without abatement—without end.

13. *Better is a poor and wise child than an old and foolish*

* Essays, *ut supra.*

King, who will be no more admonished. 14. *For out of prison he cometh to reign; whereas he that is born in his kingdom becometh poor.*

Riches were the last instance of vanity. Here Solomon affixes the stamp upon honour—man's highest condition. This is not indeed the ordinary course. God's people are often left in a low condition, while the ungodly maintain a royal elevation. But such cases do occur; and probably he had some example before his eyes of an *old and foolish king* beyond the border, raised to the throne without any fitness to reign, and shewing his *folly* pre-eminently by unwillingness to be *admonished.* For the man, who has no counsel from his own store, and refuses to receive it from another's, has an undoubted claim to the character of a fool. Indeed *old and foolish*—feebleness of mind and obstinacy linked together throw a cloud over the splendour of an earthly crown. For 'place and dignity can never make a man so happy, as his *folly* will make him miserable.' *

The contrast is minutely drawn—between *the king and the poor — the old man and the child — the foolish and the wise.* The balance is given in favour of *the child,* though *poor.* 'Such pearls are not to be slighted, though in the dust.' † For we are taught to despise not either youth (1 Tim. iv. 12) or poverty. (Jam. ii. 1–6.) Real worth is determined, not by outward show, but by solid usefulness. Royalty itself may sink in estimation, when set against attainments brought out of the lowest walks of life. From many a ragged school or wretched hovel may be dug out the richest stores of moral and intellectual wealth, compared with which the monarch's crown is the very tinsel of vanity. ' The king, *becoming poor* by his own extravagance, stalks

---

* Pemble *in loco.*					† Nisbet.

his little hour of magnificence, and then descends, the ghost of departed greatness, into the land of condemnation.' *

This comparison is confirmed by the different event happening to each. The child may for a while be in inglorious poverty. But may it not be the Divine purpose to bring, as it were, another Joseph *out of prison*,† or a Daniel out of captivity (Dan. i. 6; vi. 1), and to raise him to an honourable elevation? Wisdom may be the fruit of *the prison* discipline, and supply to *the child* what he wants in years (1 Kings, iii. 6–12); while *the old and foolish king—born* to an empire—*born in his kingdom* as his rightful inheritance—a beggar dies in obscurity. (2 Kings, xxiii. 31–34; xxiv. 12; xxv. 7; Lam. iv. 20.) 'The wisdom of the one may advance him to a sceptre; the folly of the other, as recorded experience testifies, may wrest the sceptre from his hand.' ‡

'If he, who from a dungeon shall through his wisdom be advanced to a throne, be preferred to him, who, *born in his kingdom*, is reduced to poverty by his folly; how honourable and happy will they be, who by faith in the Son of God are advanced from the bondage of sin and Satan to the glorious "kingdom that cannot be moved!"' § Joyous is the prospect of the resurrection morning—when their prison garments being changed for the glorious image of their Lord—*out of prison they shall come forth to reign—sharers of his throne for ever.*

15. *I considered all the living which walk under the sun, with the second child, that shall stand up in his stead.* 16.

---

* Dr. Chalmers' Sermon on Text. Comp. Job, xii. 18–21, 23, 25.

† Ps. cv. 17–22. Josephus mentions Agrippa as having ascended the throne *from a prison*, though with no special marks of wisdom. —*Antiq.* lib. xviii. c. 8; see also Howson and Conybeare, *Travels of St. Paul,* i. 129, second edit.

‡ Wardlaw.   § Scott.

There is no end of all the people, even of all that have been before them; they also that come after shall not rejoice in him. Surely this also is vanity and vexation of spirit.

The Preacher now turns to the people. He finds the same *vanity and vexation* as elsewhere. He takes an extensive survey, *considering all the living which walk under the sun.* Generation after generation pass before his mind's eye. All is the same character. The hereditary disease is fondness for change. Here is the king with the heir apparent—*the second* *—next to his throne, *that shall stand up in his stead.* The homage of all ranks is soon transferred to him. *There is no end* to the fickle multitude. " Surely men of low degree are *vanity,* and men of high degree are a lie; to lay in the balance they are altogether lighter than vanity." (Ps. lxii. 9.) Such was the testimony of the Preacher's father, abundantly confirmed by his own sad experience. Though he had been eminently the father of his people, how easily did *the second child* " steal their hearts from him!" (2 Sam. xv. 6, 12, 13.) Wayward Adonijah in his last days brought out the same proofs of this popular inconstancy. (1 Kings, ii. 15 with i. 6, 25.) Perhaps Solomon himself might have been mortified by some marks of the neglect of the setting, and worshipping of the rising, sun.†

This appeared to the Preacher to be the universal rule; human nature in every age alike. *There was no end of all the people.* The giddy and inconstant multitude go on from generation to generation. Solomon had seen it himself. So

---

* V. 8. *The second* does not suppose another child that is first —but implies—*second* in the kingdom, in respect to his father who reigns before him, whom he succeeded at his death —Bp. Patrick.

† See Lord Bacon's *Advancement of Knowledge,* B. II. xxiii. 5.

had others before him. So it would go on to the end. They
would abandon the present idol, as those had done, who had
been before them. The heir that is now worshipped with
servility will have his turn of mortification. *They that come
after shall not rejoice in him.* " Cease ye from man," therefore, " whose breath is in his nostrils " —is the much-
needed exhortation— " for wherein is he to be accounted of?"
(Isa. ii. 22.) The smile of to-day may be changed for the
frown of to-morrow. (Mark, xi. 8; xv. 8, 14.) The love of
change is a dominant principle of selfishness—insensible to
our present blessings, and craving for some imaginary good.
' The man is rarely found, who is not more taken up with the
prospect of future hopes, than with the enjoyment of his
present possession.'* This constant anxiety is an humbling
trial to Royalty. The crown of the brightest jewels is often
a crown of thorns.

But after all—think of our Great Sovereign —is not he
entitled to our undecaying, supreme, and devoted love? His
willing people will shew no fickleness heré. He deserves all.
He claims all. He gives all. Never, therefore, let him have
less than all. Will not every service bring an hundredfold
reward in peace — joy — salvation — heaven ?

CHAPTER V.

1. *Keep thy foot, when thou goest into the house of God ; and
be more ready to hear, than to give the sacrifice of fools ; for
they consider not that they do evil.*

THE Preacher has multiplied his illustrations of his subject—

* Lord Bacon, quoted in *Poli Synopsis.* See also Bp. Patrick

All is vanity. There is, however, one exception—the service
of God. Let us then go into the sanctuary. Precious
privileges belong to *the house of God.* Never does he fail
to cheer his humble worshippers. (Isa. lvi. 7.) 'In the word
of God and prayer there is a salve for every sore.'* Yet
even here,—alas! what a mass is there of vacant service
—of traditionary form—the copy and dead imitation—no
throbbing of spiritual life! How important therefore is the
Divine rule to maintain the vital sacredness of the service—
Keep thy foot—as with Sabbath consecration.† Let it not
be a careless step, as into an ordinary house. Begin the
holy exercise ere you leave your home. See that your heart
is engaged—not in the trifles of the moment, but in the
realizing of eternity—not in company with thy friend, but
in communion with thy Lord. Oh! it is awful to trifle at
the church door. Our business is with the High and Holy
One. He "is greatly to be feared in the assembly of the
saints, and to be had in reverence of all them that are about
him. Holiness becometh thine house, O God, for ever."
(Ps. lxxxix. 7; xciii. 5.) Utterly revolting therefore is that
service, which is not imbued with a reverential spirit. "*In
thy fear*"—says the man of God—"will I worship toward
thy holy temple." (Ps. v. 7.) If we have right views of the
Divine majesty, shall we not be as sinful worms in our own
eyes—how much more in his sight?

And is this exercise an easy work—a refuge for the

* Henry.

† Isa. lviii. 13, with Exod. iii. 5. Josh. v. 15. Mede supposes the
reference to the Eastern custom of putting off the shoes or sandals
on entering a temple for the purpose of worship. He adds—'Not
as if Solomon, or the Holy Ghost, in this admonition intended the
outward ceremony only, and no more (that were ridiculous to
imagine); but the whole act of sacred reverence, commenced in the
heart and affection, whereof this was the accustomed and leading
gesture.'—*Works*, pp. 347–349.

indolent from the harder toil of service ? Ah ! no. If it be
"good" (Ib. lxxiii. 28)—it is hardest of all—"to draw
near to God." It needs the face steadily set heavenward—
the "girding up of the loins of the mind" (1 Pet. i. 13)
—most of all—the eye looking towards that blessed mercy-
seat, where God and the sinner are at one, and where, at the
moment that we bow our knees before him, the great High
Priest stands up for our cause with Almighty pleading. (Heb.
ix. 24.) So prepared—so worshipping—we shall find "the
House of God to be the gate of heaven." (Gen. xxviii. 17.)

And here lies our preparation for profitable hearing—a
matter of no small moment. Many admit the importance of
hearing, who have little regard to that which makes the main
difference in *the house of God*—the remembrance of what we
hear. The evil to the barren professor is—that, not liking
the close personal application, he lays the burden of his
unprofitableness at the Preacher's door. Solomon's rule—
Be ready to hear, is that of our Divine Master—"Take heed
how ye hear." (Luke, viii. 18.) Prayer neglected—the
exercise of faith withers. We are disposed to ask curious
questions, but very unready to listen to practical truths.

'What miserable delusion'—observes the late excellent
Mr. Venn—'to think sermons will profit awakened and enlightened people, when they have no heart to call upon God,
and "worship him in spirit and in truth!"' Again—referring to one of his large London congregations—'I see the
people greatly inattentive to the worship, and yet hearing with
seeming earnestness. This will never do. "Worship in spirit
and in truth" must mellow the heart, and dispose it to hear
with profit; otherwise God's Spirit is grieved and withdrawn.
The preacher may be praised; but the soul will not be
profited.' Again—'While the grand business should fill
their souls, a total inattention is visible in many counte-
nances. Their entertainment seems only to begin, when the

preacher has taken his text.   Professed believers! can you
imagine you shall ever receive profit in one means of grace,
while you pour contempt on another?'*

Often indeed is there attendance without attention.   We
look for novelty, rather than for edification, forgetting that
—as Judge Hale wisely remarked—'our great object is to
be impressed and affected, and to have old and new truths
reduced to experience and practice.'† Is it not humbling to
remark, how little we realize the deep connexion of *the house
of God* with eternity? We seem to have done with the
word, as it has passed into our ears.   But the word—be it
remembered —will never have done with us, till it shall
have "judged us at the last day." (John, xii. 48.)

Truly, the hindrances press heavily.   Perhaps all (save
those connected with our physical temperament) are summed
up in one—"The word preached did not profit, not being
mixed with faith in them that heard it." (Heb. iv. 2.) Cor-
nelius and his company exhibited a fine spirit of profitable
hearing.   They were *ready to hear* —not the servant, but the
Master—"the things that are commanded thee of God."
(Acts, x. 33.) A message from God was looked for.   The
Minister's word was "received, not as the word of man,
but, as it was in truth, the word of God."   And thus it
"effectually worked in them that believed." (1 Thess. ii. 13.)
Many indeed are the hindrances to the true and profitable
hearing.   It is not to go as to a concert—"to the lovely
song of one that playeth well upon an instrument." (Ezek.
xxxiii. 32.) It is not the nice adjustment of the balances, to
determine the little proprieties of the preacher's tone, gesture,
emphasis, or attitude; as if it was of little moment what he
speaks, if only he speaks in good taste.   Nor is it "the
man, who looketh in the glass, and straightway forgetteth

* *Life and Correspondence*, pp. 404, 540.
† Bp. Burnet's *Life*.

what manner of man he was." (Jam. i. 23, 24.) Such
service can only be *the sacrifice of fools.* 'A fool is the
priest, and folly the oblation.' * For what else can it be, to
conceive that the Searcher of hearts is pleased with mere
external formalism ? or to forget that " God is a spirit," and
therefore can only be acceptably worshipped in spiritual
service and in truth? (John, iv. 23, 24.) This is indeed
vanity in its most revolting character—vanity brought into
our worship—our very religion turned into vanity. (Isa.
i. 13. Matt. xv. 7–9.) Worldly thoughts, pleasures, and
plans are brought—not only to the very door, but even to
the sanctuary itself. "Our Father's house is made a house
of merchandize." (John, ii. 16.) The truth floats across a
multitude of hearers ; but no profitable impression is left.
All is absolutely worthless—a mockery of God.

And yet, such is the self-delusion of this folly, that the
heartless worshippers *consider not that they do evil.* (Hos.
vii. 2.) But however well conceived be the outward form,
the substance is "the sacrifice of the wicked, which is an
abomination unto the Lord." (Prov. xv. 8.) Account will be
taken at the great day, not only for the commission of sin,
but for the service of duty. Alas ! who of us has not
cause to remember every step of our prayerful course, as a
deep and large ground of humiliation before God ? Indeed—
as a dying philosopher was constrained to admit—'What
would become of a poor sinful soul, but for that blessed,
all-comprehensive sacrifice, and that intercession at "the
right hand of the Majesty on high?"'† This we can plead,
and never shall we plead it in vain.

* Dr. South on v. 2.

† John Foster—*Life and Correspondence*, vol. ii. Very instructive is it to mark this gigantic mind on the brink of eternity coming
out from the dark cloud of rationalistic theology.

2. *Be not rash with thy mouth, and let not thine heart be hasty to utter anything before God: for God is in heaven, and thou upon earth; therefore let thy words be few.*
3. *For a dream cometh through a multitude of business; and a fool's voice is known by a multitude of words.*

This is a Divine Rule for prayer. We need not restrict it to public worship. Let it apply to "*all* prayer and supplication." The vanity of the heart in prayer gives full scope for this rule of discipline. Have we not cause to pray, that we might know what prayer is? How little do we know—because how little time and heart we have given to it! How much of our own spirit mingles with our intercourse with God! We admit it as a duty—Nay, do we not enjoy it as a privilege? Yet how little we realize its power—prevalence—majesty! Our business with God is infinitely greater than with all the world beside. Bright indeed is our encouragement—'nothing,' as Bp. Taylor beautifully observes, 'but desiring of God to give us the greatest and best of things we can need, and which can make us happy.' * And yet such waywardness! such ignorance! such *rash utterance of the·mouth!* such *hastiness* of spirit! "strange fire before the Lord." (Lev. x. 1.) Oh! the blessedness of realizing the Indwelling Intercessor "helping our infirmities!" There will be no more cold generalities —coming without an errand—the sure mark of an insensible heart. The Spirit brings up our real wants and concerns, frames our desires, and moulds every thought "according to the will of God." (Rom. viii. 26, 27.) 'To pray without the Spirit'—as an experimental writer observes— 'is the same as thinking without a mind, or speaking without the power of speech. In Him alone thou art a living

* *Holy Living*, chap. iv. sect. vii.

thing. Whence all thy waverings in prayer—thy discomfort after prayer—conscious of having dealt with God, yet not prevailed? Is it not this? The mind has thought, and lips have moved—without the Spirit. Better be silent altogether, than run before his motions.' *

The want of this "preparation of heart" to speak in the Lord's ear makes the heart careless and irreverent, and brings guilt upon the holy exercise. The thought of "the Lord in heaven sitting on his throne," and the defiled sinner *on earth* standing before him (Isa. vi. 5–8), the infinite distance between his greatness and our vileness—'this would keep us from that heart-nonsense, which, though the words be sense, yet through the inattention of the heart, are but as impertinent confused dreams in the Lord's ears.' † Here is a wholesome bridle to our *rashness*, but no restraint upon the Spirit of adoption. The way is open—not only to a Father's throne, but to a Father's heart.

The *few words* here directed are words well weighed— well chosen and ordered. They contrast strongly with the "vain repetitions"—such as the frantic orgies of Baal— the Romish Pater-nosters—or the Pharisees' long prayers —"thinking they shall be heard for their much speaking." ‡ But 'God hears us not the sooner for many words; but much the sooner from earnest desire, to which let apt and sufficient words minister, be they few or many.' § The *fewness of the words* is not the main concern; but whether they be the words of the heart—'whether they be gold or

---

* Mylne.   † Leighton on 1 Pet. iii. 12.

‡ Matt. vi. 7 with 1 Kings, xviii. 26. Solomon speaketh not against all length in prayer (for Christ prayed whole nights), nor against all repetition, when it proceedeth from zeal, love, and holy fervency—as that of Daniel (ix. 16–19); but of that, which is a 'vain ingeminating of the same thing without faith or wisdom.'—Bp. Reynolds.

§ Bp. Taylor, *ut supra.*

lead' *—what life there is in them. For 'nothing is more
unacceptable to God, than to hold on speaking, after we
have left off praying.' † So long as the heart and the
tongue flow together, never suppose that your Lord will be
weary of our many words. The exercise may be indefinitely
extended—the true spirit of the rule is not transgressed.
It stands indeed to remind us 'that his goodness must not
cause us to forget his greatness;' ‡ that "the throne of
grace" is a throne of majesty (Comp. Heb. xii. 28, 29,
with Deut. iv. 24); and therefore that the confidence of the
child must be tempered with the humility of the sinner.

But the *few words* imply the heart set in order before
utterance—a thoughtful mind in a spiritual habit. It is
often large and mighty prayer in a narrow compass. There
is more substance in a few minutes' real communion, than in
an hour of formal exercise. There is no artificial method—
all is full of feeling and confidence—all is sealed with
gracious acceptance.§ To maintain this tone of feeling,
ought not the Christian to study his prayers, as the minister
does his sermon? each remembering himself to be in the
awful presence of God? The keeping of the mind and
heart with God is most valuable discipline for prayer. Any
defect here restrains the holiest privileges of the Gospel. A
protracted exercise may be only empty formalism—prayer-
less prayer—*the sacrifice of fools*—routine, not vitality.
The heart is far from God.

Loose and incoherent impulses also contrast with the
few sober, recollected *words*. They are like the confused
images of *a dream*, flowing out of the hurry of distracting
business. 'As a multitude of business produces a dream,

* Nottidge's *Correspondence*, p. 419.
† Dr. South's Sermon on the Text.   ‡ Ib.
§ See Luke, xviii. 13, 14; Acts, ix. 6.

so *multitude of words* discovers the *folly.*' * And " in the multitude of" such "words"—where the tongue pours out its torrent separate from the heart—assuredly " there wanteth not sin." (Prov. x. 19.)   The indwelling word is the storehouse, that supplies the matter, and inspires confidence for prayer.   For "if ye abide in me"—saith the Saviour— " and *my words abide in you,* ye shall ask what ye will, and it shall be done unto you." (John, xv. 7.)   Prayer— such prayer as this, drawn out from the Divine treasury— is a sacred exorcist, which puts legions to flight.   Never parley with the rushing thoughts of this world's vanity, or of inner unbelief.   In a posture of resistance, all is bright- ness and energy, well poised and balanced in readiness for the conflict.

Here then is the true spirit of prayer—collected—de- liberate—pursued.   It is not advancement only, but pos- session.   Only give it permanence in the habit of faith. The Divine work will develope itself in prayer, " in newness of spirit"—with the heart in earnest.   It is in holy secrecy that the soul takes the firmest hold.   There may be no words—or only stammering words (Isa. xxxviii. 14)—little beside sighs and tears. (Ps. vi. 6. Lam. iii. 56.)   Yet is it the remedy for conscious weakness—as the dying Foster—after adverting to some matters of utter helplessness—added — ' But I can pray, *and that is a glorious thing.*' †   But let the feeling have full vent in the "intercession of the Divine Spirit with groanings which cannot be uttered;" and this, not as the result of unnatural animal excitement, but as the expression of the intense breathings of the spiritual life. (Rom. viii. 26.)

---

* Bp. Reynolds :—' Where two sentences are connected together by a copulative, there is frequently imparted a similitude between them.   Prov. xxv. 23-25, 27.' Ib.   See also Wardlaw *in loco.*
  † *Ut supra.*

4. *When thou vowest a vow unto the Lord, defer not to pay it; for he hath no pleasure in fools: pay that which thou hast vowed. 5. Better is it that thou shouldest not vow, than that thou shouldest vow and not pay. 6. Suffer not thy mouth to cause thy flesh to sin; neither say thou before the angel, that it was an error. Wherefore should God be angry with thy voice, and destroy the work of thine hands? 7. For in the multitude of dreams and of many words there are also divers vanities: but fear thou God.*

The rules in the former verses apply to the ordinary service of God. This relates to a special exercise. The warning, however, against *rashness and haste* applies here, ' lest we beg a blessing, and fall into a snare.'* Indeed this subject of vows requires a very careful and delicate treatment. A solemn engagement advisedly made with God is a transaction needing much prayer and consideration. It should rest upon the clear warrant of God's word. It should concern a matter really important, suitable, and attainable. It should be so limited, as to open a way for disentanglement under unforeseen contingencies,† or altered circumstances. It will be an hindrance or an help, according as it is the result of impulse, or of intelligence. There must be a real conviction of our total weakness, acted out in simple dependence upon Omnipotent grace; else the most sincere vow will be found too feeble an engagement for the hour of temptation, and will issue in discouragement and perplexity. The soul is rather ensnared than helped, and the enemy gains an advantage even in the very posture of resistance. And yet some special season of covenanting with God may be valuable, to strengthen the weakness of the young disciple, to remind him when he

* Bp. Taylor's *Holy Living, ut supra.*
† See Judg. xi. 30–35.

is apt to forget, and to humble him in the consciousness of short-coming or fall. The early choice is often so wavering —' convinced by the grace of God, not persuaded; and then persuaded, but not resolved; and then resolved, but deferring to begin ; and then beginning, but in weakness and uncertainty.'*

Vows however are not like prayers—our daily work, "without ceasing." (1 Thess. v. 17.) We have burdens and infirmities enough pressing upon us. Let us be careful, that we do not rashly or needlessly multiply them. The obligation indeed more fully belongs to the Old dispensation.† The "law of liberty" gives no *express* direction. We might suppose that a clear apprehension of the terms of the Gospel would render vows altogether unnecessary. For are we not bound by direct, sacred, and constraining obligation to consecrate to the Lord *all* that we are—*all* that we have—*all* that we can do—independent of an extra bond ? Here we are brought to the utmost that can be required. And yet Scriptural allowance appears to be made, in order to meet the infirmity of the case just alluded to. The Evangelical Prophet seems to connect the ordinance with Gospel times. The "subscribing with the hand to the Lord," under the outpouring of the Spirit, was evidently a special bond, and an acceptable service.‡ And even in the history of Israel's solemn covenanting with God, the "blood sprinkled upon the people" made provision for the breach of the covenant, and gives an Evangelical character to the transaction. (Heb. ix. 19, 20.) May not Sacraments also be considered, not only as the seals of God's faithfulness to us,

---

* Bp. Taylor's Sermon *on Growth in Sin*, Part ii.

† *Lawful Vows*, Gen. xxviii. 20–22 ; 1 Sam. i. 11. *Rules* to perform vows, Num. xxx. 2 ; Deut. xxiii. 21–23. *Thanksgiving Vows*, Ps. lxvi. 13, 14 ; cxvi. 12, 14–18.

‡ See Isa. xliv. 3–5. Comp. Jer. L. 4, 5.

but as the pledges of our devotedness to Him? (Comp. 1 Pet. iii. 21.)

Here, however, is not the direction to *make a vow,* but the obligation—having made it—cheerfully and instantly to *pay* it. It is an engagement we should be careful to discharge to man; much more to God. (Deut. xxiii. 21. Ps. lxxvi. 11.)   The rule is therefore emphatically repeated— *Defer not to pay it. Pay that which thou hast vowed.* Jacob's forgetfulness brought upon him the scourging rod. (Gen. xxxv. 1, 2, with xxviii. 20–22.) Hannah *deferred not to pay.* (1 Sam. i. 11, 24–28.) Instant readiness is the best proof of sincerity. Oh! my God—what is there?—is there anything —that withholds my whole heart this moment from thee? Let me live under the awful weight of the words—*He hath no pleasure* * *in fools* — ' who go about, one while to flatter him in making *a vow,* and afterwards to mock him in refusing or delaying to pay it.'† Far *better* to have refrained from *the vow,* which was a self-imposed obligation,‡ than from the payment, which is now a bond upon the soul. To refuse to enlist may be guiltless; but to desert the colours is to be guilty of death. We had need be cautious in making vows, that we may be upright in *paying* them. "Make a strait path for our feet." Go onward in singleness and simplicity of heart. There must be a living faith, not only that we may lay hold at the beginning, but hold on to the end. All depends—not only on laying hold, but holding on.

But vows contrary to God's word cannot bind a right conscience. A vow cannot make that right which is morally wrong. What is contrary to the law can never be a legitimate engagement to the Lawgiver. Herod's engagement

---

* An energy of meaning in a meiosis of expression. Comp. Ps. v. 5 ; Prov. xvii. 20.

† Bp. Reynolds.

‡ See Deut. xxiii. 22.

(Matt. xiv. 9), therefore, would have been more honoured in the breach than in the observance. ' Know'—saith Bp. Sanderson—' that neither oath, vow, nor other tie whatever, is allowed by Almighty God to bind thee to sin ! Oppose then against all thy rash promises and vows that solemn promise and vow thou madest unto God in the face of the congregation, and tookest the holy sacrament upon it in thy baptism—" to keep his holy commandments, and to continue his faithful soldier and servant unto thy life's end." Let equity teach thee, that the first bond should be first discharged; and reason, that if an oath or a vow must stand, the first should rather.' *

Every member—so active is the principle of sin !—stirs the whole body. The *rashness of the mouth causes the flesh* —the whole corrupt mass—*to sin*. To how many inconsiderate and unwarranted vows does this warning apply ! (Judg. xi. 30. 1 Sam. xiv. 24.) Never *suffer thy mouth* to promise what thou canst not, and oughtest not to perform. This is to bring sin upon us, by seeking occasion for it, when God has left us free. (Acts, v. 4.) The vow of celibacy, without the gift of continency—what a torrent of *sin* has it poured in upon the Church ! It might often occur under the Jewish economy, that a man—greedy of eminence in the Church—would vow before the priest beyond his power and intention ; and when the claim was pressed (see 1 Sam. ii. 13), he would attempt to deny the extent of his engagement. Many a modern hypocrite hath laid this snare for himself. To stand high with his brethren, he sets apart "that which is holy." His carnal appetite subsequently "devours it," and "*after* vows he makes enquiry" to avoid the obligation.† *Let him not say before the angel,‡ that*

---

* Sermon on *Presumptuous Sins*.   † See Prov. xx. 25.

‡ Lampe considers here a reference to the Angel of the covenant. Mede seems to take it collectively—more than one—

it was an error—a thoughtless mistake. Oh! clothe not the hateful sin with so slight a name. Let it be seen in its fearful colours — its heavy aggravations. The Omniscient Searcher of hearts strips off the flimsy cover— *God is angry at his voice ; and destroys the work of his hands.* Such awful mockery the God of Truth could never pass by with impunity.

The fruit of this deceit proves its source. No steady purpose can flow from half-hearted principle. *All such words* and professions therefore have as little substance, as *the multitude of dreams. In many words* how fruitful is the harvest! A single thoughtless *word* lights up the fire. A *word* of discontent stirs the troubled waters. *Many words—divers vanities.* " The Lord knoweth the thoughts of men, that they are but vain" (Ps. xciv. 11)— multiplied provocations ! But the remedy is before us. *Fear thou God.* Here is the grand fundamental of godliness — inseparably linked with every Christian grace — not impulse, but principle — the " bit and bridle" to repress the *rashness of the flesh* — the habit of holy discipline to frame the spiritual service — " Sanctify the Lord God in your hearts. And let him be your fear ; and let him be your dread." (Isa. viii. 13.) Let him have the best — not the dregs. Let him have the whole confidence—the whole heart.

But be sure that every exercise—ordinary or special—

and considers the cherubim of glory on the mercy-seat, and the carved cherubim on the walls of the temple, all to signify that where God's sacred memorial is—the ensign of his covenant and commerce with men —there the blessed angels out of duty give their attendance.'—*Works,* book ii. 345. However ingenious this exposition may be, the more probable reference is to the priest, because it was his express duty to receive the vow in God's stead, and to give dispensation, acceptance, and discharge as the matter might require. See Lev. v. 4-8 ; also xxvii. 11, 12. See also the name of angel or messenger of the Lord given to the priest, Mal. ii. 7. Comp. Rev. i. 20.

has the one distinctive character of " a living" and " spiritual sacrifice." (Rom. xii. 1. 1 Pet. ii. 5.) All ascends upwards on one ground—through one way of access (Heb. xiii. 15) —with one plea for acceptance.   And here sins of infirmity, no less than sins of presumption, when confessed and repented of, are covered, cleansed, and blotted out for ever. (Ib. x. 19-22.) What do we know of vital religion, unless we come to God by this his own—his only—way of acceptance ?

8. *If thou seest the oppression of the poor and violent perverting of judgment and justice in a province, marvel not at the matter ; for he that is higher than the highest regardeth, and there be higher than they.*

We need not in this book always expect continuous connexion. It is not the regular dissertation upon a given subject, but a rapid survey of the different points in the great sphere before him.   Yet this verse falls in with one great object of the Book, which is to compose the minds of the servants of God to stillness and confidence under his inscrutable dispensations.   Solomon supposes a wide extent of unjust *oppression*— not a village—town—city—but *a province* under *perverting* influence.   This is truly a dark page in providence, which exercises " the patience and faith of the saints" (Ps. lxxiii. 12, 13. Jer. xii. 1), stumbles the ill-instructed, and opens wide the caviller's mouth.

But—as Bp. Butler wisely remarks—'there may be the wisest and best reasons, why our happiness and misery should be put in each other's power in the degree in which it is.'*

* *Analogy*, part i. c. iii. 'It is not necessary we should justify the dispensations of Providence any further than to shew, that the things objected against may, for aught we know, be consistent with justice and truth—not only consistent with justice, but instances of it.'—Ib. part ii. c. viii.

There is therefore no cause to *marvel at the matter,* as if it were unexpected, to allow hard thoughts of God, to complain of his dispensations, or to be weary of his service. There is an appeal to a higher court. All will be set right there. If the oppressor be high, *the Higher than the highest regardeth.* (Ps. x. 11–14; xii. 5. Prov. xxii. 12, 13.) He does not look on as an unconcerned spectator. If he "keeps silence," his forbearance is not forgetfulness.* He is only waiting— as in his dealings with the chosen nation—his own best and fittest time for their deliverance. (Exod. iii. 7–9.) Messiah's kingdom is brightened with the sunbeam—" He shall deliver the needy when he crieth; *the poor* also, and him that hath no helper." (Ps. lxxii. 12–14.)

High and lofty as the *oppressors* of the Church may be, let us look upward. " *The Lord reigneth.*" Here is our present stay. (Ib. xlvi. 10; xcvii. 1, 2; cxlvi. 7, 10.) " I know that the Lord will maintain the cause of the afflicted, and the right of the poor." (Ib. cxl. 12.) His angelic messenger— *higher than* the oppressors—may be the swift invisible instruments of vengeance. (Ib. ciii. 20; civ. 4, with 2 Kings, xix. 35 ; Acts, xii. 20.) *The Lord cometh*—Here is our "blessed hope." He will assert his own sovereign right, and remove all inequalities. (Tit. ii. 13. Mal. iii. 5 ; iv. 1–3.) " Rest " to the *oppressed* will be the joyous consummation of *that day.* (2 Thess. i. 7.)

9. *Moreover, the profit of the earth is for all; the King himself is served by the field.*

Moreover—connects this statement, though somewhat obscurely, with the preceding.† Perhaps the supremacy of God, giving to *all* an equal interest in *the earth,* was in-

---

* See Ps. L. 21. † See *Poli Synopsis.*

tended as a memento, that common interest and mutual dependence should check unjust *oppression*.

Gradation of rank is indeed the ordinance of God, evil only, when the higher abuse their elevation. Yet there is a level, where "the rich and the poor meet together." (Prov. xxii. 2.) The curse upon the ground is so far mitigated, that while "bread" is still "eaten in the sweat of the face" (Gen. iii. 17) there is profit—directly or indirectly—*for all*. The many live by it. The highest cannot live without it. *The King himself is served by the field.* He is more dependent upon the labourer, than the labourer is on him. He has more need of the labourer's strength, than the labourer has of his royal crown. Agriculture was an ordinance of God before the fall.* 'And of all the arts of civilized man, it is transcendently the most essential and valuable. Other arts may contribute to the comfort, the convenience, and the embellishment of life. But the cultivation of the soil stands in immediate connexion with our very existence. The life itself, to whose comfort, convenience, and embellishment other arts contribute, is by *this* to be sustained, so that others without it can avail nothing. In their dependence on *the field* all are equal. The prince and the peasant are alike *served of it.*† Humility, therefore, is the lesson for the rich; contentment for the poor. All of us may be reminded of the important truth, with its daily responsibilities—that all are members of one body—parts of one great whole. Indepen·dence is man's proud delusion. The desire of this prerogative was his fall and ruin. (Gen. iii. 4, 5.) Gracious therefore and wise is the dispensation, that sweeps it away. The highest cannot say to the lowest—"I have no need of thee." (1 Cor. xii. 21.) No man lives for himself, but for the body. Mutual helpfulness contributes to the increase and prosperity of the whole. (Eph. iv. 15, 16.)

* See Gen. ii. 15.   † Wardlaw.

10. *He that loveth silver shall not be satisfied with silver; nor he that loveth abundance with increase. This is also vanity.*
11. *When goods are increased, they are increased that eat them, and what good is there to the owners thereof, saving the beholding of them with their eyes.* 12. *The sleep of a labouring man is sweet, whether he eat little or much; but the abundance of the rich will not suffer him to sleep.*

The tempter may paint a brilliant prospect of happiness. But fact and experience prove, that *he that loveth silver* or any worldly *abundance* will be satisfied neither with the possession, nor *with the increase.* The appetite is created—not satisfied. The *vanity* of this disease is coveting what does not satisfy when we have it. Hunger is satisfied with meat, and thirst with drink. But hunger or thirst for this world's wealth is as unsatisfied at the end, as at the beginning.* 'Could you'—says a lively expositor—'change the solid earth into a single lump of gold, and drop it into the gaping mouth of avarice, it would only be a crumb of transient comfort, a cordial drop, enabling it to cry a little louder, 'Give—give.' '† So true is it, that " a man's life"—his real comfort of life—" consisteth not in the abundance of the things which he possesseth." (Luke, xii. 15.) ' Nature is content with little, grace with less, but lust with

* Classic testimony confirms the declaration—
 ' Crescit amor nummi, quantum ipsa pecunia crescit.'
                    Juven. *Sat.* xiv. 139.
 ' Creverunt et opes, et opum furiosa libido,
   Et cum possideas plurima, plura petunt.'—Ovid, *Fasti.*
   'Semper avarus eget.'—Hor. Lib. i. Ep. 2.
The two words used in the New Testament identify themselves with each other—φιλαργυρία, the love of money (1 Tim. vi. 10)—πλεονεξία (Col. iii. 5), the desire for more. For who would desire more of that which he did not love?
 † Hamilton's *Royal Preacher*, Lect. xi.

nothing.' * *Silver* can neither give peace, nor make up for
the loss of it.   Be it however remembered, that the evil lies
in the *love*—not the possession *of silver.*   Abraham had
abundance of it, but with an heavenly heart. (Gen. xiii. 2 ;
xxiv. 2, with Heb. xi. 9, 10.) David's treasures were almost
countless.   Yet they were not his portion, but his talent—
always felt to be not his own—laid up joyfully for God.
(1 Chron. xxviii. 10–19 ; xxix. 1–16.)   It is the *love* of
money—the "will to be rich—enlarging the desire as hell,
and as death, which cannot be satisfied" (Hab. ii. 5. Comp.
Isa. v. 8)—the making riches the idol—the all—the
treasure—here are the "snares and temptations, that drown
men in destruction and perdition."†   'The whole system of
heathen idolatry furnishes no more complete renunciation
of God.   He who makes a god of his pleasure, renders to
this idol the homage of his senses.   He who makes a god
of his wealth, renders to this idol the homage of his
mind ; and he therefore of the two is the more hopeless and
determined idolater.   The former is goaded on to his idolatry
by the power of appetite.   The latter cultivates his with wilful and deliberate perseverance, consecrates his very highest
powers to its service, fully gives up his reason and his time,
and all the faculties of his understanding, as well as all the
desires of his heart, to the great object of a fortune in this
world.'‡   "Thou, O man of God, flee these things." (1 Tim.

* Henry.
† 1 Tim. vi. 9, 10. Luther's last will and testament strongly contrasts the gain of godly contentment, vv. 6–8. 'O Lord God, I thank
thee, that thou hast been pleased to make me a poor and indigent
man upon earth. I have neither house, nor land, nor money to leave
behind me.   Thou hast given me a wife and children, whom I now
restore to thee.   Lord, nourish, keep, and preserve them as thou
hast me.'   See also Scott's valuable *Practical Observations on Agur's
Prayer.*   Prov. xxx. 7–9.
‡ Chalmers's *Commercial Discourse on Job,* xxxi. 24–28.

vi. 11.) For when our desires are running before our wants,
it were far better to sit down content where we are, than
where we hope to be in the delusion of our insatiable desire.
A portion in this life is therefore far more to be dreaded than
to be envied. Success is enough to frighten a sober, intelligent mind. It is often connected with the disease of
spiritual consumption—insensible to present danger. Every
way, therefore, the verdict flashes upon us. *This is also vanity.*

Nor is it to be forgotten, that an *increase of goods* is fol-
lowed with a corresponding *increase* of consumers. Solomon's expensive establishment kept pace with his increasing
treasures. (1 Kings, iv. 22–26.) In all similar cases the
multitude of retainers increases. A certain appearance must
be maintained. *The owner* may be a poorer man, than when
he had less riches, and fewer mouths to feed. The only
good is the mere empty pleasure of *beholding with his* eyes,
and saying, 'These are mine.' 'The poorest artizan in
Rome, walking in Cæsar's garden, had the same pleasures
which they ministered to their lord. The birds made him
as good music; the flowers gave him as sweet smiles; he
there sucked as good air, and delighted in the beauty and
order of the place, for the same reason, and upon the same
perception as the prince himself: save only that Cæsar paid
for all that pleasure vast sums of money, the blood and treasure of a province, which the poor man had for nothing.' *
' I have no comfort in all these things'—said one, who had
made for himself a princely Elysium—'because I meet
death in every walk.' 'Ah! David, David'—said Dr.
Johnson to Garrick, when shewing him his Twickenham
Villa—'these are what make a death-bed terrible!'

Even in the common comforts of life—is not the balance

* Bp. Taylor's Sermon on *The Foolish Exchange.* See also the
same lively description, Bp. Sanderson's *Fifth Sermon on Philip.*
iv. 11.

often in favour of *the poor?* Having little to lose, they have but little fear of losing. *Their sleep* is therefore the natural fruit of weariness without care ; whereas *the abundance of the rich* is often a sleeping weight. When the last thoughts are of the world, and the heart centred there, carefulness is the atmosphere of the day, and hurried restlessness often the weariness of the night. Thus are sleepless nights connected with anxious days. Perhaps Shakespeare's royal picture may paint the anxieties of a worldly heart, as well as the trouble of a guilty conscience—

> "How many thousands of my poorest subjects
> Are at this hour asleep," &c.

Grandeur often pays a nightly penance for the triumph of the day.' *

This is the evil of covetousness—an " easily besetting sin." Multitudes condemn it in others, who little suspect its influence in their own hearts. ' It is a fleshly desire— something that has got into the place of God—a deep, desperate, plausible, but damning sin. Men are accustomed to give it a softer name, such as prudence ; but there is no sin more hardening, and stupefying to the conscience.' †

It is an awful thought, that this habit does not necessarily bring an outward blot upon the Christian profession. We may " err from the faith" under this deadly principle

---

* Hamilton, Lect. xi. Elwes the millionaire is said to have often started from his sleep, and to have been found in the dead of night wandering through his house, mourning over the loss of five pounds. Mr. Cecil finely contrasts his own case in extremity with this wretched drudge—'Sitting in my blankets with this Bible before me, I seem like old Elwes with a bushel of Bank - notes and India Bonds ; but with this difference—*that he must have all his taken away*, and *I shall take all mine with me.*'—Fragment written in illness.

† Cecil's *Original Thoughts on Scripture*, pp. 182, 183.

(1 Tim. vi. 10), without changing one atom of our Evangelical Creed. We may slumber in the delusion of our varying religious feelings, while the cankering habit is fixed in the world hidden within. Oh! what need of deep searchings of heart—"of watchfulness unto prayer!" Well does an old commentator remark—' He is rich—not who possesses much, but who desires little'*—we may add—whose treasure is in his God and Saviour. For where—but in Him—can the vast desires of our souls be satisfied? If he loves us, he will not lose us. Yet he will use his rod to the end, rather than suffer that to abide in us, which his soul abhorreth.

13. *There is a sore evil, which I have seen under the sun, namely, riches kept for the owners thereof to their hurt. 14. But those riches perish by evil travail; he begetteth a son, and there is nothing in his hand. 15. As he came forth from his mother's womb, naked shall he return to go as he came, and shall take nothing of his labour, which he may carry away in his hand. 16. And this also is a sore evil, that in all things as he came, so shall he go; and what profit hath he that hath laboured for the wind? 17. All his days also he eateth in darkness, and he hath much sorrow and wrath with his sickness.*

Another illustration of the utter vanity of riches. This profound book discloses many humbling secrets. Is the man repining about his hard lot, and ready to envy his more wealthy neighbour? Let him study here the lesson set before him, and return with a contented—yea—with a thankful heart—' Thank God! I have blessings with less care, temptation, and disappointment.'

On no side can we look, but we *see a sore evil under*

---

* Brentius.

the sun—painful to the eyes—much more to the heart.
Can we wonder at it? The seed produces the harvest.
" Whatsoever a man soweth, that shall he also reap." (Gal.
vi. 7.)   Mark this picture of grovelling vanity—Bunyan's
Muckrake drawn to life.   *Riches* centred in selfish aggrandizement, and therefore *kept for the owners thereof to their
hurt.*   And grievous indeed is the *hurt.*   Such strong
temptations to pride, vain-glory, love of the world, forgetfulness of God—so many bye-paths to perdition (1 Tim. vi.
9, 10)—so many mighty hindrances against entering into
the kingdom ! *   They are always a temptation.   So often
a rise in the world is declension or apostacy from God.   It
is only when they are consecrated to God, and laid out in the
service of our fellow-creatures—that they become a blessing.

Here, however, the fortune which the miser had heaped
up, has *perished* by some kind of *evil travail.   There is
nothing in his hand.*   He leaves his child a beggar, and *he
returns to his mother's womb naked as he came forth.* (Job, i.
20. 1 Tim. vi. 7.)   This may seem a commonplace picture.
But what if the reality had its due practical influence?
What a substance of the truest happiness would there be in
living for eternity !   The miser's present course is indeed *a
sore evil*—all his *profit* of pouring out his heart upon the
world will be found at last to have been only *labouring for the
wind* (Hos. viii. 7 ; xii. 1)—'embracing a shadow; grasping
the air; wearying himself for that, which hath no substance
of true felicity in it.' †   *Sickness and sorrow* shadow his path
to a clouded eternity.   And what will be the forlorn despondency in awakening to the consciousness—'I have
wasted all the golden opportunities that can never be recalled, of gaining grace, and winning heaven—wasted them

* Matt. xix. 23.   *Those that trust in riches.*   Mark, x. 24.
† Pemble.

in the most senseless of all objects—heaping up treasure
for no other end than the splendour of my own name?'
"Horror taketh hold of me" in the thought of the last
passage—'even when cold in death, his hand remaining
clenched in the last convulsive grasp, with which he sought
to retain his darling treasure'*—*wrath* from above!—terror
from within!—a *dark* eternity of unspeakable torment!—
one everlasting night! He "shall never see light!" (Ps.
xlix. 19.)

18. *Behold that which I have seen; it is good and comely for*
one to eat and to drink, and to enjoy the good of all his
labour that he taketh under the sun all the days of his life,
which God giveth him; for it is his portion. 19. *Every*
man also, to whom God hath given riches and wealth, and
hath given him power to eat thereof, and to take his por-
tion, and to rejoice in his labour—this is the gift of God.
20. *For he shall not much remember the days of his life,*
because God answereth him in the joy of his heart.

A bright vision comes before the wise man, in contrast
with the frowning cloud just before. He calls our earnest
attention to it. It is a matter that he can vouch for. *Be-*
hold that which I have seen. There is a school among us
who are fond of describing religion by its sorrows, and who
forget, or seem to forget, their overbalancing joys. In their
view it is as if we were 'humbled and degraded, with only
not despair; sorrowing with a perpetual sorrow.'† But
Solomon shews us the reality of happiness even in a world
of sin and sorrow. "All things are ours—things present,"
as well as "things to come." (1 Cor. iii. 22.) And *good*

* Wardlaw.
† Sewell's *Christian Morals*, p. 408.

and *comely* is the privilege of connecting our present blessings with the enjoyment of God.*

Is this the picture of mere worldly happiness? as if we
might plead against over-strictness, and in favour of more
indulgence. Shall the libertine plead it in excuse for his own
lust? We think not. The law of discipleship in the Old
and New Testament is substantially the same—self-denial
—taking up the cross. Solomon only insists that the true
servant of God is really the happiest of men—that "God
giveth him richly all things to enjoy" (1 Tim. vi. 17)—
that he has a goodly *portion* in the world—though not the
world for his portion—something really to be enjoyed,
allotted by him, who in temporals, as well as in spirituals,
"divideth to every man severally as he will." *This is the
gift of God*—every day of our life a new *gift*—specially
to be employed for his glory and in his service.

It is difficult to maintain a just appreciation of the *gifts*
of God. 'We err either in excess or in defect.' † 'A
Christian'—as has been well said—'knows the value of the
good creatures of God. But he does not put them in the
place of God.' ‡ It is most important to set out Christian
liberty, while we inculcate Christian mortification. We
must be careful not to give unworthy views of the real happiness to be found in the world—not primary indeed, yet
valuable, though subordinate. Let there be no cloud upon
the glory of the Divine beneficence. Let godliness throw a
sunbeam upon all temporal enjoyments. Let us carefully
adjust the balance. We have seen that riches well-nigh
shut us out of heaven (Matt. xix. 23)—and that "the love
of them drowns men in destruction and perdition." (1 Tim.
vi. 9, 10.) Must we not then cast them away? The

* See 1 Tim. iv. 3–5. Comp. chap. ii. 24 ; iii. 12, 13, 22.
† Lavater.   ‡ Cecil's *Original Thoughts*, p. 609.

Preacher gives the due balance. They are not essentially evil. The evil is in their abuse—as we have said—in their love, not in their possession. The true difference is not in the gift, but in *the power* to use it—*to eat thereof.* The gift may belong to the ungodly. *The power* is the exclusive privilege of the Christian. He 'is not the slave of his worldly goods, but truly the master of them.' * God 'giveth him bodily health, joy of spirit, occasions of content, peace, and liberty, of possessing, and enjoying, and other the like favours, without which goods are useless to men; and yet they depend only upon God's good-will, and riches cannot give them; nor man of himself gain them.' †

And what of the ungodly? His days drag heavily. *The remembrance* is clouded. The road before him dark and wearisome. But what with him, who 'lives in God's grace?' God *answereth him* in the joy *of his heart* ' by the comfort of his Spirit.' ‡ With him time flies on with angels' wings. *The remembrance of the days of his life* are " few and evil." (Gen. xlvii. 9.) The glowing anticipation melts away the past. For how soon will every spring of sorrow be dried up for ever! (Isa. xxxv. 10.) How bright does the eternity of joy contrast with " the affliction but for a moment!" (2 Cor. iv. 17.) " Pleasures" ever new are his portion " at God's right hand for evermore." (Ps. xvi. 11.)

* Bp. Patrick. † Diodati. ‡ Ibid.

CHAPTER VI.

1. *There is an evil, which I have seen under the sun ; and it is common among men.* 2. *A man, to whom God hath given riches, wealth, and honour ; so that he wanteth nothing for his soul of all that he desireth thereof ; and yet God giveth him not power to eat thereof ; but a stranger eateth it. This is vanity, and it is an evil disease.*

THIS evidently continues the last chapter. Covetousness—that odious lust—is again before us. ' Covetousness'—says Bp. Taylor—' makes a man miserable, because riches are not means to make a man happy. And unless felicity were to be bought with money, he is a vain person, who admires heaps of gold and rich possessions.' * The man—like Solomon himself †—*wanted nothing for his soul of all that he desired thereof.* But here was the contrast—and *the case was common among men.* The gifts of God abounded to overflowing. But here *God gave not the power to eat thereof.* Sickness, affliction, or worldly disappointment, restrained the blessing. It seems to have been a judicial infliction. He did not use the gifts of his bountiful Father for their rightful purpose. Most justly therefore is he deprived of their blessing. " From him that hath not shall be taken away even that which he hath." (Matt. xxv. 29.) ' Because he has not the will to serve God with it, God denies him the power to serve himself with it.' ‡ His portion *a stranger eateth.* Some artful interested person has smoothed his way into the miser's good graces, and melted

* *Holy Living,* chapter iv. sect. viii.   † See chap. ii. 10.
‡ Henry.

away his substance. Thus "he heapeth up riches, and cannot tell who shall gather them." (Ps. xxxix. 6.)   Here is another show of *vanity*—truly *an evil disease*.   Blessed indeed are the gifts of God to us, when we own them to be his property!   But never let us forget the responsibility which they bring with them—"Occupy till I come." (Luke, xix. 13.)   We all have our responsibilities.   And we are happy just in the proportion that we acknowledge them. Selfishness blasts the harvest.   As well might we look for it from the seed-corn laid up in the granary, instead of being cast into the ground.   Our real happiness, therefore, is the thankful improvement of God's own gifts—acknowledging his prerogative to give the power of enjoyment, no less than the blessing to be enjoyed.   As for the riches, wealth, and honour—'though it be but an image, if it be a golden image, all people, nations, and languages, will fall down and worship it.'*   A mercy—a special mercy is it to be delivered from Mammon idolatry!—to be restrained in our worldly desires—and, above all things, to "lay up for ourselves treasures in heaven"—treasures, that we can never lose—that never spend, and never perish.†

3. *If a man beget an hundred children, and live many years, so that the days of his years be many, and his soul be not filled with good, and also that he hath no burial, I say, that an untimely birth is better than he.   4. For he cometh in with vanity, and departeth in darkness, and his name shall be covered with darkness.   5. Moreover he hath not seen the sun, nor known anything; this hath more rest than the other.   6. Yea, though he live a thousand years twice told, yet hath he seen no good.   Do not all go to one place?*

In the case here supposed two of nature's fondest desires

        * Henry.   † See Matt. vi. 20.

are alluded to—a quiver full of children,* and *the days of many years.* Yet if the *soul is not filled with good,* nothing would be of avail for our happiness. As a proof of the ill esteem in which he is held, his life may end with obloquy —no respect paid the miser at his burial—his death unhonoured, unlamented.† Sordid accumulation is a dark cloud upon his name to the last. The Preacher decides without hesitation upon this case. *Better* not to have been born at all—or if born, to have died at the birth—to have gone at once from the womb to the grave. 'Better is the fruit that drops from the tree before it is ripe, than that which is left to hang on till it is rotten. Job in his passion thinks the condition of *an untimely birth* better than his when he was in adversity. (Job, iii. 1–16.) But Solomon here pronounces it *better* than the condition of the worldling in his greatest prosperity, when the world smiles upon him.' ‡

'*I say,* then'—concludes the wise man—'*that an untimely birth* § *is better than he. He cometh in with vanity,*' seeming to have been born to no purpose. *He departeth in darkness*—leaving no trace or remembrance behind—*his name*—if indeed he can be said to have a *name*—*is covered with darkness*—he is immediately forgotten. He *hath not seen the sun, nor known anything.* His pleasures are momentary ; yet unalloyed. He neither *sees nor knows anything* to connect him with a world of sorrow. It is a nega-

---

* Ps. cxxvii. 5. Comp. Ps. xvii. 14—*an hundred children*—a definite for an indefinite number. See 1 Sam. xviii. 10. Prov. xvii. 10. 1 Cor. xiv. 19.

† The importance attached to burial is often alluded to.   Deut. xxviii. 26. 1 Kings, xiv. 11–13. Isa. xiv. 19, 20. Jer. xxii. 18, 19, &c. The picture does not describe the literal want of burial, but the absence of all suitable and affectionate honour paid to his remains. —See *Pictorial Bible* in loco.

‡ Henry.

§ See Chap. iv. 3. Ps. lviii. 8.

tion of enjoyment—a peaceful shadow of existence without guilt, disgrace, pain, or punishment. He had rest in the womb, and now in the grave (Job, iii. 17)—*rest more than the other,* who is still, as the man of avarice, tossed about still in restless misery—*seeing no good*—a mere blank—a cumberer of the ground. Surely it is not life, but enjoyment that gives value to existence, and makes the vital difference.* *Life, though a thousand years twice told,* without *seeing good,* is only protracted misery. The longest inhabitant of earth— as well as he that *hath not seen the sun*—*do not all go to one place?* " The small and great are there. All are of the dust, and all turn to dust again." (Job, iii. 19. Chap. iii. 20.)

But may we not look at this picture on an higher level? All hangs upon this point—*the soul*—the whole man— *filled with good.* And what *good* is there that will *fill* the man? Only when as a sinner he finds a reconciled God in Christ—his way to God—his peace with God. Never was a more refreshing truth, than from one who found the witness and seal of it in contact with heathen misery. 'The sweet savour of Christ'—writes an Indian missionary—'is the only antidote to the wretchedness of man.'† Put aside this high privilege—or neglect it—and then to die with all the unfulfilled responsibilities of a long life upon his head— who can calculate the issue for eternity?—Truly *an untimely birth is better than he.* " Good were it for that man, if he had not been born!" (Matt. xxvi. 24.) Sinner! there is time yet to pause—to pray—to consider—" Work while it is day." For the faithful worker eternity has no cloud. Hell is closed against thee by the blood of Jesus. Heaven will be thy home—the infinite reward of grace. 'Thy best

* See 1 Pet. iii. 10.

† Rev. A. H. Frost, Church Missionary in Bombay.—*Missionary Record,* April 1859.

rest'—as a pious expositor remarks—'will be in the arms
of thy Saviour.' *

7. *All the labour of man is for his mouth, yet the appetite is
   not filled.*   8. *For what hath the wise man more than the
   fool ?   What hath the poor, that knoweth to walk before
   the living ?*

The labour of man is ordinarily *for his mouth*—for his
whole body—for the support of life.   Such is the ordinance
of God—the curse of the fall—" In the sweat of thy face
thou shalt eat bread." (Gen. iii. 19.)   If the curse be removed, the cross remains.   Man can do no more by his *labour*
than satisfy his bodily wants.   " He that laboureth, laboureth
for himself; for *his mouth* craveth it of him." (Prov. xvi. 26.)

Yet with all our *labour the appetite is not filled.*   The
same natural cravings return from day to day.   Worldly
desires are no less unsatisfied.   The covetous man—the
more he has, the more he wants.   'Vain indeed'—says Bp.
Taylor—'is the hope of that man, whose soul rests on
vanity.' †   Strange delusion, to suppose that more of this
world would bring increase of happiness !   This is indeed to
seek where it is impossible to find, and where the insatiable
appetite is continually crying " Give, give." (Prov. xxx. 15.)
This lust is indeed an universal disease.   *For what*—in respect of satisfaction—*hath the wise man more than the fool?*
In real substance—" Wisdom excelleth folly, as far as light
excelleth darkness." (Chap. ii. 13.)   But in outward circumstance (*the only point to which Solomon is adverting*)—there is
no pre-eminence.   Riches, 'lest they should be thought to

* Geier.
† Sermon on *The Foolish Exchange.*

be evil, are given also to the good ; and that they should not be esteemed great, or the chiefest jewels, they are given also to the bad.' *

The last clause is obscure. † But a careful consideration of the statement will bring out a satisfactory meaning. As *the wise man hath nothing more than the fool;* so neither hath *the poor — knowing to walk before the living* — any advantage above his more simple neighbour. The same fruit of their *labour* provides for them both. In fact, man's external condition *in natural satisfaction* is far more equalized than appears on the surface. Each has his station and his work. Happy indeed are they, who *labour* in dependence upon him, who alone can bless their work. And thrice blessed are they, who are *labouring* for eternity, and who yet receive the reward of their *labour* as the free gift of their Divine Master. (John, vi. 27.)

9. *Better is the sight of the eyes than the wandering of the desire : this is also vanity and vexation of spirit.*

The sight of the eyes is the reality before us. *The wandering of the desire* is the longing pursuit of some unattainable object — some phantom only imagined — never reached. The fruitless search only ends in *vanity and vexation of spirit.* *Better* therefore to enjoy what we have in possession, than to be roving up and down in anxious weariness. For what can be more wretched, than when the false pictures of the world palm themselves upon us for realities, when the shadows begin to pass away, and there is no substance to supply their place ! 'The true good that a man can have in this life, is to enjoy that which he hath in peace and rest,

---

* Augustine, quoted by Serran.
† See *Poli Synopsis* and Bp. Patrick.—Holden.

and not to *wander* in the straying and unsatisfied desires after that which he hath not.' * The *wandering desire*— "Loving to wander"—is indeed our nature. † But under Divine Teaching the light is clear and strong; the eye and heart are fixed. One object fills every desire—" Whom have I in heaven but thee? and there is none upon earth that I desire besides thee." (Ps. lxxiii. 25.) Everything is unreal, when placed beside this glorious treasure. Our position is not so much looking up to heaven from earth, as looking down from heaven to earth. And it is when we thus realize our rightful standing in heaven (Comp. Eph. ii. 6; Philip. iii. 20) we rise above the dying vanities of earth. " The way of life is above to the wise, that he may depart from hell beneath." (Prov. xv. 24.) There is no *wandering* here. But if we do not find our rest here, truly it is a sickening picture. Our comforts are dashed with bitterness. Our whole sky is darkened with despondency.

And yet this steady discipline of our *desires* is a Christian habit of no easy attainment. When the pilgrims passed through 'Vanity Fair'—it was only the earnest cry— " Turn away mine eyes from beholding Vanity" (Ps. cxix. 37), that could maintain their singleness of purpose, and repress the constant *wandering of the desire*. And this must be our prayer every day—all the day. We cannot—we must not—forget it. Xerxes is said to have promised a great reward to the inventor of a new pleasure. How prolific is our great enemy in his inventions! The world is the grand instrument of his bright delusions. Volumes might be written upon the subtle wiles, by which he labours to keep God out of sight—out of heart. But in the posture of prayer and watchfulness, we lay claim to all the promises of the Gospel; and—however vehement the conflict—we come off " more than conquerors." (Rom. viii. 37.)

* Diodati.   † See Isa. liii. 6. Jer. xiv. 10; l. 6.

But often it is the spark within. How fearful the con-
flagration from one *wandering desire*—one flesh-pleasing
indulgence! How often is our wise and loving Father constrained to make the creature a grief, because we are so disposed to make it a god! 'Thou hast made us for thyself'—
said the pious Augustine—' and our heart is restless, until it
finds rest in thee. Who shall give me to rest in thee, that
thou mayst come into my heart, and inebriate it; that I may
forget my own evils, and embrace thee, my only good?
Behold! the ears of my heart are before thee. O Lord,
open them, and " say unto my soul, I am thy salvation!' " *

10. *That which hath been is named already, and it is known
that it is man; neither may he contend with him that is
mightier than he.*

The Preacher is here reviewing the result of his long and
extensive enquiry. *That which hath been*—the whole of
what can be obtained from all sources—wisdom—pleasure
—honour—riches—all—*has been already named.* All have
opened before us, as so many shades of vanity—*known* to be
that little word of great meaning—*Man.* For " verily man
at his best state is altogether vanity." (Ps. xxxix. 5.) His
original dignity only serves to set out more vividly his present
degradation. Let him be ever so high in his own eyes, or in
worldly estimation, the stamp of vanity is indelible. *It is
known that it is man*—at best but man.

His religion is self-wrought. Whatever it be, it never
brings him close to God. It always therefore leaves him
short of peace with God. Man is its centre. What is
wanting is the teaching of humility. 'Remember'—

* *Confessions*, book i. Ps. xxxv. 3.

speaks Bp. Taylor in his own eloquence—'what thou wert before thou wert begotten. Nothing. What wert thou in the first regions of thy dwelling, before thy birth? Uncleanness. What wert thou for many years after? Weakness. What in all thy life? A great sinner. What in all thy excellences? A mere debtor to God—to thy parents—to the earth—to all the creatures!'*

A being—thus fraught with infirmity and corruption—a very worm in utter weakness and helplessness—can he *contend* with his Maker—infinitely *mightier than he?* (Isa. xlv. 9.) Can he implead him, and call him to account? "Nay, but, O man, who art thou that repliest against God?" (Rom. ix. 20.) Learn the lesson of prostrate submission. Take thy proper place—"laying thine hand on thy mouth" (Job, xl. 4), and thy mouth in the dust. To *contend* is to add madness to folly. To submit is thy security and thy rest.

11. *Seeing that there be many things that increase vanity, what is man the better? For who knoweth what is good for a man in this life all the days of his vain life, which he spendeth as a shadow? For who can tell a man what shall be after him under the sun?*

Let us look at the point to be demonstrated. No fruit of happiness can be found in this world's *vanity*. The several parts have been brought out before us, and *the many things* have been proved to *increase,* instead of removing, the *vanity.* Past, present, and future—all partake of the same *vanity.* Nor is it the infirmity of our bodily nature—"of the earth, earthy." (1 Cor. xv. 47.) It is the result of the fall, burying us under an almost infinite number of carnal appetites—keeping us down to earth. Every day's experience

* *Holy Living*, chap. ii. section iv.

brings painful proof of this degradation. So that the godly
expositor suitably reminds us—'Humbly acknowledge thy
state. Fly from the fleeting vanities of the world. Look
for all goodness in Christ and in heaven.'*

The question, therefore, is clearly decided—*What is man
the better*, in regard to his true happiness, for any—for all—
of them? Every form of happiness is but a phantom. He
is, therefore, no *better*—no happier—no richer—for having
more opportunities than others to follow such shadows.
(Chap. i. 2, 3.)

A sickening prospect, if this world be our all! We
may well then ask—*Who knoweth what is good for a man?*
Hard is it to know. What we think *good* may be evil. What
we think evil may be substantial *good*. What a hazard we
run in making our own choice! Lot's well-watered meadows
brought him an harvest of misery.† Oh! my God, while
I am *"walking in a vain show,"* let me be grasping the everlasting substance. Save me from 'the foolish exchange' ‡—
eternity for trifles. While the future is clouded in darkness,
and no man can *tell me what shall be after me;* let me lie
passive in thy hand, and be active in thy present work, and
all will be peace. Whatever be, let it be thy choice for me;
not mine for myself.

> Thy way, not mine, O Lord,
> However dark it be!
> Lead me by thine own hand;
> Choose out the path for me.
>
> I dare not choose my lot;
> I would not, if I might;
> Choose thou for me, my God,
> So shall I walk aright.

Bonar's Hymns, p. 258.

---

* Geier.   † See Gen. xiii. 10, 11, with xiv. 12. 2 Pet. ii. 7, 8.
‡ Bp. Taylor.

One way is open to us all to *know what is good*. Many
are asking with restless enquiry—" Who will shew ?"   Let
our prayer be—" Lord ! lift thou up the light of thy countenance upon us." (Ps. iv. 6.)   Reconciliation and acceptance
realize the blessing with perfect, never-ending satisfaction.
Nothing is wanting for the present, but what he largely
supplies.   Eternity will be our home with him, and we " shall
go no more out." (Rev. iii. 12.)

CHAPTER VII.

1. *A good* name is better than precious ointment, and the
day of death than the day of one's birth.*

'As we have proved life to be such a mass of vanity, and
exposed to so many troubles—shall we then cast it away ?
Far from it !   Rather let us order it so as—partly at least—
to escape some of its many evils, and to gather all the fruit
that may be obtained from it.' †

We are now coming to a somewhat brighter atmosphere.
The varied shadows may have led Solomon to bring out
something lasting—precious in itself, more precious, because
lasting.   *A good name* is a substantial good ; it brightens a
man's life, and embalms his memory. (Ps. cxii. 6.   Prov. x. 7.)
' It both tarrieth behind him on earth, and goeth with him to
heaven, and will crown him with glory at the last day.' ‡
A good name is better than a great *name*, that flimsy—
worthless vanity—of great account with the world.   But,

---

* Literally *a name*—put for *a good name*.   Comp. Prov. xviii. 22 ;
xxii. 1.   Ps. xxxvii. 23.

† Beza.   ‡ Grainger.

Lord, teach us to remember — "That which is highly esteemed among men is abomination in the sight of God." (Luke, xvi. 15.) The real treasure is 'the true and solid *name* of faith and holiness' * — a glorious crown, though stamped upon men, who "are made as the filth of the world," and "of whom the world is not worthy." (1 Cor. iv. 13. Heb. xi. 38.) But let there be no pluming upon outward merit or adorning. Remember — the appearance may be cast away with revolt, and yet the idol may be secretly worshipped. 'Let thy face, like Moses', shine to others. But make no looking-glasses for thyself. Take no content in praise, when it is offered thee. But let thy rejoicing in God's gift be allayed with fear, lest this good bring thee to evil.' †

Solomon could form a just estimate of this *good*. He had known both its possession and its loss. Elsewhere he compares it with "great riches," and found it far excelling. ‡ Here he weighs it against precious *ointment* — a treasure highly valued. 'The *name* is good' — says Bp. Sanderson — 'and the ointment good; but of the two goods, *the good name is better than the good ointment*.' §

To some, indeed, it is a matter of no moment what the world say or think of them. But ought it not to be a care? The Apostle counted "it a very small thing to be judged of man's judgment." But how strongly did he inculcate the obligation to "be blameless and harmless, the sons of God without rebuke, in the midst of a crooked and perverse

* Diodati.

† Bp. Taylor's *Holy Living*, chap. ii. section iv.

‡ Prov. xxii. 1. The Son of Sirach heightens the balance — and prefers it 'before great treasures of gold.'—Ecclus. xli. 12, 13.

§ *Sermon on Text*. Comp. Ecclus. xlix. 1. We find *precious ointment* among Hezekiah's choice treasure. 2 Kings, xx. 13. Isa. xxxix. 2. Comp. also John, xii. 3.

nation, among whom we shine as lights in the world!"*
The value of this *good name* is every way manifest. It gains
esteem and confidence. It gives force to counsel, authority
to reproof, weight to example.

The second clause must obviously be taken with its limit.
To the apostate Judas—and with him—to all the ungodly
heirs of the second death—the judgment is awfully clear and
decisive. "Good were it for them, if they had not been
born." (Matt. xxvi. 24. Rev. xxi. 8.)   But where the *name*
is adorned with "the beauties of holiness," it is a name in
" the Lamb's book of life"—" sealed unto the day of redemption." (Rev. xiii. 8. Eph. iv. 30.)   The possession is assured.
The prospect draws nearer every day.   Joyous therefore as
was *the day of one's birth* (John, xvi. 21), *the day of death* will
be infinitely *better*.   Is not the day, that will deliver us from
sin and sorrow, far *better* than the day that brought us into
them ?   Does not the "voice from heaven" proclaim this
blessedness with the attesting seal, " Yea, saith the Spirit ?"
(Rev. xiv. 13.)   Does not every returning birthday rejoice the
heart with the remembrance—a year nearer home ?   The
conflict then ended for ever !   The term of exile from the
Lord then finished !   (2 Cor. v. 6–8.)   How complete will be
the consciousness—"To die is gain !   To depart, and to
be with Christ is far *better*." (Philip. i. 21, 23.)   Born an
heir of trouble (Job. v. 7), crowned an heir of glory !   Who
can doubt but the coronation-day must be *the better* day—
the day of unspeakable and everlasting joy !†

2. *It is better to go to the house of mourning than to the house*

* 1 Cor. iv. 3, with Philip. ii. 15.   Comp. iv. 8 ; also 2 Cor. viii. 21.

† It was the bright shining of this *better day*, that stirred up the
triumphant faith of a Christian mother—who, seeing her beloved
child depart for glory—looking up to heaven, exclaimed—' I wish
you joy, my darling !'—*Life of Mrs. Isabella Graham.*

of feasting: for this is the end of all men, and the living will lay it to his heart.

A heap of paradoxes are rising before us, like the beatitudes which preface the Sermon on the Mount. But the paradoxes of the Bible open out valuable truths. Here is no dream of theory or imagination—no difficult point of controversy—but a page of daily history. Experience only brings us to these conclusions. These are the words of sober wisdom. Thousands of Christian mourners—all who are chastened *as sons*—have responded and borne testimony to their truth. Our heavenly Father, even when using his sharpest rod, so accompanies it with the whisper of his love,* that the child almost dreads the removal of the discipline—lest he should lose so rich a blessing. Yet this is not the judgment of the world. They do not love to be brought into contact with realities, or to be reminded of the coming "days of darkness." (Chap. xi. 8.) There is an unwelcome message to their conscience—Art thou ready to meet this solemn—this hastening season? The wise man does not say that it is sweeter, but that *it is better to go to the house of mourning.*

'It will do us more good to go to a funeral, than to go to a festival.'† Not that either of them are wrong. Our blessed Lord attended both. 'He adorned and beautified with his presence and first miracle' a marriage-feast.‡ And he was found groaning and weeping at the grave of Lazarus. (John, xi. 33–35.) In both places we may glorify him, and follow his footsteps. May it be in his spirit!

The value of *the house of mourning* is in the lesson it teaches. Here is the *end of all men.* What *better* lesson can there be? If anything will set the thoughtless to think,

* See Rev. iii. 19.   † Henry.
‡ *Marriage Service.* See John, ii. 1–11.

this will be it.   It is what all must expect—what all must
arrive at—"going the way of all the earth." (Josh. xxiii. 14;
Heb. ix. 27.)   It is the grand design of *the house of feasting*
to destroy recollection—*The house of mourning* makes the last
scene palpable.   It is the Divine ordinance to bring *the
living* to thoughtfulness; and far gone must they be, if they
do not *lay it to heart,* and fasten it there.

A mercy indeed it is to be brought to think!   A greater
mercy still to be led to pray.   When the solemn messenger
knocks—when his entrance spreads a pall over the joyous
house, then indeed does he speak to the heart—seal his impression there—and stir up the enquiry—'How may I meet
the crisis in peace, confidence, and acceptance?'   And
then comes in sight the remedy—most welcome, because
most fitting to the sinner's case.   'Sin his disorder; Christ
his physician; pain his medicine; the Bible his support;
the grave his bed; and death itself an angel, expressly sent
to release the worn-out labourer, or crown the faithful
soldier.'*

3. *Sorrow is better than laughter; for by the sadness of the
   countenance the heart is made better.   4. The heart of the
   wise is in the house of mourning; but the heart of fools is
   in the house of mirth.*

'How earnestly'—as an excellent commentator observes†
—'does Solomon persevere in drawing our hearts from the
vain and perilous joys of the world!'   Still he continues his
paradoxes—*Sorrow is better than laughter.*   So valuable, so
needful is it, that we doubt whether it be safe to be without *sorrow,* till we are without sin.   Christiana was well
reminded on the outset of her pilgrimage—'The bitter is

---

* Cecil's *Visit to the House of Mourning.*   † Geier.

before the sweet, and that also'—she added—'will make the sweet the sweeter.' This is not therefore the sentiment of a sour misanthrope. It is that of one, who looks beyond the momentary ebullition of the *sorrow* to the after-abounding and largely-compensating results. What if there be a "need be" for the present "heaviness?" How bright the end — "Found unto, praise and honour and glory at the appearing of Jesus Christ!"* (1 Pet. i. 6, 7.) Meanwhile—waiting for this glorious end—*the house of mourning* is *the wise man's school.* Here we are disciplined to lessons of inestimable value. We obtain the knowledge of that dark mystery— our own hearts. We learn the Christian alphabet, and spell out in the Lord's dealings the letters of wisdom, forbearance, faithfulness, and love. We study the Christian dictionary, and often find such views of the character of God and his ways presented to us, as a whole life of ordinary study and contemplation could not have set forth. We find the Bible to be a book of realities. We cannot but bear our witness to it. We have felt its power. "I believed, and therefore have I spoken." (Ps. cxvi. 10. 2 Cor. iv. 13.)

Often when our sky is bright, we forget that the clouds may quickly form. And here the sight of *sorrow* brings us to a right recollection ; and we can bless our God, that he is leading us through a wilderness, and not through a paradise. We seem to be bereaved. But the main matter is untouched. Enough is left for "a song in the house of our pilgrimage." (Ps. cxix. 54.) If we look at the medicine, we take it from him as exactly fitted to our case. It is weighed out by his own hand. We see how the different ingredients "work *together*" (not the sweet alone without the bitter) "for good." (Rom. viii. 28.) If we complain of the cross as a fainting burden, we will carry it to him. Cannot he who appointed, support us under it, and carry us through it ?

* Ponder carefully Heb. xii. 10, 11.

Now then let us take the balance, and see—Is not *sorrow better than laughter?* It is not only a school of instruction, but the house of consolation. *By the sadness of the countenance the heart is made better.* Here is " meat to eat that" the world " know not of." " Thanks be to God, who causeth us *alway*"—in *sorrow* not less than in comfort— " to triumph in Christ." (2 Cor. ii. 14.) We hear our Father's voice. We live upon his promise. We assure ourselves with undoubted confidence in his power to make every promise good—to perform it even more than we had anticipated. And our answer to the question—" Is all well?" is joyfully given—" All is well." (2 Kings, iv. 26.)

> Bless my trials, thus to sever
>   Me for ever
> From the love of self and sin.
> Let me through them see thee clearer,
>   Find thee nearer,
> Grow more like to thee within.
>
> Tersteegen, *Lyra Germanica*, 2nd Series.

This *sorrow* is no sudden flash—vanishing, and leaving no impression behind. It is a solemn tender spirit—meek humiliation of soul. Nothing but Almighty grace can produce it. ' Philosophy'—as our great moralist* lays it down —' may infuse stubbornness. But religion only can give patience.' The one may force the confession—" Thy will be done." But it is the other only, that puts stillness and submission into the words, and makes them real. The Divine Sovereignty—reverently acknowledged and applied—at once silences and satisfies.

Yet there is much exercise for the child of God. He is in a training school for heaven—the school dignified by the humbling experience of the Son of God, who, "though a Son," condescended to "learn obedience by the things which he suffered." (Heb. v. 8.) The lessons of the school are

* Dr. Johnson.

costly. Yet if they seem to be severe—be it remembered—
it is the education of the Heir of a crown. We are made to
feel, that had we not leaned so strongly on our earthly props,
they might not have broken under us. But if our Father
takes away *our* all, does he not give *his* all—infinitely richer
and more enduring? Still it may be a school of paradoxes.
Yet to humility and faith all will be made plain in our
Father's best and most fitting time.

But no wonder, that with such lessons to be learned, and
such consolations to be enjoyed, *the heart of the wise should
be in the house of mourning.* To *the house of mirth* we may
go. But *our heart* can never rest there. The world can
never be our home. Its resources are too poor for our wants.
Solid satisfaction—bearing us up, when all is sinking around
—a balm for every sorrow, when worldly 'joys are all packed
up and gone'—these are the treasures of *the house of mourning.* The refined exercise of sympathy—the sufferings of
our fellow-creatures stirring up thanksgivings for our own
mercies—the sunbeams of heaven darting their rays within—
all this is bright. But how much brighter and more joyous
is the prospect of *the house* without *mourning*—where "the
days of our *mourning* shall be ended" (Isa. lx. 20)—where
"there shall be no more sorrow, nor crying, nor any more
pain, for the former things" shall have "passed away!"
(Rev. xxi. 4.)

In this true resting-place is *the heart of the wise.* But
where is *the heart of the fool?*—where he can try to forget
himself—gratify his corrupt taste—get rid of unwelcome thoughts—put away God and eternity—all reality
blotted out of his mind—'O my soul, come not thou into
his secret.' (Gen. xlix. 6.) 'In the midst of *his laughter* the
heart is sorrowful, and the end of *that mirth* is heaviness.'
(Prov. xiv. 13.)

5. *It is better to hear the rebuke of the wise, than for a man to hear the song of fools.* 6. *For as the crackling of thorns under a pot, so is the laughter of the fool ; this is also vanity.*

In many things we all offend. (Jam. iii. 2.)   None of us therefore are above the need of rebuke.   But do we all value it ?   It is naturally unpalatable.   And it is often hard to receive it from another, even "when our heart condemns us." But as many sweet things are poison, so many bitter things are medicine.   Let me then bring home this probing point. Are the "faithful wounds of a friend" welcome to me ?   Do I heartily admit his "open *rebuke* to be *better* than secret love" (Prov. xxvii. 5, 6)—yea, an exercise of true and Christian love ? (Ps. cxli. 5.)

But it is *the rebuke of the wise* alone that carries weight (Prov. xxv. 12)—carefully regarding the mind, manner, measure, and temper of the individual ; avoiding needless irritation in the exercise of Christian faithfulness.   David felt the value of this *rebuke*, and recorded it as a special mercy from his God. (1 Sam. xxv. 32, 33.)   And who of us, who have reaped its fruit in a tender conscience (Prov. xv. 32), but will come to a clear judgment—*It is better to hear the rebuke of the wise, than for a man to hear the song of fools ?*

Ah ! that atmosphere of poison—be it ever far from us ! It is only a reckless determination to fill the mind, so as to leave no room for the thoughts of death and of eternity. Again we insist—"*Sorrow is better than laughter.*"   'He that makes this mirth and he that likes it—both are fools, and their pleasantness will soon have an end.' *   For what after all is this *laughter of the fool,* but the *crackling of thorns under a pot*—a mere blaze for the moment? (Ps. lviii. 9; cxviii. 12.) ' It has answered—and even that in appearance only—the care-killing end of the moment.   But the subsequent dullness

* Pemble.

and *ennui* are only the deeper.'* Whether. it be the intoxi-
cation of the drunkard—the foolishness of the trifler, the
nonsense which amuses by its wit or rather folly—it only
brings out more fully the conviction—*This is also vanity.*
Indeed what other fruit could be found in pleasure pursued,
possessed, enjoyed—without God? Let the joy be admitted.
But how short-lived! Nothing left to reflect on! Solemn
is the warning from a voice of love. "Woe unto you that
laugh now; for ye shall mourn and weep." (Luke, vi. 25.)

7. *Surely oppression maketh a wise man mad, and a gift destroyeth the heart.*

The wise man bids us notice his special emphasis—*Surely.*
Often is he dwelling on the evils of oppression. (Chap. iii.
16; iv. 1; v. 8.) 'All of us are either subject to the power
of others, and therefore in danger of *oppression;* or we are
invested with power, and therefore tempted to oppress.'†
Oppression may be either the active power of inflicting suffering, or the passive enduring of it. The latter would seem to
be the more natural meaning—wrong cruelly inflicted—the
misery of being beaten down by tyranny. In the oppressor
himself it is an ebullition of selfishness (Ps. lxxiii. 8)—a
galling chain to his victims—sometimes *making* even *a wise
man mad.* (Exod. v. 21.) More than once has it thrown the
man of God off his sober balance, and hurried him into a
state nearly allied to *madness.*‡ How tender and considerate
is the dispensation—which, while it permits "the rod of the
wicked" to come, forbids it to "*rest* upon the lot of the
righteous!" The reason given is as here—lest it should
make the wise man mad—"lest the righteous put forth their
hands into iniquity." (Ps. cxxv. 3.)

---

* Wardlaw.   † Cartwright.
‡ Jer. xx. 7–18, with Job, iii. 1. Comp. Deut. xxviii. 32–34.

But the evil falls back upon the oppressor himself. One selfish principle naturally begets another. The act of *oppression* is often traced to *the gift* tendered as the price of the *oppression—destroying his heart*—blotting out every principle of moral integrity, rendering him callous to suffering, and deaf to the claims of justice. (Prov. xvii. 23.) Good reason was there for the Mosaic veto, restraining the influence of *gifts*. (Exod. xxiii. 8. Deut. xvi. 19.) There is indeed peril on both sides. Tyranny forces to irrational conduct ; bribery to lack of feeling. The standard of the Bible is the only security. " He that ruleth over men must be just—ruling in the fear of God." (2 Sam. xxiii. 3.)   When the Bible is reverenced as the Book of God—the sole rule of faith and practice, " a man's wisdom will make his face to shine" (Chap. viii. 1); and godliness will enrich the land with the precious fruit of "whatsoever things are honest, just, pure, lovely, and of good report." (Philip. iv. 8.)

8. *Better is the end of a thing than the beginning thereof;*
    and the patient in spirit is better than the proud in spirit.

The first clause is not indeed an universal maxim. Sometimes—and that in the most important of all matters *—*the ending* is far worse *than the beginning thereof.* Yet it often holds good. Solomon had already given an example (v. 1). In the instance just adverted to (Comp. also Prov. xx. 21), the *oppressor* may appear to have the advantage at first ; but *the end* may bring him low. The ordinary trials of the Christian life are grievous in *the beginning*; but fruitful in *the end*.† Therefore—whatever be the trial of faith—never despond. Never look at the present dark face of things, except in connexion with the will of God's love. We say

---

* See Matt. xii. 45. 2 Pet. ii. 20.
† See Heb. xii. 11. 1 Pet. i. 6, 7.

emphatically—*the will of his love.* Because—as Charnock finely observes—'God does not act anything barely by an immutable will, but by an immutable wisdom, and an unchangeable rule of goodness.'* Things might have been otherwise arranged; and they doubtless would have been so, had not this arrangement been the very best that could have been made. How many valuable discoveries in Christian experience has *the end of the thing* laid open, which at *the beginning* had only been imperfectly developed! The later mercies that flow out of early trials—how multiplied are they! 'It may be'—said Bp. Taylor—'that thou art "entered into the cloud," which will bring a gentle shower to refresh thy sorrows. God, who in mercy and wisdom governs the world, would never have suffered so many sadnesses, and especially to the most virtuous and wisest men, but that he intends they should be the seminary of comfort, the nursery of virtue, the exercise of wisdom, the trial of patience, the venturing for a crown, and the gate of glory.'†

When the aged Patriarch said—"All these things are against me"—he looked only at *the beginning.* Yet he lived to see the sun bursting out of the dark cloud. And at *the end* he saw that the things which he judged to be "against him," were not the evil that he had feared, but the "evil from which he was redeemed." Evil turned out to be substantial good—beyond all his expectation. (Gen. xlii. 36, with xlviii. 16.) Such also was the issue of the wilderness wanderings — "good" opened out "at the latter *end.*" (Deut. viii. 16.) And when "the Lord blessed the latter *end* of Job more than his *beginning,*" our special attention s turned to it as the cheering manifestation of *the end of the*

---

* Charnock on *The Immutability of God.*
† *Holy Living,* chap. ii. section vi.

Lord—that the Lord is very pitiful, and of tender mercy. (Job, i. with xlii. 12. Jam. v. 11.)

Evidently therefore things are better known by *the end*, than by *the beginning*. ' When the whole contexture and web of providences about the Church, and every individual member thereof, shall be wrought out, and in its full length and breadth (as it were) spread forth in the midst of all the redeemed, perfected, glorified, and triumphant company of saints standing round the throne, and with admiration beholding it; there will not then be found one misplaced thread, nor any wrong-set colour in it all.'*

The second clause of our verse naturally contrasts *patience* with *pride*. *Pride* is the source of impatience, as humility is the principle of gentleness and endurance. Our *patience* harmonizes with the will of God, and ministers to our comfort, as *pride* does to our trouble. ' Blessed grace !' exclaimed the saintly Martyn—' how it smooths the furrows of care, and gilds the dark paths of life ! It will make us kind, and enable us to do more for God and the Gospel, than the most fervid zeal without it.'† Every way therefore *better is the patient in spirit than the proud in spirit*. The one waits for *the end*. The other in the impatience of self-will revolts. " Let him make speed, and hasten his work, that we may see it." (Isa. v. 19.) There may be a determined purpose for God. And yet uneasy questionings, such as we may find it hard to answer—may afterwards arise, whether we took time to wait, before the impulse to act. Here then *patience*—committing the case to God, and doing his present will— brings a peaceful issue of the matter, even though fresh perplexities should arise after the decision.

Patience is the child of faith. " He that believeth shall not make haste. Surely there is an end, and thine expec-

---

* Durham—a valuable Scotch Puritan writer.

† *Life*, Part i.

tation shall not be cast off."* Let the Lord take his own course, as certainly he will. But trust him for *the end* in his own time and way. We can only improve his dispensations, as we walk with him in them, to know his mind. Beware of fretfulness in walking through the rough and thorny path. Does not he make it the way home—the way to glory? Never forget that we are most incompetent judges of his purposes. This only we know—and we know it from his own mouth—that the thoughts which he thinks towards us are thoughts of peace, and not of evil, to give us an expected *end*. (Jer. xxix. 11.)

Meanwhile we "have need of *patience*." (Heb. x. 36.) And not to value its work—hastily to give up good purposes because of difficulties—would prove us to be poor novices in the Christian life. *Proud* self-confidence expects to carry all before us, and after repeated failures sinks down in despondency. *The patient in spirit* is content—if it must be so—with feeble beginnings, poor success, and many repulses. He 'suffers in submission, and waits in hope, bearing the evils inflicted by man, in the remembrance that men are but God's hand; and resting in tranquil expectation, that *the end will be better than the beginning*.'† Deeply indeed do we need this daily cross—this practical homage of

---

* Isa. xxviii. 16. Prov. xxiii. 18.

"Wait the result ; nor ask with frantic rage,
  Why God permits such things ? His ways, though now
  Involved in clouds and darkness, will appear
  All right, when from thine eyes the mist is clear'd ;
  Till then, to learn submission to his will,
  More wisdom shews, than vainly thus t' attempt
  Exploring what thou canst not comprehend,
  And God for wisest ends thinks fit to hide."
                          Choheleth : Paraphrase.
            † Wardlaw.

the will. * But *the end* compensates for all. "After we
have done the will of God, we receive the promise." (Heb.
x. 34.) 'It is now the school-time, the season of the lesson
and the rod; then will be the eternal holiday. It is now
the season of the plough and harrow; then will be the pleasant harvest home; "they that sow in tears shall reap in
joy." ' † (Ps. cxxvi. 5.)

**9. *Be not hasty in thy spirit to be angry; for anger resteth in
the bosom of fools.***

A most important rule! So deeply affecting our happiness, and not less the beauty and consistency of our Christian
profession. It is indeed possible to conceive of "being
angry, and not to sin." (Eph. iv. 26.) Anger is an holy passion in the bosom of Jehovah. (Nah. i. 2.) It was displayed in the pure humanity of the Divine Saviour. (Mark,
iii. 5.) It was the intense sensibility of sorrow in the man
of God, when he witnessed the debasing idolatry of the
chosen nation. (Exod. xxxii. 19.) And yet it would be
most dangerous to presume upon this rare purity, when in
the infinite majority of cases, it is the ebullition of pride,
selfishness, and folly.

The impulse of *anger* here forbidden is *hastiness*—'a distemper, which seizes men on the least occasion in the world,
and perpetually without any real reason at all.' ‡ A quick
word—the veriest trifle—what a rude extinguisher it is for

---

* Luke, ix. 23.

> " As much we need the cross we bear,
>   As air we breathe, or light we see.
> It draws us to thy side in prayer ;
>   It calls to seek our strength in thee."—*Anon.*

† Robert Hall's *Sermon on the Heavenly Assembly.*

‡ Bp. Butler's *Sermon on Resentment.*

the moment! a sudden gust, that puts all holy feelings to flight! And alas! where is the atmosphere—even in the Church of God—where this damper to spirituality is not sensibly felt? *

The sad influence of this *hasty spirit* is deeply to be deprecated. We must "lift up holy hands without wrath." (1 Tim. ii. 8.) 'Anger'—as Bp. Taylor observes—'is a perfect alienation of mind from prayer; and therefore is contrary to that attention, which presents our prayers in a right line to God. For so'—adds he in his exquisitely beautiful picture—'have I seen a lark rising from his bed of grass, and soaring upwards, and singing as he rises, and hopes to get to heaven, and rise above the clouds. But the poor bird was beaten back with the loud sighings of an eastern wind, and his motion made irregular and inconsistent. Descending more at every breath of the tempest than it could recover by the libration and frequent weighing of its wings, till the little creature was forced to sit down and pant, and stay till the storm was over; and then it made a prosperous flight, and did rise and sing, as if it had learned music and motion from an angel.' †

Often does Solomon graphically mark this evil in his practical code. "He that is soon angry dealeth foolishly." (Prov. xiv. 17.) Commonly he contrasts it with its opposite grace—"He that is slow to wrath is of great understanding; but he that is hasty of spirit exalteth folly. A wrathful man stirreth up strife; but he that is slow to anger appeaseth strife. He that is slow to anger is better than he that taketh a city." (Ib. xiv. 29; xv. 18; xvi. 32.) The Apostolic rule is to the same purport, and of universal ap-

---

* David, 1 Sam. xxv. 21.   Elijah, 1 Kings, xix. 4.   Job, iii. 1. Jeremiah, xx. 7–18. Jonah, iv. 1–9. The disciples, Luke, ix. 54. The great Apostle, Acts, xxiii. 3.

† *The Return of Prayers.* Works, i. p. 638.

plication. "Let *every man* be slow to speak, *slow to wrath.*" (Jam. i. 19.) Physical temperament may sometimes call for a forbearing judgment. Yet as a general rule, let the excitement never be excused, or looked upon otherwise than as a sin hateful to God. If there be not at least some measure of command over the tongue and the temper, it may fairly be asked—'What is the Gospel worth? What evidence is there of its power upon the heart?' A present Saviour is the display at the front of the Gospel.* But you say 'I cannot help it.' You can, if you will—not of yourself—but "through Christ that strengtheneth you." (Philip. iv. 13.) Is not the power in him for you?—ready for every moment's application—sufficient for every emergency? Remember your God's high claims upon you, that "your light should shine to his glory." (Matt. v. 16.)

At all events, if *anger* rushes in by some sudden power, or at some unwary moment, take care that it does not *rest.* † It may *pass through* a wise man's heart. But *the bosom of the fool* is its home. The indulgence of causeless *anger* is the mark of *a fool*. Take care that we do not open our *bosom* to receive what we are forbidden to foster there. Its unrestrained power may be murderous outrage. The contemplation of the Saviour is the mysterious secret of victory. When did an "unadvised" word ever drop from "his lips?" When did mockery or scorn ever ruffle his spirit? When did sudden provocation ever for a moment cloud the bright sunshine of his holiness? Look then, and be what you behold. Look, and be like him. The likeness grows on us as we look. He is the holiest man, who looks most steadily at the mirror of glorious perfection. (2 Cor. iii. 18.)

---

* See Matt. i. 21.

† Cain, Gen. iv. 5–8. Jacob's sons, Gen. xxxiv. 7, 25. Absalom, 2 Sam. xiii. 22, 28, 32. Haman, Esth. iii. 5, 6. Herodias, Mark, vii. 19.

10. *Say not thou, What is the cause that the former days were better than these? for thou dost not enquire wisely concerning this.*

Impatience often produces a querulous spirit. 'How much brighter were the days of our fathers! Never shall we see the like again.' Yet be it remembered, we know *the former days* only by report. Present days are a felt reality. Under the pressure it is natural to believe, that *the former days were better than these.* Not indeed that the comparison in all cases is proscribed. A worldly failure implies the fact, and naturally excites *the enquiry —* *What is the cause?* It may also be a home question in Christian experience — Is there not a cause? "Let a man examine himself, and prove his own work." (1 Cor. xi. 28. Gal. vi. 4.) In the wider field some ages of the Church or the world may doubtless be *better* than others. The eras of civilization, and of extended religion, *are better* than the barbarous and unenlightened ages. This would suggest the legitimate application of the *enquiry.*

But the rebuke is evidently directed against that dissatisfied spirit, which puts aside our present blessings, exaggerates our evils, and reflects upon the government of God as full of inequalities, and upon his providence, in having cast us in such evil times. Do we ask — *What is the cause?* Let the fact first be proved. It could not apply to Solomon's time. No *former days* would compare with those best *days* of Israel's prosperity. (1 Kings, x. 27.) In other cases there may indeed be substantive materials for the proof. National changes may bring national declension. Increasing wealth and luxury may relax the tone of public morals. But — it may be asked — 'Is it not the ordinary habit of the old men of the generation to give

undue worth and weight to the records of bygone days?' *
Has not each succeeding generation left a protest against
the degeneracy of its predecessor? Yet in a general view
'God has been always good, and men have been always
bad,' † and "there is nothing new under the sun." (Ch. i.
9; iii. 15.)

The case therefore involves 'a doubtful problem and a
foolish question.' ‡ *For thou dost not enquire wisely concerning this.* The picture of a golden age, and the loveliness and purity of the primitive era, are now confessedly
only the day-dreams of imagination. Take then the broad
features of the present *day*. After due allowance has been
made for the fearful discoveries of ignorance and depravity
—yet mark the spread of true religion—the large provision
for the temporal comfort of the poor—the widely-diffused
blessings of Scriptural education—the influence of civil and
religious liberty—and, above all, the extended circulation
and preaching of the glorious Gospel throughout the world
—Would it not be hard to produce *former days better than
these?* " Blessed are the eyes that see the things that ye
see!" (Luke, x. 23, 24.)

After all—'it is folly to cry out of the badness of the
times, when there is so much more reason to complain of the
badness of our hearts (if men's hearts were better, the times
would be mended); and when there is such reason to be
thankful that they are not worse; but that even in the
worst times we enjoy many mercies, that help to make them,
not only tolerable, but comfortable.' §

The question has been well asked—'If the times are
bad, what are we doing to mend them?' Have not we

* Thus Horace's old man—
        "Laudator temporis acti."—*De Arte Poeticâ.*
† Henry.
‡ Dr. South's Sermon on Text.   § Henry.

helped to make them bad? And do not murmuring complaints make them worse? Could we change clouds for sunshine, would it be for our real good? Is not the arrangement of the infinitely wise and gracious Father more for
our true advantage than the dictates of our poor human
folly? It was not our lot to be born in *former,* and—as
is supposed—*better days.* But surely it is our duty to
gather all good out of the seeming evil, and cheerfully to
submit to what we cannot change.* " Murmurers and
complainers" belong to every age. Leave God's work to
him, and let us attend to our own work, which is—not
so much to change the world, but to change ourselves
—to "serve our own generation by the will of God," and
to 'let the badness of the age in which we live make us
more wise, more circumspect, more humble.'† Brighter
days are before us—each day brightened with the hope of a
near-coming salvation. O Christian! "Salvation nearer."
What a quickening glow! (Rom. xiii. 11.) Faith, hope,
diligence, perseverance, watchfulness—all stir up the bottom springs of the heart. (1 Pet. i. 13.) The earnest is
"joy unspeakable." What will the consummation be?

11. *Wisdom is good with an inheritance* (as good as an in-
    heritance—yea better too, marg.); *and by it there is
    profit to them that see the sun.* 12. *For wisdom is a
    defence, and money is a defence* (shadow, marg.); *but the
    excellency of knowledge is, that wisdom giveth life to them
    that have it.*

The reading in the text marks the *profitable* use of *wis-*

---

* 'Submission either removes or lightens the burden. Giving
way either avoids or eludes the blow; where an enemy or affliction
is too strong, patience is the best defiance.'—*Dr. South,* ut supra.
    † Bp. Reynolds.

dom with an inheritance, directing the most valuable use of a
responsible talent.   And doubtless—as good Bp. Hall
observes—'if a man have a great estate, and *wisdom* to use
it, he may do great matters, and is very happy therein.' *

Perhaps, however, the weight of authority is on the side
of the marginal reading.† *Wisdom is better than an inheritance,* and *is profitable* unto mankind. The proof is manifest.   *For*—not only does it provide *a shadow* from many
temporal evils, but specially it *giveth life to them that have it.
Money is* indeed *a shadow.* ‡ It surrounds with friends, pro-
tects from foes (Prov. xix. 4; x. 19), and secures many
external blessings.   Thus " the rich man's wealth is his
strong city.   The ransom of a man's life are his riches."
(Ib. x. 15; xiii. 8.) But they " profit not in the day of
wrath." (Ib. x. 2.) Here lies the superlative value of wisdom 'as that, which both can safe-guard the present life,
and give a better to the owner of it.'§   The smallest atom
of this *wisdom and knowledge is life* eternal. "Whoso findeth
me findeth life." (John, xvii. 3. Prov. viii. 35.) Natural
wisdom—the world's idol—leaves us blind and dead. Here
is *life* revealed, proposed, possessed, secured.

What then is my deliberate choice—my vital knowledge ? " We know that the Son of God is come, and hath
given us an understanding, that we may know him that is
true; and we are in him that is true—even in his Son
Jesus Christ.   This is the true God, and eternal life."
(1 John, v. 20.) Here is the One that gives the true

* *Hard Texts.*

† See Bp. Patrick—Geier—Holden—Scott—and Wardlaw.

‡ In the original the words go thus—'For in the shadow of wisdom, and in the shadow of money—but the excellence of *knowledge*,'
&c. An obvious ellipsis remains therefore to be supplied. 'A man
resteth, or is sheltered.'—See Bp. Reynolds. Our free translation
gives the clear meaning.

§ Bp. Hall.

knowledge. Here is the treasure, that ensures every other blessing. *Life and knowledge* from any other source, *so far as eternity is concerned*, is utter vanity.

And yet how often do we see intellectual wisdom separated from *this life-giving knowledge!* How much laborious trifling has been expended upon the letter of the Bible by those, who have been wholly ignorant of its real spiritual meaning! In the argument of Christian evidences the infidel has been often confuted by the unbeliever. The demonstration of the truth is irresistible. But the reality and influence is little known. The outposts are successfully defended. But the citadel is uncared for.*

Since the advantage of this true wisdom is so vast, let the diligence in seeking it be proportioned. If it is worth seeking at all, it is worth seeking *first*.† And if it be not sought *first*, it will not be sought at all. 'Specially let us take care, lest being destitute of faith—the only *wisdom* of Christians—we be found dead in sin—and this life ended —in eternal death. Although thou be poor in this world's substance, so long as thou art wise in the Lord, thou wilt be nevertheless in good mind from the hope of eternal life in heaven.' ‡

We cannot but mark how this Divine *knowledge* opens the deepest mysteries in the simplest forms. Admirably does Bp. Taylor contrast the man of nature with the man of God. 'The one understands by nature; the other by grace. The one by human learning; the other by Divine. The one reads the Scriptures without; the other within. The one understands by reason; the other by love. And therefore he does not only understand the sermons of the Spirit, and perceives their meaning; but he pierces deeper, and knows the meaning of that meaning—that is, the secret of the

---

* By such critics as Grotius—such champions as Lardner.
† See the Rule, Matt. vi. 33.   ‡ Geier.

Spirit—that which is spiritually discerned.' * Where is the Divinely-instructed scholar, who does not long for clearer light, and more energy in the Christian life?

13. *Consider the work of God; for who can make that straight, that he hath made crooked?*

"The works of the Lord are great, sought out of all them that have pleasure therein. His work is honourable and glorious." (Ps. cxi. 2, 3.) Such is the Psalmist's commendation. Who will not respond to it? Solomon here places *the work* of Providence before us, and bids us *consider* it. And truly a most interesting and enriching study it is. "Whoso is wise, and will observe these things, even they shall understand the loving-kindness of the Lord." (Ps. cvii. 43.) Difficulties will start up before us. But all is in perfect harmony. He makes no mistakes; but "he giveth not account of any of his matters." (Job, xxxiii. 13.)

There is indeed no want of conformity to his own Divine standard. Yet there are many things *crooked* in man's eye, because they cross his own will, and thwart his own imaginary happiness. It is needful discipline that there should be—as has been said—'a crook in every lot.' Man's will goes one way—God's dispensation another. In every part of his course man must expect to meet with his crook—specially perhaps in his most tender—because most needed part. And hard is it to bear, till the spirit is thoroughly tamed to bear it.† 'Yet no power of man can *make it straight;* only he that made can mend it.'‡

* Sermon before the University of Dublin.

† See Jer. xxxi. 18.

‡ Boston. See Job, ix. 12; xxxiv. 29. Isa. xliii. 13. Lam. iii. 37. Dan. iv. 37.

But we must not forget, how often we are the framers
of our own troubles. How hard it is to love the creature,
and not over-love it! And yet if the Lord loves our souls,
he will remove our idols. Children, too closely fastened to
the heart, will be either continued as a thorn in the flesh, or
pass away from our eyes as a shadow. Either way our
sweetest comforts will become our deepest afflictions.

Most profitable therefore is it carefully to ponder the
dealings of God with us. Let us command our judgment
and reason to stand by, that we may with reverence, submission, and faith, *consider the work of God.* The vision in
his own time will speak for itself. We can see light and
order above, when all seems confusion below. Meanwhile
let us mark his hand, rest and stay upon his will, and
gather up carefully all the instruction of his discipline.
When the whole *work* shall be complete—every particle
will be seen to have fallen just into its own proper place.
And all will then appear One Great Whole every way worthy
of God—the eternal manifestation of his glory.

14. *In the day of prosperity be joyful; but in the day of
adversity consider. God also hath set the one over against
the other, to the end that man should find nothing after
him.*

Consider the work of God. Here—Christian—is thy
refuge and thy rest. Here enjoy quiet communion—satisfied confidence. And here learn that 'man's wisdom consists in observing God's unalterable appointments, and
suiting himself to them.' * Mark the wise and gracious
balancing of his dispensations. Surely in Providence—no
less than in grace—" he hath abounded toward us in all

* Scott.

wisdom and prudence." (Eph. i. 8.)   "He giveth us richly
all things to enjoy." (1 Tim. vi. 17.)   He means therefore
that we should enjoy them—not wantonly, or selfishly, but
as opportunities of glorifying him, and doing good to our
fellow-creatures.   His rule therefore is—*In the day of prosperity be joyful.*   'In the day of good be thou in good.
When God gives thee *prosperity,* do thou enjoy it with a
cheerful and thankful heart.' *   "Not to serve him with
joyfulness" was under the legal dispensation charged upon
Israel as a heavy indictment—as an ungrateful return for
undeserved mercies." (Deut. xxviii. 46, 47. Comp. xvi. 11 ;
xxvi. 1–11.)   How much more constraining is the obligation under the Gospel, when love infinitely greater and
more free, has been so gloriously displayed !   Ill does it
become us to walk before our Father with a wrinkled brow,
doubting, desponding.   No, rather—let us give him his just
right in an affectionate and delighting confidence.

And yet if we be *joyful,* must we not rejoice with
trembling ? (Ps. ii. 11.)   Is it not *a day of prosperity,* a
time of special temptation ?   How hard to maintain an
honourable walk, and the enjoyment of Christian privilege,
in the atmosphere of ease !   Never in times of ease is the
prayer out of season—'In all time of our wealth, Good
Lord, deliver us.'†

And yet—'let me be rich—great—honourable'—is
the cry on all sides.   Ah ! could the deluded votary realize
the consequence of this wish—the gratification of this
heart's desire !   In how many cases would it be Satan's
great—perhaps fatal—advantage !   Humility—godly watchfulness—weanedness of heart—this is the safe—the consecrated path—the path to "glory, honour, immortality."
Wise indeed therefore is the appointment, that makes

* Bp. Reynolds. Comp. Chap. iii. 4 ; viii. 15 ; ix. 7–9.
† Litany.

the day of prosperity to be not our *entire* lot.   It is
hard to hold a full cup steady.   There is a valuable balance
of *the day of adversity*, equally of Divine appointment.
For " shall we receive good at the hands of the Lord ?   And
shall we not receive evil ?"* This *day* is indeed most important, not only as our school of discipline, but as the test
of our improvement in this school.   For ' if *prosperity* doth
best discover vices, *adversity* doth best discover virtue.'†
The diligent improvement‡ of this *day* brings with it a
mighty blessing.   The internal malady is checked.   Creature
dependence is put away.   In the darkest hour of *the day* we
can look up with confidence and enjoyment.   All is passing
away, and withering.   But " thou art my portion, O Lord."
(Ps. cxix. 57.)   Give me faith to believe all thy love to me.

   We do not however always connect the two things
— being in *the day*, and knowing how to act in it.
When the resolution is thoroughly carried out — never more
to question, complain, fear, or faint ; when second causes —
those sharply-piercing thorns — have been wholly cast out,
rich fruit has been already gathered.   We have learned in
the school training-lessons of incalculable value.   Our *joy*
is not crushed.   It is only tempered with sober and most
profitable *consideration*.   We are taught to mark the hand
and character of God (Deut. viii. 5) — the humbling cause
(Job, x. 2. Ps. xxxix. 11) — the gracious end§ — how to obtain

   * Job, ii. 10. Comp. Isa. xlv. 7. Amos, iii. 6.

   † Lord Bacon, Essay v.

   ‡ We insist upon *diligent improvement*.   For Abp. Whately
wisely reminds us, ' Let no man flatter himself, that anything
external will make him wise or virtuous, without his taking pains
to learn wisdom or virtue from it.   And if any one says of any
affliction—' No doubt it is all for my good'—let him be reminded
to ask himself, whether he *is seeking to get any good out of it.*'
Notes on Bacon's Essay, *ut supra*.

   § Heb. xii. 10. Jam. v. 11. 1 Pet. i. 6, 7.

support (Ps. l. 15; lxxxvi. 7)—how to realize more fully
the enriching blessing (Ps. xciv. 12, 13)—how to assure
ourselves of deliverance (1 Cor. x. 13)—how to anticipate
complete and eternal compensation.* Precious teaching!
Child of God—this is thy present privilege—sustaining
thy confidence—rejoicing thy heart.

Thus the brightest *prosperity* is found in nature's darkest
adversity. We all know how the vicissitudes of the natural
seasons—*set over against each other*—conduce to the healthi-
ness of the atmosphere. Hence the adoring acknowledgment
—"Thou hast made summer and winter" (Ps. lxxiv. 17)—
and the merciful promise—that "while the earth remaineth,
they shall not cease." (Gen. viii. 22.) Not less necessary is a
measure and proportion of each of these seasons to maintain
the Christian temperament in healthful vigour. Either
without the other would be defective in operation. *The day
of prosperity* would be dangerous exaltation (2 Cor. xii. 7)
—*the day of adversity* fainting despondency. (Ps. cxxv. 3.
Isa. lvii. 16.) *The one set against the other* is therefore
Divine perfection of arrangement.† The proportions of each
vary according to the sovereign will and wisdom of the
Great Disposer (Ps. xc. 15); "and his work is perfect."
(Deut. xxxii. 4.)

And yet is it not wonderful, that, when the adjustment
is made with such unerring skill, that balance should always
be on our side? This is the more wonderful, when we
remember that we have not deserved one moment of the
prosperity vouchsafed, and that we have deserved far more
than all *the adversity* that we have suffered. On the one
side—may we not say with the Patriarch—"We are not
worthy of the least of all thy mercies" (Gen. xxxii. 10)
—on the other side—with the godly scribe (Ezra, ix. 13),

* Heb. xii. 11. Zech. xiii. 9. Rev. vii. 14.
† See Bp. Reynolds' beautiful note.

"Thou, O God, hast punished us less than our iniquities deserve?" Practical and experimental religion is only learned in that extremity, that brings us to contrite prayer, and casts us in unreserved trust upon our God. Is then the godly man mournful? At least he need not—save by his own fault—be miserable. The Lord has never appointed temporal prosperity as the undoubted seal of his love. "All things come alike to all." (Chap. ix. 2.) His covenant, while it includes the rod for his child, secures him from the curse.* And when the soul is at peace, temporal *adversity* will be—comparatively at least—little felt. It may cloud the physical enjoyment. But it will not shake the solid foundation, nor touch the blessedness of Divine acceptance. 'Give up the doctrines of Jesus Christ'—said Mr. Cecil in his last illness—'all is pitch darkness without it—dark as a Socinian—dark as a moralist. There is no light, but what Christ brings. All important truth is in the Bible, and I feel that no comfort enters sick curtains from any other quarter.'†

Surely then God has so wisely disposed these changes, and so accurately appointed their several proportions, *that a man shall find nothing after him*—nothing superfluous, defective, or irregular. If *a man* should take upon himself to review the work *after him,* and conceive that a greater or less degree of *prosperity or adversity* would have been better—or that either would have sufficed, without the balance of the other—he only stands before us in all the folly and presumption of fancying himself to be wiser than God. What God has done, he has done best. He has indeed kept his own time, and used his own means—not ours. But he has made us to see in the end, that his time and means were better than ours. Whatever seems to oppose or to perplex—remember—it is our Father's work;

* See Ps. lxxxix. 30–35.　　　† *Memoirs* by Mrs. Cecil.

and let us learn to take a cheerful view of that lot, which he has ordained *solely* for our happiness, and which under his guidance will turn to the best account. Oh! think of the many now before the throne, who are blessing God to all eternity for that wise, providential dealing, which under Divine grace prepared them for their home, and brought them to it with everlasting joy.

15. *All things have I seen in the days of my vanity. There is a just man, that perisheth in his righteousness; and there is a wicked man, that prolongeth his life in his wickedness.*

Solomon was a man of vast observation. His whole life indeed at best was made up *of days of vanity**—how much more his time of apostasy from God. Yet he had employed it in making an extensive survey of the world before him. Often has he mentioned the sight before his eyes (Chap. iv. 1-4; v. 8)—so stumbling to the ignorant, and staggering to the faith even of the children of God (Ps. lxxiii. Jer. xii. 1)—*the just man perishing in his righteousness.* This was the first record from the fall (Gen. iv. 8). And all successive records of the Church confirmed the testimony. "He that departeth from evil maketh himself a prey." (Matt. xxiii. 35, with Isa. lix. 15.) The Divine dealings with *the wicked man* shew also a mysterious exercise of Sovereignty. Sometimes he is not permitted to "live out half his days." At other times he "*prolongeth his life in his wickedness.*" (Job, xxi. 7, with Ps. lv. 23.)

Yet after all—"Say ye to the righteous—'It shall be well with him.'" (Isa. iii. 10.) Where is the servant of God, that would exchange the most abject poverty for the highest

* See Chap. vi. 12; ix. 9.

prosperity of *the wicked?* If *the just man perisheth,* "he shall enter into peace." (Isa. lvii. 1, 2.) If *the wicked prolongeth his days,* continuing in sin, surely the very sight of him excites —not our envy—but our deepest compassion. We can only tremble, lest this *prolongation* should be the righteous and merciful God " enduring him with much long-suffering as a vessel of wrath, fitted for destruction." (Rom. ix. 22.)

There is therefore no reason to be stumbled either at the calamities of *the just man,* or at the continued prosperity of *the wicked.* Divine teaching expounds the dark chapter of Providence (Ps. lxxiii. 16–20), and shews them to be displays of wisdom and love. Soon will all mysteries be eternally cleared up. " Clouds and darkness" will melt away. "Righteousness and judgment" will be fully manifested to be "the habitation of the throne" (Ps. xcvii. 2) of the Great Sovereign of the Universe. And the everlasting song of the hosts of heaven will be—" Alleluia ! for the Lord God Omnipotent reigneth." (Rev. xix. 6.)

16. *Be not righteous over-much ; neither make thyself over-wise; why shouldest thou destroy thyself?* 17. *Be not over-much wicked ; neither be thou foolish ; why shouldest thou die before thy time?* 18. *It is good that thou shouldest take hold of this ; yea, also from this withdraw not thine hand; for he that feareth God shall come forth of them all.*

The two strange things that had fallen under Solomon's observation — *the righteous perishing in his righteousness, and the wicked* escaping with impunity — suggested double cautions. On the one side the externally *righteous* need to be guarded against a false religion ; and even the upright against a false display of true religion. On the other — *the wicked*—escaping for a time—let them not presume upon continued security.

The first caution— *Be not righteous over-much*—is the
sheet-anchor of the profane—the ungodly—the formalist !
What havoc does the great deceiver make with Scripture—
shooting God's arrows from his own quiver ! —teaching his
deluded victims to "wrest the Scriptures to their own
destruction !" And how strange is it to see, that, while they
hate the grand truths of the Bible, and wholly repudiate it
as their rule of faith and practice, they will gladly quote it
—nay—they will insist upon its authority, when at any
point it *seems* to bear upon their side !

We cannot wonder, therefore, that this should be one of
their favourite texts—held in high estimation. However
clear may be its true meaning, it seems to admit of so many
shades of interpretation, as if it would allow any man to fix
his own rule and standard. The insincere professor finds an
excuse for loving the world in his heart, and meeting it half
way in his practice. He may have a plea for avoiding all
the offence of the cross. He may revolt from the most
spiritual doctrines and exercises of the Gospel. He has one
answer at hand against every warning. 'There is an express
rule from God. Its authority therefore is undoubted.
We must not carry matters too far. Everything must have
its place. There are certain proprieties of life—conventional
usages of good society—that must be regarded. Religion
must keep to its proper place, and its proper time. The
direction is plain— *Be not righteous over-much.'*

Such is the rule, as expounded by the votaries of the
world. But is it really possible to transgress it, so as to
have too much of the substance of religion ? A sinful being,
"in whom dwelleth no good thing" (Rom. vii. 18) —too
good ! *righteous over-much !* Impossible to conceive a warning of God against this danger ! 'Too religious—in the
proper sense of the word,' Abp. Whately well reminds us*

* Annotations on Bacon's *Essays*, xvii.

—'we cannot be. We cannot have the religious sentiments and principles too strong, if only they have a right object. We cannot love God too warmly, or honour him too highly, or strive to serve him too earnestly, or trust him too implicitly; because our duty is to love him with *all* our heart, and *all* our soul, and *all* our mind, and *all* our strength.' It is surely absurd to warn the carnal man against an excess of spirituality—the earthly-minded man against *over-much* seeking of heavenly things. The danger obviously lies in defect, not in excess; in stopping short, not in going too far. Strip this perverted caution of its false cover; and too often at last it means— Be not righteous *at all*. For unquestionably its advocates have more sympathy with men of no religion, than with those, whose high and heavenly character condemns their own worldly profession.

To whom then, and to what, does the admonition apply? We have seen that it does not warn us against true *righteousness*. But it is a wholesome caution against the 'vain affectation of it.' * Every right principle has its counterfeit. We have monkery and celibacy as the shadow of Christian perfection— penances and self-imposed austerities in lieu of the true mortification of the flesh—the name for the reality —the skeleton for the living man. Here 'the name of the mean is given to the extreme.' † That which in sobriety is *righteousness* often carries its name beyond the true boundary. It includes—what the heavenly Martyn dreaded in himself— 'talking much, and appearing to be somebody in religion.' ‡ Details may be easily multiplied. Religion is made to consist mainly in externals. Self-conceited professors insist upon their own Shibboleth,§ without regard to the different

* Lord Bacon, quoted by Bp. Patrick.
† Bp. Reynolds. See also Mercer, *in loco*.
‡ *Life*, Part i.
§ See Judg. xii. 5.

judgments of their brethren. Christian duties are pressed
beyond their due proportion, interfering with immediate
obligations, and making sins, where God has not made
them. Scrupulosity in matters indifferent takes the place
of the free obedience of the Gospel. In the exercise also of
Christian graces there may be danger of extremes. Boldness may verge to rashness, benevolence into indiscriminate
waste, candour into weakness. In all these and many other
details the Scriptural line seems to be passed, and the warning is justly applied — *Be not righteous over-much.*

Even ' in well-doing there may be over-doing,' * and
this over-doing may inadvertently progress towards undoing.
Indeed much of this is not religion, but superstition, which
' is not the excess of godliness ' (as Abp. Whately remarks)
' but the misdirection of it — the exhausting of it in the
vanity of man's devising.' † It is important that our religion should be reasonable, consistent, uniform — not a matter of opinion, but of the heart. Great indeed is our need,
and constant should be our prayer — " O let me have understanding in the way of godliness." (Ps. ci. 2.)

But we are warned against another extreme. Neither make
thyself *over-much wise* — a wholesome practical rule ! Avoid
all affectation or high pretensions to superior wisdom. Guard
against that opinionative confidence, which seems to lay
down the law, and critically finds fault with every judgment
differing from our own. The Apostle gives this warning
with peculiar emphasis and solemnity — " This I say, through
the grace given unto me, to every man that is among you,
not to think of himself more highly than he ought to think,
but to think soberly, according as God has dealt to every

* Henry.

† *Ut supra.* So an old Expositor writes — ' Religion is one
thing — superstition is *another — not the excess of the same thing.*'
Brentius *in loco.*

man the measure of faith." * 'The more humble thou art, the more wary and circumspect thou wilt be ; and the more wary the more safe.' †

A question is put to give energy to the warning — *Why shouldest thou destroy thyself?* Men may be martyrs to trifles magnified unduly. They may bring needless trouble upon themselves, by making conscience of doubtful or subordinate matters. And thus, unless the exercise of wisdom is tempered with humility and reverence, it may be the "pride that goeth before *destruction.*" (Prov. xvi. 18.) To be wise *up* to that which is written, is diligence — a bounden obligation. To be "wise above that which is written," ‡ is presumption, as if affecting to be acquainted with the whole of Divine truth. To intrude into God's province of "secret things" — is *over-wisdom* — passing the boundary line — "vainly puffed up by the fleshly mind." (Deut. xxix. 29. Col. ii. 18.) It may be provoking the judgment of our own *destruction.*

Another caution — and a remarkable one — is added from the opposite quarter — *Be not over-much wicked.* Not as if one particle of *wickedness* could be tolerated by Him, who is "of purer eyes than to behold iniquity." (Hab. i. 13. Comp.

---

* Rom. xii. 3. 'Not to be wise above what he ought to be, but to be wise unto sobriety.'—Professor Scholefield's accurate version. *Hints for an Improved Translation.*

† Bp. Reynolds.

‡ 1 Cor. iv. 6. 'It is for us to seek to know as much, and to be content to know *only* as much, of heavenly things as Scripture tells us, and to remain willingly ignorant of what our All-wise Master does not think fit to teach us.'—*Abp. Whately's Lessons on Morals,* p. 64. Again — most wisely—'We should study to be wise — not above Scripture, but in Scripture—to learn—not the things which God hath concealed, but what he has revealed.' Again, 'To dare to believe less, or to pretend to understand more, than God has expressly revealed, is equally profane presumption.'— *Detached Thoughts,* p. 60.

Ps. v. 4.) Every degree of *wickedness* is *over-much*. We must shun the least sin as a very pestilence. But many— so far as ordinary causes are concerned—might have lived longer, but for their wickedness. Take care not to loosen the reins of sin. This were folly in its fullest extent. Flagrant sin hurries men on towards destruction of body and soul. The murderer by his *over-much wickedness dies before his* natural *time*. The drunkard, by wasting his constitution, prepares it for premature ruin. Haman's malice (Esth. vii. 10) and Herod's pride (Acts, xii. 23) hastened their end. Sin is therefore rash presumption—the forerunner of certain destruction. It is to "*run* upon the Almighty—even upon his neck—upon the thick bosses of his buckler." (Job. xv. 25, 26.) Let the sinner stop, ere his course of wickedness rise to presumption—ere the forbearance of God have an end. What if his next plunge—his next wilful indulgence —should harden his heart in *foolishness,* and close his day of grace for ever! Perdition will come soon enough. Why should he provoke his God, that it should come *before his time?* How near may he be to the depths of hell—whence there is no escape—where there is no hope! How fearful not to learn the truth, till he learns it there!

We have therefore valuable cautions against all extremes. It is wise for us to "make strait paths for our feet" (Heb. xii. 13) — to preserve the mean of a sober scriptural *righteous-ness*—to cultivate 'that gracious humility, which hath ever been the crown and glory of a Christianly-disposed mind'* — and to guard against a headlong and presumptuous course. *It is good* indeed *to take hold of this* — never to lose thy hand-fast—never to *withdraw thine hand from it.* Lay it up in thine heart as a certain truth— that the *fear of the Lord* is the keeping of his children—the fear of the Lord sustaining them against the deadly influence of the

* Hooker, Pref. chap. i. 3.

fear of man. Learn to be truly *righteous*—wisely *righteous*. Never be satisfied with the standard of the world. Press onward in the path of the Bible—marking, and closely following, "the footsteps of the flock." Never shrink from the confession of principle. But do not court needless offence. Be determinately—not fanatically—singular. A religion of impulse, novelty, fashion, or eccentricity, will never practically influence. What is wanted is the religion of reality—the stamp of God upon the heart of man. Any other religion is a cold—cheerless—wintry atmosphere—chilling the healthy glow of the Christian life. No sunbeam sheds its radiance within.

It may seem scarcely possible always to preserve the golden mean in the narrow path. But in "the fear of the Lord is strong confidence." (Prov. xiv. 26). *He therefore that feareth the Lord comes forth of all these* opposite temptations victorious, and untainted—in all the honour of Christian consistency—in all the glow of Christian liberty, guarded on every side from unholy licentiousness.

This well-balanced religion is of essential moment. Admitting the full weight of the caution—*Be not righteous over-much,* we must fully acknowledge the Scriptural standard —a religion of works, as well as words. It is fearful hypocrisy to profess the Gospel, and yet to restrain the full allegiance which our Divine Master claims at our hands; to seek a private walk, instead of the broad manifestation of godly exercise. Soon will "the fire try every man's work of what sort it is." (1 Cor. iii. 13.) How much profession will then be burnt up, that now makes a fair show even in the Church of God!

19. *Wisdom strengtheneth the wise man, more than ten mighty men, who are in the city.* 20. *For there is not a just man upon earth that doeth good, and sinneth not.*

Solomon never seems to have wearied in his commendation of *Wisdom*. He had just pronounced it to be *better* than riches. (vv. 11, 12.) Now he prefers it to *strength*— as the principle of Christian courage—energizing the whole soul. This *wisdom* is evidently identified with *the fear of the Lord*, which had just been pronounced to be an effective cover from unscriptural extremes. There was therefore *good* reason to *take hold of it*. It has more *strength* than mere physical courage — *more than ten* * *mighty men* in defending *the city*. This he elsewhere proves by an instance, that had probably come under his own knowledge. (Chap. ix. 16–18.) Once and again he confirms the maxim, that the "wise man is the strong one,—so 'strong,' that he scaleth the city of the mighty, and casteth down the strength of the confidence thereof." (Prov. xxiv. 5 ; xxi. 22.) And in truth—the man that is walking with God is sheltered by Omnipotence. "The eyes of the Lord run to and fro throughout the whole earth, to shew himself strong in the behalf of them, whose heart is perfect towards him." (2 Chron. xvi. 9.) Under such a cover, what assault—whether of malice or subtlety—need we fear ? † Fearless composure will be the fruit of the realized vision of faith— "They that be with us are more than they that be with them." (2 Kings, vi. 15–17.) Feeble we may be in natural power. "But he that is feeble among us shall be as David," when with a dauntless front he dared Goliath to the combat. (Zech. xii. 8. 1 Sam. xvii. 39–47.)

We have indeed good reason to cherish this upholding principle. *For there is not a just man upon the earth that sinneth not*, and therefore who doth not need the *strength* of this *Divine wisdom* in his spiritual conflicts and temptations.

We must not overlook this humbling testimony to the universal and total corruption of the whole race of man.

---

* An indefinite number. Comp. Gen. xxxi. 7 ; Num. xiv. 22 ; Neh. iv. 12 ; Job, xix. 3.

† See Ps. xxvii. 1–3.

This important statement lies at the foundation of all right views of truth. Till the plague is known, the need of a remedy will never be felt, and the only true remedy will be worthless in our eyes. In heaven indeed *just men* are made perfect. (Heb. xii. 23.) *On earth there are just men that do good.* But there is not one that doeth good, and *sinneth not*—"no—not one." * Every work—even the best—has the taint of the evil nature. (Isa. lxiv. 6.) "The lust of the flesh" defiles the purest "working of the Spirit." There is not only guilt in the many sins that we commit, but in the very best principle of our good. Yet the true exposition of this case need not give the Christian any discouragement. 'The pain felt is not from increased sinfulness, but from increased consciousness of it ; not from his conduct having become worse, but from his moral judgment being more enlightened, and his perception of what is wrong, and his abhorrence of it, being stronger than before.'†

Solomon in his brightest days had made the same humbling confession. (1 Kings, viii. 46.) Scripture biography gives its sad confirming testimony. ‡ There is always defect, if not wilfulness; defilement, if not omission. The same testimony has been given in every age by Christians of the highest maturity in Grace. 'I cannot pray'—is the oft-quoted confession of Bp. Beveridge—'but I sin. I cannot hear or give an alms, or receive the sacrament, but I sin. I cannot so much as confess my sins, but my very confessions are still aggravations of them. My repentance needs to be repented of; my tears want washing; and the

* Ps. xiv. 3. The Romanists insist on one exception—that no one is without venial sin, except Christ, *and the most Blessed Virgin*.—Lorin on vv. 19, 20. But how could her "spirit rejoice in God her *Saviour*" (Luke, i. 47), if she was not conscious of sins that needed that *Saviour* ?

† Abp. Whately's *Lessons on Morals*, Lesson ix. § 1.

‡ Abraham, David, Solomon, Peter, &c.

very washing of my tears needs still to be washed over again
with the blood of my Redeemer.' *

Child of God! is there no response from your heart?
Does not every defect in your fellow-sinner read a fresh
lesson of your own helplessness? Can you anticipate the
time *on earth*, when, " if you say that you have no sin, you"
will not " deceive yourself?" (1 John, i. 8.) " If thou, Lord,
shouldest mark iniquities, O Lord, who shall stand?" (Ps.
cxxx. 3.) Only he, whose eye is upon the High Priest
" bearing the iniquities of the holy things." (Exod. xxviii.
38. Comp. Rev. viii. 3, 4.) There is no peace—no security
—against deeper sin, but an instant and continued application
to him. 'Always a sinner'—is the Christian's name to the
end, and therefore with godly Nehemiah we will combine
with the consciousness of sincerity the cry for sparing mercy
(Chap. xiii. 22)—with the reverend Hooker in deep prostra-
tion we will 'plead—not our righteousness, but the forgiveness of our unrighteousness.' † With holy Leighton—
'instead of all fine notions, we fly to—Lord, have mercy on
me—Christ, have mercy on me.' ‡ The publican's prayer
will suit to the very last breath—nothing better—contri-
tion for sin—confidence in the propitiation. §

21. *Also—take no heed* (give not thy heart, marg.) *unto all
words that are spoken, lest thou hear thy servant curse*

---

* *Private Thoughts.* A devout Romanist Expositor observes on
this place, 'The Hereticks will gain nothing here in defence of their
perverse dogma'—'A just man sins in every good work.'—Lorin
in loco. Very differently writes a pious Protestant Expositor—
'We are *all* corrupt. We are *altogether*—so corrupt, that the *just
man* in any good work is not without sin. Hence'—he adds—
'penitently deplore thy corruption.'—*Geier.*

† Walton's *Life.*

‡ Letter to Rev. James Aiard.

§ Luke, xviii. 13. ἱλασθητι—not ἐλεησον.

thee. 22. *For oftentimes also thine own heart knoweth,*
that thou thyself likewise hast cursed others.

Also — This seems to point to an admonition suggested
by the statement just given of man's universal corruption.
Even *the just man* in his frailty, much more the careless
and ungodly, may "offend in word." (Jam. iii. 2.) The
wise counsel therefore to avoid the vexation of this evil world
is — not to resent. *Take no heed — Give not thy heart unto*
all words that are spoken. Some words perhaps spoken "unadvisedly," or in a passion. They were not intended for us,
and we have no right to hear them. Listeners, standing
upon the tip-toe of suspicion, seldom hear good of themselves.
Lord Bacon therefore well advises 'the provident stay of
enquiry of that, which we would be loth to find.' * It
were far better not to work out matter for our own mortification. Saul took the prudent course against the taunts
of "the children of Belial," when he "held his peace" (1
Sam. x. 27) — regarding them not. David in the same wisdom "was as a deaf man, and heard not — as one, in whose
mouth were no reproofs." (Ps. xxxviii. 13, 14.) It is often
a matter of prudence, not to examine things too closely —
not to be too eagerly inquisitive — not curiously to search
into every crevice, or to affect to hear everything. Some
truth may be learned from the saying of the Great Frederick
(though the morality be doubtful), — 'He knows not how
to govern, who does not know how to dissemble.' 'He that
will have peace' — said Bp. Hall — 'must put up with many

---

* *Advancement of Learning*, B. ii. xxiii. 5. 'Never listen' —
writes Bp. Taylor, adverting to this text — 'at the door or windows ;
for besides that it contains in it danger and a snare, it is also in-
vading my neighbour's privacy, and a laying that open, which he
therefore enclosed, that it might not be open.'—*Holy Living*, chap.
ii. sect. vi. Comp. chap. x. 20.

injuries of the tongue,' * else we shall always be in contention—never in quiet. The Bible is a household book; and
happy is the house that is disciplined by its wisdom. We
may hear, that our names, characters, and concerns have
been lightly spoken of in our household. Nay—we may
hear our own servant in a moment of hasty provocation
curse or rail upon us. How indignant we feel! How ready
to reprove, and to give way to angry feelings! But the
Bible rule is—*Take no heed to all the words.* Turn in to
thine *heart* for a motive to forbearance, and a lesson of
charity. Well does it *know, that thou thyself likewise hast
cursed others.*

Few—if any—of us can plead ' Not Guilty' to this indictment of Evil-speaking—slandering and back-biting ' are
all associates and kindred, which are to be cast away together.' † If we recall our conversation at the end of the
day, how many breaches of the law of love! how seldom
are our words free from that, which we should not like to
have repeated! If it does not amount to *cursing,* yet it is
something said to the disparagement of another—and said
with a sort of gratification, which we do not feel in the same
degree, when we are speaking in another's praise. Why is
this, but from the " root of bitterness?" Oh! the infinite
evil of an unbridled tongue—an unloving heart!

After all—how valuable is the lesson of forbearance in
the remembrance of our former selves! The recollection that
" we ourselves were sometimes hateful and hating one another"—*our hearts knowing,* and bearing witness to the fact
—furnishes the most constraining motive "to speak evil of no
man, shewing all meekness to all men." (Tit. iii. 2, 3.) We
cannot condemn others, when we are so conscious of having
been so guilty ourselves. We cannot expect too much from

* *Hard Places.*
† Barrow's *Sermons on Evil Speaking.*

our brethren, when we are still under the conviction of our own weakness. The rule of humility and love will be— Deal tenderly with others—severely with ourselves. Our Master's pattern illustrates the rule, and sheds light on every step of our path.

23. *All this have I proved by wisdom. I said—I will be wise; but it was far from me.* 24. *That which is far off, and exceeding deep, who can find it out?* 25. *I applied mine heart* (I and my heart compassed, marg.) *to know, and to search, and to seek out wisdom, and the reason of things, and to know the wickedness of folly, even of foolishness and madness.*

The Preacher turns again to his own history. He had first exercised his wisdom in intellectual research. Here he soon found his bottom. Notwithstanding all his advantages of a comprehensive understanding—all his extensive and multifarious resources—*when he said he would be wise,* it was *far from* him—*far off*—deep, *deep—exceeding deep.* He was always opening some new vein in the golden mine. Yet even his powerful mind was made to feel its limits, and to cry out— *Who can find it out?* "Such knowledge is too wonderful for me; it is high, I cannot attain unto it." (Ps. cxxxix. 6.)

Heavenly wisdom teaches the same lesson, only with a deeper and more practical impression. Our highest knowledge is but a mere atom, when compared with the unsearchable extent of our ignorance. The more we know of God—his nature (Job, xi. 7)—his works (Ps. xcii. 5)— his dispensations (Rom. xi. 33), the more we are humbled in the sense of our ignorance. What Calvin wisely calls 'a

learned ignorance'*—a well-instructed contentment to be
ignorant of what God has covered from us—this is at once
our duty and our rest.   There is much that *is far off*—not
only from our senses, but from our understanding—*exceeding deep* to men—even to angels. (1 Pet. i. 12.)   Nay—
the plainest surface needs Divine teaching for the practical
knowledge of it.

Solomon's disappointment could not be attributed to any
want of heart in his object.   Nothing could exceed his inde-
fatigable industry in its pursuit.   He heaps word upon
word to attempt some adequate conception of the intensity of
his ardour.†   '*I and my heart* turned every way—left no
means unattempted exactly to discover wisdom'‡—persevering in despite of all difficulties.   He was far more stimulated
by the grandeur of his object, than disheartened by the difficulty of attaining it.   Nor was he content with the mere
knowledge of facts.   He would *seek and search out* principles
—*the reason of things*, tracing effects to their causes.

But his interest was mainly fixed in *knowing the wickedness of folly*—specially of that sin, which bears upon it the
peculiar stamp of *folly* (Gen. xxxiv. 7)—yea—that well
deserves the name of *madness*.   For what is man living for
his own lusts, but the picture of man having lost his understanding ? (Hos. iv. 11.)   But in this unhallowed track he
plunged himself into perilous hazard.   Far better (as our
first parents found too late) to *know* nothing of evil, than to
learn it experimentally.   Far better would it have been for
Solomon to have *known foolishness and madness* by observation, by the records of conscience, by the testimony of the
word, than by the terrible personal experiment.   Who has

* *Instit.* lib. iii. c. xxi. § 2.   Afterwards he speaks of the eager
appetite for hidden knowledge as a species of *madness*, c. xxiii. § 2.
—See Hooker's *Admirable Statements*, B. i. § 2.

† See also Chap. i. 13–17 ; viii. 16, 17.   ‡ Bp. Reynolds.

not need of the prayer—" Keep thy servant also from presumptuous sins?"* (Ps. xix. 13.)   Practical godliness is the
keeping of the soul.   "He that is begotten of God keepeth
himself, and that wicked one toucheth him not." (1 John,
v. 18.)

26. *And I find more bitter than death the woman, whose heart
is snares and nets, and her hands as bands: whoso pleaseth*
(he that is good before, marg.) *God shall escape from her;
but the sinner shall be taken by her.*

We have had many striking pictures of the vanity of the
world, and its utter insufficiency for our happiness.   We are
now turning over to another page to see the vileness of sin —
its certain tendency to our misery and ruin.   Solomon had
often drawn this graphical picture for the warning of others.
Here he describes the apparatus of a fowler as the picture of
the heart of the unprincipled woman.   Such a tissue of
snares, nets, and bands!—too subtle even for himself—the
wisest of the wise—to *escape!*   It is an affecting record in
the after-page of sacred history—that " among many nations
there was no king like him, who was beloved of his God;
nevertheless even him did outlandish women cause to err."
(Neh. xiii. 16, with 1 Kings, xi. 1–8.)   But mark the
mighty power of the temptation!   Such a multitude of
devices!   Such consummate skill in the application of them!
the spell of enchantment chaining her deluded victims with
irresistible influence!
    What then is the escape from this extreme peril?   Man's
highest moral sense—all his strength of resolution—is absolutely powerless.   The Sovereign grace of God is Omnipotent.
Prayer brings this secure cover, and spreads it over those

* See Prov. ii. 18, 19; v. 2–5; vi. 26; vii. 21–29; ix. 18; xxii.
14; xxiii. 27, 28.

who, like Joseph in similar temptation (Gen. xxxix. 9, 10) *are good before him.* ' He that displeaseth God by walking in the bye-paths of sin, God shall withhold his grace from him, and he shall be tempted, and foiled.   But *whoso pleaseth God* by walking in his holy ways, God shall so assist him with his grace, that when he is tempted, *he shall escape.*' *

But the sinner shall be taken by her (Prov. ii. 19; xxii. 14)—described so fearfully—*more bitter than death!*   We read of the bitterness of death (1 Sam. xv. 32); and of a worse bitterness.   "The end of a strange woman is bitter as wormwood, and her steps take hold on hell." (Prov. v. 4, 5.) ' Death may be sweetened and sanctified, made a welcome and desirable thing to a believer.   But the bitterness of hell is incurable.   Death may be honourable, to die in a good cause, to go to the grave in peace, lamented, desired, with the sweet savour of a holy life, and many good works to follow one.   But for a man to putrefy alive, under the plague of impure lust—to make shipwreck of his honour—to put hell into his conscience—to bury his name, his substance, his soul and body—in the bosom of an harlot—this is a *bitterness* beyond that of death'†—not only separating the soul from the body, but separating soul and body eternally from God.

Such is the poor deluded sinner! and on the brink of such frightful ruin—when he loses his only safe keeping—watchfulness over himself—dependence upon his God!   Let us once more take this valuable lesson from one, who eminently practised it himself, and therefore was the better fitted to inculcate it upon us.   "I keep under my body"—said the great apostle—"and bring it into subjection; *lest* that by any means, after I have preached to others, I myself should be a cast-away." (1 Cor. ix. 27.)

* Bp. Sanderson, *Sermon on Prov.* xvi. 7.
† Bp. Reynolds.

27. Behold! this have I found (saith the Preacher) counting one by one to find the account. 28. Which yet my soul seeketh, but I find not; one man among a thousand have I found; but a woman among all those have I not found.

Behold! a sad testimony he is about to give. Conceive him looking at the multitude of his courtiers standing before him—*counting one by one to find the account* how many faithful and true—*his soul seeking, but not finding* it clearly to his judgment. Yet the result, as he could obtain it, *found one man among a thousand* only—of godly *women among them not* even *one.* What a contrast to his father's house and court! " Mine eyes"—said the man of God—" are upon the faithful in the land, that they may dwell with me." (Ps. ci. 6.)

We cannot suppose, that Solomon's judgment of woman was an universal sweeping condemnation. He had no difficulty to find female virtue in its own legitimate sphere. And many were the testimonies which he has given of its value.* Who would scruple to adopt Luther's judgment, that ' there is nought on earth so lovely as a woman's heart, with God's grace to guide its love?' But here his view was evidently confined to the walls of his own harem. (Comp. 1 Kings, xi. 3.) And among the *thousand* " strange women" (Ib. v. 1) dwelling in that crowded seraglio he himself living in the open breach of God's law (Ib. v. 10)—in the gross violation of marriage purity—and casting away all the domestic happiness of endeared affection and undivided love—how could he expect to find " the virtuous woman," whom he so beautifully portrays—" her price far above rubies?"† Here therefore he only informs us, that, looking where he had

* Prov. xii. 4 ; xiv. 1 ; xviii. 22 ; xix. 14 ; xxxi. 10–31.
† Ib. xxxi. 10–31, *ut supra.*

no warrant to find the jewel—the result was unmingled
disappointment. And such will always be the fruit of sin.
Child of God! Be thankful for the bitterness of the draught
from the "broken cistern," as the weaning discipline, that
turns your heart back to your God.

> 29. *Lo! this only have I found, that God hath made man
> upright; but they have sought out many inventions.*

This is a most important verse. It opens up to us an
hidden mystery—man's original, and his awful apostasy
from it—how *God made man*—how man unmade himself.
Lo! Thus the Preacher calls our attention to his humbling
discovery. All his other discoveries were absorbed in this
one. *This only have I found.* All the streams of wickedness
were beyond the ken of his sight. But he saw enough to
trace the direful fall as the fountain-head of corruption.
Man is indeed 'very far gone'—as far as possible—'from
original righteousness.'* 'When the progenitors of our race
came from the forming hand of their Creator, they were the
subjects of perfect intellectual and moral rectitude. There
was no distortion in the understanding, no obliquity in the
will, no corruption in the affections. There was perfect
truth in the mind, perfect purity in the heart, perfect practical holiness. They were "made in the image and likeness
of God" himself, which, according to the apostle, consisteth
"in knowledge, righteousness, and true holiness." Otherwise than this man could not be made by a pure, holy,
and benevolent Being.'†

Such was *man—made upright.* Yet "being in honour,
he abideth not. How is the gold become dim, and the most
fine gold changed!" (Ps. xlix. 12; Lam. iv. 1.) How dif-

* Art. ix. Quam longissime.
† Wardlaw; Gen. i. 26, 27, with Eph. iv. 24; Eph. iv. 24.

ferent from the holy creature which came out of his Maker's hands! Why he decreed his fall, so that without this decree of his will it could not have been—we dare not ask. Suffice it to know, that if he so far permitted, as not to prevent it, he was in no degree the cause of it. He did not drop the poison. Nor did he withdraw from him the original gift of integrity. On the other hand, he was not bound unchangeably to confirm him in this gift, to restrain his will, or to force upon him that Omnipotent grace, of which he felt no need, which he had no desire to seek; yet which — had he sought it—might have been his victory. ' It was therefore as clear, that God was without fault, as that man was the maker of his own evil.'*

We have entered upon this trackless path with fear and trembling. 'I sought'—said the godly Augustine— 'whence evil should be, and I sought *ill*. Nor did I see that evil, which was in that very enquiry of mine.'† All we know is—" An enemy hath done this." (Matt. xiii. 28.) The origin of the evil was in Satan's heart. Man's responsibility was his consent to it—his abuse of his own free will, not—like God's— unchangeably holy, but *mutable* — even in its highest strength of *uprightness*. Here therefore was a voluntary act—the free choice of his independent will; and therefore wilful apostasy from God. Thus man in the exercise of his own free will became the author of his own ruin.

Nor let us suppose that we, under more favourable circumstances, might have prevented the evil. *They sought out* — our first parents, and their whole posterity with them. For the whole race was in their loins, as Levi was in the loins of Abraham.‡ All therefore were made

* Beza.   † *Confess.* b. vii. c. 5.
‡ See Heb. vii. 8, 9.

responsible, as sharers of the corruption.* The judgment
was pronounced—not only on the individual offender, but
upon the guilty race to the end.   As punishment is the
consequence of sin, how could they be punished in Adam, if
in some way they had not sinned in him?† We cannot
dispute against facts. We see the present punishment of
Adam's sin in every child of his race—a punishment, which
we trace back clearly to the moment of his fall.   As
Pascal remarks—'Without this incomprehensible mystery,
we are ourselves incomprehensible to our own mind. The
clue which knits together our whole fortune and condition,
takes its turn, and plies in this amazing abyss; insomuch
that man will appear no less inconceivable without this mystery, than this mystery appears inconceivable to man.' ‡

They have sought out many inventions to fall away from
God.   Man's discontent with the happiness which God hath
provided for him—this was his first *invention.*§ Hence he
fancied a higher perfection than that in which he had been
confirmed. Hence he yielded to follow the new way, which
Satan and his deceived heart had placed before him—
despising his Creator's law—suspecting his truth—nay,

---

* 'We hold it for certain, that in regard to human nature, Adam
was not merely a progenitor, but, as it were, a root, and that accord-
ingly by his corruption, the whole human race was deservedly
vitiated. From a corrupt root corrupt branches proceeding, transmit
their corruption to the branches which proceed from them.'—*Calvin's
Institutes*, b. ii. c. i. 6, 7. 'Our first parents would needs follow the
desires of their own hearts ; and we, their sinful posterity, do nothing
but devise further means of our own ruin.'—*Bp. Hall.*

† Gen. ii. 17, with Rom. v. 12 ; 1 Cor. xv. 22.

‡ *Thoughts*, chap. iii.

§ 'He hath entangled himself with an infinity of questions.'—
Douay Version. 'They seek dyverse sotylties.'—*Coverdale.* Taylor's
Hebrew Concordance gives our version—'invention, Ecc. vii. 29'—
something newly found—a principle in his nature unknown before
—some new mode of obtaining happiness.

even aspiring to share his Sovereignty. This first *invention* was the parent of the *many*—all marked by the same falsehood, folly, and impiety—all flowing out of the bottomless depths of the heart alienated from God, full of windings and turnings—" turning every one to his own way." (Isa. liii. 6.) All sin is only a form of self-love, instead of the love of God. The *many inventions* take the throne in turn. Former vanities soon produce the weariness of disappointment, others step into their places, so that this usurped dominion is changed only, not subdued. Man is constantly meddling with endless questions instead of the path of duty—the way of safety—the one only way to God. Never can he charge God. Let him cast all the blame upon himself, and cast himself upon the second Adam for restoration.

But what is the present picture? No ruin is to be compared with this sad sight—man's original *uprightness* ' in his great fall utterly robbed and spoiled.'* The whole evil is in the man, and the whole of man is in the evil. If the people, who had seen the glory of the first temple, wept when they beheld the glory of the second, only because it was inferior in external magnificence; † might there not well be " a fountain of tears" drawn out by the sight of the first spiritual temple in its " perfection of beauty"—totally defiled—yea, made a temple of Satan?

Blessed be God! He has provided—not restoration only —but complete security. ' To Adam he gave the power to live, *if he* would. To the faithful he has given the will, that they might live. To him he gave a happiness, from which he could fall. To us he has given a state of grace and happiness, which we cannot lose.' ‡

And then—it will not always be as now. "We, according to his promise, look for new heavens and a new earth,

---

* Bp. Reynolds *On the Passions*, chap. xxxvi.
† Ezra, iii. 12, 13.　　　　　　　　　　　‡ Cartwright.

wherein dwelleth righteousness." (2 Pet. iii. 13; Rev. xxi. 1–4.) Man will then be, as before, the temple of God; only in undefiled holiness, and inconceivable glory. If our first state was good, even when mutable; how much more blessed, when it shall be confirmed in unchangeable standing, and infinite enjoyment!

CHAPTER VIII.

1. *Who is as the wise man? And who knoweth the interpretation of a thing? A man's wisdom maketh his face to shine, and the boldness of his face shall be changed.*

Two things Solomon had desired to *seek out*—*wisdom and folly* (chap. vii. 25.) The latter he had known to his cost, and most faithfully has he described it. He now adverts to the former—*Who is as the wise man?* There is no one to be set by him, however splendidly endowed, rich, noble, or learned. " Wisdom is the principal thing" (Prov. iv. 7)—worth all the pains of prayer and diligence to gain and to hold fast. If it is anything, it is everything. A matchless gift! The Preacher cannot restrain his burst of admiration —*Who is as the wise man?*

But it is the practical quality that we chiefly regard —to *know the interpretation of a thing.* The Apostle distinguishes between " the gift of tongues, and the interpretation of tongues." (1 Cor. xii. 10.) To have the gift of communicating the treasure is far more valuable than the mere personal benefit. *The interpreter*—one who can expound the mind, the word, the ways, the works of God—is " one among a thousand" (Job, xxxiii. 23)—one very rarely to be found. In the field of science the gifts of *wisdom and interpretation* are distinct. Many a man may see clearly through his own optics; but he has no talent to remove the cloud, that obstructs his brother's vision.

The *wisdom,* here so highly commended, as a mere intellectual quality has no practical influence. But as a heavenly principle, *it makes the face to shine* from intercourse with a brighter world. There is not indeed — as in the cases of Moses and Stephen (Ex. xxxiv. 29; Acts, vi. 15) — any external glory. But the Lord fulfils his own promise — I "will beautify the meek with salvation" (Ps. cxlix. 4.) " Holiness to the Lord" stamps the profession with a Divine lustre. Godliness is never long without making itself seen. If it be too humble to court the eye, it is too active to escape it. Are we not all more or less moulded into the spirit of our society? What a moulding of holiness must there be in fellowship with God — ' walking in the light, as he is in the light ! ' * What a weight of holy character must be the result ! This is indeed a religion — not only convincing by its consistency, but attractive by its loveliness.

Lord Bacon beautifully describes the diversified influence of this practical principle — ' If a man be gracious and courteous to strangers, it shews that he is a citizen of the world, and that his heart is no island cut off from other lands, but a continent that joins to them; if he be compassionate towards the afflictions of others, it' shews that his heart is like the noble tree, that is wounded itself when it gives the balm ; if he easily pardons offences, it shews that his mind is planted above injuries, so that he cannot be shot ; if he be thankful for small benefits, it shews that he weighs men's minds, and not their trash : but above all, if he have St. Paul's perfection, that he would wish to be an anathema from Christ for the salvation of his brethren, it shews much

* See 1 John, i. 3–7.

of a Divine nature, and a kind of conformity with Christ himself.'*

One display of this Divine transformation may be seen in the *change of the boldness of our face.* Once it was hard and stern loftiness. Now, without losing one atom of its firmness, it melts down into humility. Moses, when occasion warranted, could shew *the boldness of his face.* Yet his habitual course was *the change of this boldness,* as one, who " was very meek above all the men which were upon the face of the earth" (Ex. xxxii. 26–28, with Num. xii. 3.) How fine and perfect the contrast in our Divine Master, when *the boldness of face* awed the buyer and seller in the temple; and yet he could *change* it for the exercise of a Teacher "meek and lowly in heart?" (John, ii. 15, with Matt. xi. 29.) It is however only when *the face shines* under heavenly influence, that the sturdiness of Christian confidence will be fully set out. The combination is perfect—'heaven upon earth to have a man's mind move in charity, rest in Providence, and turn upon the poles of truth.'†

2. *I counsel thee to keep the King's commandment; and that in regard of the oath of God.*

Having commended *wisdom* in its bright shining beauty, he now enforces some of its practical rules. Loyalty is a component part of Christian obedience. (Tit. iii. 1.) The command — " Render unto Cæsar the things that are Cæsar's," stands upon the same ground as—"Unto God the things that are God's." (Matt. xxii. 21.) The preacher speaks

---

* *Essays On Goodness.* See further examples, Job. xxix. 8–10. Dan. vi. 4, 5.

† Lord Bacon's *Essays On Truth.*

with authority—*I counsel thee* to keep the King's command-ment*—to observe the mouth of the King (Heb. Ps. ciii. 20, 21), as 'the angels behold the face of God,' the mark of their constant readiness to execute his first commands. This obedience has respect to *the oath of God.* If there be no outward covenants, as in days of old;† the solemn obligation still remains to those who stand to us in the place of God. 'All Authority'— Bp. Taylor reminds us—'descends from God, and our superiors bear the image of the Divine power, which God imprints on them; which whoso defaceth shall be answerable for the defacing of the King's image. And in the same manner will God require it at our hands, if we despise his authority, upon whomsoever he hath imprinted it.'‡ This was St. Paul's argument for our obedience—" The powers that be are ordained of God." (Rom. xiii. 1–5. Comp. 1 Pet. ii. 13.)

Yet no earthly sovereign can claim the right of absolute obedience. ' The law of the land ought not to be made our standard of moral right and wrong.'§ (Dan. iii. 16–18; vi. 10. Acts, iv. 19; v. 29.) The Babylonish confessors, and the Apostles of Christ, shewed themselves to be servants of God by their very act of disobedience to man. The service of man must ever be subordinated to the supreme claims of the service of God. To God, *the oath* of allegiance is bound indissolubly. Soul and body are alike the purchase of the Son of God. (Ps. cxix. 106, with 1 Cor. vi. 19, 20.) Where therefore man's command is contrary, we must shew respectful but unflinching determination.

---

* An ellipsis—something to be supplied — implying special emphasis.— Comp. Ps. cxx. 7, v. 2.

† Comp. 1 Chron. xi. 3; 2 Chron. xv. 12–15; Neh. ix. 38; x. 29; 1 Kings, ii. 43.

‡ *Holy Living,* c. iii. s. 1.

§ Abp. Whately's *Lessons on the British Constitution.*

' The case'—as a valuable Christian writer determines—
' does not admit of argument. The course is distinct and
clear. The will of God is the simple and absolute rule.
Whatever is not in exact consistency with this is sin. God
alone is worthy of homage. His law is the supreme and
only guide, from which there is no appeal, and which admits
of no rival.'* The throne must be for the Great King.
The second place would be, as if we cast him out, and
" would not have him to reign over us." (Luke, xix. 14.)

3. *Be not hasty to go out of his sight ; stand not in an evil*
   thing, for he doeth whatsoever pleaseth him.   4. Where
   the word of a King is, there is power : and who may say
   unto him—What doest thou ?   5. Whoso keepeth the
   commandment shall feel no evil thing : and a wise man's
   heart discerneth both time and judgment.

These wise and important rules have a special reference
to despotic power—The standing daily before the King
(1 Kings, x. 8 ; Esth. i. 14) was the mark of obedient readiness. *Hastiness* therefore *to go out of his sight* would be an
insolent or disrespectful taking offence, seeming to fling
off all allegiance. If there has been *an evil thing*—inadvertently or wilfully— *stand not in it.* There is little hope
of escape. The same rule he elsewhere gives— " If thou
hast done foolishly in lifting up thyself, or if thou hast
thought evil, lay thine hand upon thy mouth." † ' Kings, as
the Proverb says, have many eyes, many ears, many and
long hands.'‡ Instant confession is far better than *standing*

* Dr. Abercrombie's *Essays and Tracts*, p. 299.
† Prov. xxx. 32. See also Chap. x. 4.
‡ Lavater *in loco.*

out. *Where the word of a King is, there is power.* The Autocrat—whether he be good or bad—whether he be a Solomon (1 Kings, ii. 29–46) or an Herod (Matt. xiv. 9, 10) is without control.* *He doeth whatsoever pleaseth him,* and *who may say unto him—What doest thou?* A conscientious counsellor is bound in faithfulness to his Sovereign and to the interests of his country. He may therefore in cases of wilful or inadvertent wrong, be constrained to a firm protest at all hazards—*What doest thou?*† But in the ordinary course—quiet obedience—*keeping the commandment,* and marking the time—is the best security. Thus Esther in prudent submission preferred her anxious request. And "by the good hand of her · God upon her," she was preserved from *feeling evil,* and honoured as the Saviour of her people. (Esth. v. 1–8.) Indeed the indemnity from *evil* gives great encouragement to this path of godly confession. Moses *felt no evil* from Pharaoh—nor Samuel from Saul—nor Elijah from wicked Ahab. And even the exceptive cases—where outward injury was sustained, could not be said to have been charged with *evil,* when the crown of martyrdom was the result.

'The Apostolical precepts'—as has been well observed— 'are just those of Solomon in a more extended form. The same counsel is given. It is enforced by the same considerations of "wrath and conscience." And the same means are prescribed for shunning the severity of the ruling powers —called by Solomon *keeping the commandments*—by Paul —"doing that which is good."'‡

But we speak—not only of the courtiers, or the im-

---

* Prov. xxx. 31; Dan. v. 19.

      Sic volo; sic jubeo; stat pro ratione voluntas.

'I will this—I command that—No hesitation—my will is law.' —Dr. A. Clark, *in loco.*

  † See 2 Sam. xxiv. 3.   ‡ Wardlaw, with Rom. xiii. 1–7.

mediate attendants of the earthly Sovereign. Who of us
does not lie under a primary obligation to the " King of
Kings ? " If it be an honourable "happiness" (Comp.
1 Kings, x. 8) to stand continually before him; yet what
carefulness—what reverence—what implicit subjection—
what ready obedience is required! Never for a moment let
us *stand in the evil thing*—" I have sinned against heaven
and in thy sight" (Luke, xv. 21) : let this be the breathing
of instant and hearty confession. Think of *the power of
the King's word*, "who can destroy both body and soul in
hell." (Ib. xii. 4, 5.) Think of his absolute—sovereign rule
—" all the inhabitants of the earth" (such was the confession of the Heathen Monarch) " are reputed as nothing ;
and he doeth according to his will in the army of heaven,
and among the inhabitants of the earth ; and none can
stay his hand, or say unto him, What doest thou ?" (Dan.
iv. 35. Comp. Job, ix. 12.)

This path of *keeping the commandment* will preserve us
from *feeling evil*. Every *command* bears the stamp of infinite
tenderness and love. Not one is supernumerary. Yet our
course must not be one command standing upon the ruins
of another ; but the exercise of godly wisdom—just where
the Lord has marked out our path, there to lay ourselves
out for him. And this indeed is a most precious means
of grace, opening to us the mystery of the Christian's joy.*
'This *keeping God's commandment*,' writes Bp. Taylor—'is
rewarded with *keeping God's commandments.*† And in this
world God hath not a greater reward to give. For so the
soul is nourished up to life; so it grows up with the increase
of God; so it passes on to a perfect man in Christ; so it is
consigned for heaven; and so it enters into glory. For glory
is the perfection of grace, and when our love to God is

---

* See Isa. lxiv. 5.   † See Ps. cxix. 55, 56.

come to its state and perfection, then we are within the circle
of a diadem, and then we are within the regions of felicity.'*

Indeed the most trifling details of our every-day obedience become the stepping-stones to our highest Christian
privileges. Difficulties will arise, as the exercise of needful
discipline, and calling for sound judgment to guide us
through them wisely and practically. *The King's commandment*—when to *keep*—when to resist it—the right
manner of *keeping* or resisting—this is sometimes a *time and
judgment* calling for great *discernment*. It is not man's
natural prudence that sufficeth. It is *the wise man's heart*
—the heart enlightened by the knowledge of God and his
will—the heart possessed by " the Spirit of wisdom"—here
alone is the safe *discernment*.

Too often in the ordinary course we encumber the path
with difficulties of our own framing. Sincere Christians are
not always wise. The husbandman never fails to *discern the
time*. He never mistakes the season for the plough, the
seed-time, and the harvest. But in " God's husbandry "
(1 Cor. iii. 9) how few seem to *discern* the value of the season!—how much the well-timing—whether in saying or
doing—adds to beauty and effect! (Prov. xv. 23 ; xxv. 11.)
The command—" Be instant" (2 Tim. iv. 2), is with many
Christian professors rather an excuse for being " out of
season" than a motive for being " in season." They feel
it quite enough to have acted rightly in the substance of
a duty, and they have little care about the wrongness of
time and manner in doing. We may therefore sometimes
feel evil even in the profession of *keeping the commandment*.
Want of *discernment* may bring us into some of the many
bye-paths of self-will or self-delusion. There may be danger
in fleeing from the temptations of the world, of fleeing
from its duties. We may possibly be neglecting immediate

* *Apples of Sodom.*

duties for extraordinary service; forgetting that the soldier's place is in his ranks, and that no impulse of his own courage can justify him in rushing out of his own proper position for some unexpected occasion of exploit. So many indeed and so plausible are the devious paths, that can we help feeling the daily need and value of the prayer—"Teach me good judgment and knowledge; for I have believed thy commandments?" (Ps. cxix. 66.) Carefulness of others will often cast the light of holy simplicity upon our own path. In the calculations of the day, always take trials into the account. They will come as one view—one exercise—of his love; not to consume, but to prove and purify, our faith. They will come too with the precious promise—"If any man lack wisdom, let him ask of God, who giveth to all men liberally, and upbraideth not; and it shall be given him." (Jam. i. 5.)

6. *Because to every purpose there is time and judgment, therefore the misery of man is great upon him. 7. For he knoweth not that which shall be; for who can tell him when it shall be?*

Solomon had already shewn—that there is *a time and judgment to* every *purpose*—a special time, and a special application.* All things are in the hand of a wise Sovereign. 'There comes to be a critical nick of time, into which such and such things must fall, and into no other.' † *A wise man's heart discerneth,* and therefore improveth *this time.* But the mass of mankind—through weakness or perverseness—discern it not. And therefore in the neglect of improvement it becomes the occasion of *greater misery.* Great indeed is the mischief of this neglect. In common life

* See Chap. iii. 1–8.
† Howe's *Principles of the Oracles of God,* Works, vii. 212.

valuable opportunities of improvement pass away without a harvest. The future is under a cloud. *He knoweth not that which shall be.* If God does not teach, *no one can tell him when it shall be.*

All concerning us is determined in the counsels of God, and all in *judgment.* The time is the best time, because it is God's time. It is a solemn thought to us all—most precious to the Christian—that each of us has been in the mind of God—the subject of the thoughts of God—from all eternity. Every particle of our being—every trial—every step in our journey—the most minute as well as the most important—everything has been marked with the stamp of the Divine *purpose.* And what a dignity does it give to the veriest trifle of circumstance or work! Yet what can be called a trifle, that is a link in the purpose of the great Sovereign ?

But how little does man conceive the responsibility of indifference to the purpose of God! The evil of this wilful ignorance in the concerns of eternity is ruinous beyond all calculation—God's *time* of mercy—his "accepted time"* —how bright is the sunshine of every moment ! But let it be neglected—*great* indeed *will be the misery.* "The door" once "shut," is shut for ever. (Matt. xxv. 10. Luke, xiii. 24–28.) Friends all gone—left alone with devils—no hope —no rest—nothing but eternal despair! The soul, capable of the eternal enjoyment of God, lost beyond remedy ! Better never to have had the time, than to have had it, and not known it. One can hardly imagine tears too bitter—groans too deep—fears too awful. We seem to shrink from the conviction of what we know to be the fact and history of every moment—Souls lost for eternity !

We long to sympathize with the Saviour's weeping

* Ps. xxxii. 6. Isa. lv. 6. 2 Cor. vi. 2.

lamentation—" If thou hadst known!" (Luke, xix. 41, 42.)
The sentence is left unfinished, as if the tears interrupted
his speech, or melted it away in more speaking silence.
And were these vain and causeless tears? They dropped
from the most intellectual and comprehensive eye—from
the most tender, bleeding heart. They told how *great the
misery of* man, despising or neglecting his *time*—his day
of grace. Oh, sinner! be persuaded to turn now. To-
morrow is with God—in eternity.

Much indeed of the future is far beyond the keenest and
most sagacious eye. *What or when it shall be*—is our present exercise. But prayer and diligence will bring the
light in God's fittest time. Meanwhile this ignorance does
not touch our security, or cloud our confidence. " *We
know* that all things"—including the whole universe—the
mightiest as well as the weakest movement—the chastening
as well as the healing—the sharp as well as the gentle—
all combine for the one grand issue—our present and eternal
good. (Rom. viii. 28.) Rich indeed must be the portion,
that includes death in its treasures—not as a bar to keep
us out, but as a bridge, by which we pass over, and possess
our inheritance. Thus the certainty of death assures the
certainty of heaven. Both worlds are provided for—" things
present, and things to come—all are ours." (1 Cor. iii. 22.)
Whatever be the threatening trial, ' the sure testimony of
God, received in humble, realizing, obedient faith, is the
only remedy for the evil.' *

8. *There is no man that hath power over the spirit to retain
the spirit; neither hath he power in the day of death; and
there is no discharge in that war, neither shall wickedness
deliver those that are given to it.*

* Scott.

One event—specially stamped with uncertainty, but linked with the Divine purpose, is—"a time to die." (Chap. iii. 1, 2.) This most momentous event in man's history hangs upon the Almighty Fiat. *Who can tell a man when it shall be?* But the word once given—*who hath power over the spirit, to retain the spirit?* Such is the uncontrolled government of God. Man—after all his mightiest efforts to make himself independent of God—cannot retain his spirit in its tabernacle prison a single moment beyond the time. Nay, *he hath no power at all in the day of death.* The king is as impotent to resist as the beggar. 'The power, that sways millions with a nod, fails here. The wealth, that procures for its owner all that his heart can wish, fails here. The might of the warrior, which hath slain his thousands, and which no human arm could withstand, fails here. The most earnest desire of life, and the tears, and the wailings, and the fond caresses of disconsolate affection—all fail here.' * Only one of the children of Adam has ever claimed this dominion over his life. And he, while he thus asserted his prerogative, was pleased—for our sake—blessed for ever be his name!—to wave it. "No man"—declared the Divine Redeemer—"taketh my life from me; but I lay it down of myself. I have power to lay it down; and I have power to take it again." (John, x. 18.)

A man therefore, *having no power to retain* his life, hath of course *no power in the day of his death* to repel the stroke. The physician's skill may seem to put off this day. But he is only the instrument, and his success or failure only serves to mark the Divine purpose hitherto hidden. Giant strength is powerless before "the king of terrors." In other *wars a discharge* may place us beyond the reach of danger. But no such *discharge* is here. The Christian hero

* Wardlaw.

of an hundred fights can claim no privilege as *miles emeritus.**
The mighty one must be met in single combat. No help
will be given from earth or heaven. The struggle may be
long or short. But the issue is certain. Each falls in turn
before him. The word has gone out—" It is appointed
unto men once to die." (Heb. ix. 27.)

No truth is more certain—perhaps none more often repeated; yet none more practically forgotten. Men live as
if they were never to die—as if they were exempted from
the universal law. *The wicked* " strengtheneth himself in
his wickedness." (Ps. lii. 7.) But he can neither outwit
nor outbrave the enemy. *Given to his wickedness,* he will
find that it is no *deliverance* for him. His " covenant with
death and with hell shall be disannulled." He " shall be
driven away in his wickedness." (Isa. xxviii. 14–18. Prov.
xiv. 32.)

Child of God ! thou must enter into *the war* with this
great enemy. But thou shalt not be alone in the awful
crisis. Thine unseen Friend—" Jehovah thy Shepherd "—
walks with thee in the valley—thy cover from all evil (Ps.
xxiii. 1–4.) " The Captain of thy salvation" (Heb. ii. 10)
hath entered into the conflict for thee. He hath come out
victorious—He " hath abolished death." (2 Tim. i. 10.)
" He hath destroyed him that had the power of death."
(Heb. ii. 14.) His victory by faith is thine. Shrink not
then from the conflict. To thy Saviour it was most bitter
trouble. To thyself it will be only the dismissal from thy
prison—the entrance into everlasting joy.

But—Reader—prove thy security. Not to have an interest in him, is to be under the power of death. To be
vitally united to him, is to be safe for eternity. On one
side is death—on the other, victory and life eternal. (Isa.
xxv. 8. 1 Cor. xv. 55–57.)

* The soldier, whose services have entitled him to *a discharge.*

9. *All this have I seen, and applied my heart unto every work that is done under the sun. There is a time, wherein one man ruleth over another to his own hurt.* 10. *And so I saw the wicked buried, who had come and gone from the place of the holy; and they were forgotten in the city, where they had so done. This is also vanity.*

' To encourage confidence in his statements, Solomon tells us once and again, that they were the result of his own careful observation over the vast field of Divine Providence and Government.'* In the corresponding field of Creation he had been a diligent and successful student. (1 Kings, iv. 33.) But ' they that would judge aright of any one of the Lord's dispensations, must be careful students of them all. They must not slight any work of his, because all, though they be many to us, make but one entire work in God's hand. And every part of that work is a commentary, clearing the nature and use of the whole, and God's intent therein.' † Solomon's views were not on the surface; nor were they the views of a philosopher merely, or of a theorist. Man in all his various relations was the object of his study —at this moment with a special reference to the ordinance of God, in which he himself bare a part—*one man ruling over another.* Often had he seen this rule perverted from its legitimate end—exercised *to the hurt*—not of the ruled only, but of the *ruler.* So wide a sphere for the mighty striving of self-will must be peril—a pinnacle of fearful danger. Thus was Pharaoh "raised up" to a throne, only that his fall might be more tremendous. (Exod. ix. 16.) Well may "the rich rejoice, in that he is made low." (Jam. i. 10.) Especial mercy is it to be kept upon humble ground; not seeking to mount, but thankful to be kept watchful in godly fear.

* Cartwright.   † Nisbet.

But let us follow Solomon in his field of observation. *Wickedness*—so far from being a *deliverance*—becomes an occasion of *hurt*. *The wicked* may have *come and gone* in pomp and ceremony *from the place of the holy.** But the great leveller comes without respect of persons. The splendid pageant of a funeral passes before us—*I saw them buried.* Their hypocrisy is laid open.† Instead of being embalmed in memory, soon the miserable object is out of mind—*forgotten* —even *in* his own *city.* For "the memory of the wicked shall rot." (Prov. x. 7.) 'Whereas in their life they would be as gods, they died like men, and were soon *forgotten* as beasts.'‡ The wise man's father had painted the picture in strong colours, as it passed under his own eye—" I have seen *the wicked* in great prosperity, and flourishing like a green bay-tree. Yet he passed away, and lo! he was not; yea—I sought him, but he could not be found." (Ps. xxxvii. 35, 36.) Is not this another exhibition of this world's *vanity?* And yet this is the best portion that earth can give, but such a portion as the poorest child of God would utterly despise.

---

* The best expositors have considered *the place of the holy* to be "the place of judgment" (chap. iii. 16), counted *holy* as the place where "God sat by his representatives pronouncing judgment." (Comp. Ps. lxxxii. 1 ; Deut. i. 17 ; 2 Chron. xix. 6.) The application to wicked rulers seems to point this way. The individual case (v. 9) is probably put for the whole race of oppressive rulers. The whole verse Mercer calls— *valde intricatus* (very intricate). But the received translation is well warranted by authority.

† See Luke, xii. 1, 2.   ‡ Grainger.

> . . . . . 'Nor mine eyes
> Have those unrighteous ministers escaped
> Who on the judgment-seat exalted high,
> Were honour'd once as gods.   What fun'ral pomp
> Attends their obsequies !   How soon forgot !
> Their glory with them to the grave descends
> There everlasting darkness blots their names
> As if they'd never been.   So vain a thing
> Is human grandeur !'—*Choheleth.*

Who that has ever grasped the substance could bear to be put off with such a shadowy inheritance?

11. *Because sentence against an evil man is not executed speedily, therefore the heart of the sons of men is fully set* in them to do evil.*

Wondrous are the dispensations of Divine mercy! But not less wondrous is the wickedness of man in turning all this world of mercy into an occasion of deeper sin. *Sentence against an evil work* is instantly *passed*—"Woe unto the wicked; it shall be ill with him:"† Why then—reason would ask—is it not *speedily executed?* Why does he not crush him at once by his stroke? The glorious perfection of Divine long-suffering must be displayed.‡ Adam therefore lived more than nine hundred years under the *sentence* passed—*not executed.* (Gen. ii. 17; v. 5.) "The long-suffering of God waited in the days of Noah." (1 Pet. iii. 20, with Gen. vi. 3.) The ordinary course is to give the sinner time and space for repentance—to open to him a day of grace—"An accepted time, leaving him in the neglect of it without excuse." (Luke, xix. 42.) Were the execution instantly to follow the sentence, how many glorious manifestations of grace would have been lost to the Church! We might have known Paul as "a blasphemer, and a persecutor, and injurious;" but not as the "chief of sinners, who obtained mercy," as a special display of "*all* long-suffering; and for a pattern to them which should hereafter believe." (1 Tim. i. 13–16.)

* 'The phrase noteth an height of confidence and resolvedness on sinful courses, called in the Scripture madness, excess, greediness,' &c.—Bp. Reynolds.
† Isa. iii. 11. Comp. Jer. xviii. 11; Mic. ii. 3; Gal. iii. 10.
‡ See Exod. xxxiv. 5, 6; Ps. ciii. 8; Joel, ii. 13, 14.

As to the bold and presumptuous sinner—if he expected the thunderbolt to fall upon his head in the very act of sin, would he not turn pale at the thought? But *because sentence is not speedily executed*—because the threatened destruction seems to loiter—he goes on secure, because he goes unpunished. He dares not say so with his lips; but "he hath said in his heart, Thou wilt not require it." (Ps. x. 13. Comp. Luke, xii. 45.) He does not really believe that God will be true to his own word. He has often sinned—So have his neighbours—No evil consequence has come—The *Sentence* is gone forth; but there is a *chance* whether it will be executed. And upon this hazardous *chance* all the momentous interests of eternity are rashly staked! The sinner takes his plunge—"I shall have peace, though I walk in the way of my own heart." (Deut. xxix. 19.)

Mark the emphasis of this presumptuous sin. *The heart* —as if it were but one common *heart of the sons of men*— the bent of one purpose acting in every man in the world— this *heart is set*—*fully set*—it is not only yielding to sin under some special assault, but one wilful—habitual—determined resolution—without remorse—all—*to do evil*. It is "man drinking up iniquity like water—*setting* himself in a way that is not good (the meiosis figure—speaking less than is meant), putting themselves to hard labour—" drawing iniquity with cords of vanity, and sin as it were with a cart-rope."* Such is the picture of man in rebellion against his God!

But *because sentence is not speedily executed*, it is not the less sure for the delay. The scoffer asked in contempt— "Where is the promise of his coming?" But the promise *did* come in God's time, and swept them away. (2 Pet. iii. 3–6. Luke, xvii. 26–29.) 'It comes'—as good Bishop Reynolds remarks—'with feet of wool; but it will strike with

* Job, xv. 16. Ps. xxxvi. 4. Isa. v. 18.

hands of lead.' And yet the wickedness of man abuses the
long-suffering of God, as an occasion of more desperate
rebellion. Awful indeed is the sight. How he "despiseth
the riches of God's goodness, and forbearance, and long-
suffering, not knowing that the goodness of God leadeth him
to repentance!" Yea—" after his hardness and impenitent
heart, he treasureth up unto himself wrath against the day
of wrath and revelation of the righteous judgment of God."
(Rom. ii. 4, 5.) What 'venom must there be in the
ruption of our nature, that can suck such poison out
such a sweet attribute as the patience of God!'* Never
let it be supposed that God's patience is the proof, that he
thinks lightly of sin. There is indeed a treasure of wrath,
and hour by hour, yea—moment by moment—has the
impenitent sinner been adding to the heap. How soon
the cup may be full! Who knoweth but he may be at this
moment exhausting the last drop of the appointed patience
of God? We live only by the mere act of grace. And yet
we would burden his forbearance, because it is so great, and
load him with the weight of sin, only because he is so slow
to avenge himself.† The devils might have been capable of
this aggravated sin, of thus trampling upon the mercy of
God; but guilty they could not be, simply because their
instant punishment precluded them from the opportunity.

This awful revolt is not reached at once. The habit,
that entrenches the sinner so firmly in his own delusion, is
not formed in a day. Conscience will stir, and remonstrate
—specially in the early stages—and not without a severe
struggle will this 'Deputy of the Supreme Judge be *wholly*
silenced.' ‡ Bishop Taylor has accurately drawn the grada-
tions and progress of this mighty principle of evil—' Vice

* Cotton.
† See those astonishing declarations, Isa. xliii. 24. Amos, ii. 13.
‡ *Sermon on Text*, by Rev. R. Walker, Edinburgh.

first is pleasing ; then it grows easy ; then delightful ; then
frequent ; then habitual ; then confirmed ; then the man is
impenitent ; then he is obstinate ; then he resolves never to
repent ; *and then he is damned.'* Beware of the first steps
—the first taste of the poison—the first lust after its sweetness—the first consent of the will—the first yielding of the
heart to anything but to God. If the lust has been indulged, at least shew beginning of repentance—believing the
indulgence to be thy shame. Awful indeed is the thought
—'He that blushes not at his crime, but adds shameless-
ness to his shame, hath no instrument left to restore him to
the hopes of mercy.' †

Who can tell our infinite obligation to this glorious perfection—the long-suffering of God ? It is the silence of his
justice, and the first whisper of his mercy ‡—the time of his
"endurance of the vessels of wrath " (Rom. ix. 22)—the
assurance that he is "not willing that any should perish "
(2 Pet. iii. 9)—the display, as we have just remarked, of
his sovereign grace. (1 Tim. i. 16.)

12. *Though a sinner do evil an hundred times, and his days be
prolonged ; yet surely I know that it shall be well unto
them that fear God, which fear before him.* 13. *But it
shall not be well with the wicked ; neither shall he prolong
his days, which are as a shadow, because he feareth not
before God.*

The sinner's heart is so *fully set to do evil,* that he *may do
it an hundred times,* ' never so often.' § Instead of the
thunderbolt of vengeance, *his days may be prolonged.* He

---

* *Sermon on the Deceitfulness of the Heart.*
+ Ib. *Holy Living,* chap. ii. s. 5.
‡ See 2 Pet. iii. 15.   § Bp. Reynolds.

may even grow bolder than ever in sin. He may be exalted in outward prosperity, while the children of God are crushed in affliction. The sanctuary expounds the difficulty, and solves the apparent contradiction. The end shews all to be infallibly right,* and (to use the simile of a quaint commentator) 'as with a sponge, the ground of offence is wholly taken away.'† At the great day, there will be a clear discernment between the righteous and the wicked—between him that *feareth*—and him that *feareth not—before God.* (Mal. iii. 18.)

The two classes—mark emphatically, *two only*—are before us. They are known by the influence or the want of that 'Divine quality—a holy, filial *fear* of offending God' ‡ —*fearing before him*—before his face—as their present God —the witness of all their doings—always in his sight. With those that thus *fear* (Heb.) *before him it shall be well.* It may often seem to be ill with the godly, and *well* with the sinner. We see Joseph in the pit (Gen. xxxvii. 24), Job in the ashes (chap. ii. 8), Lazarus at the rich man's gate (Luke, xvi. 20, 21). We may see Haman in power (Esth. iii. 1), the foolish in prosperity (Ps. lxxiii. 3). But the statement on both sides stands firm. "Many indeed are the afflictions of the righteous." (Ps. xxxiv. 19.) But "thou hast given them the heritage of those that *fear* thy name." (Ib. lxi. 5.) How rich that heritage must be, where every loss turns to our gain, and is overruled for our real and eternal good. This heritage is no other than the Lord himself (Ib. xvi. 5.) — ' a God'—as Pascal beautifully describes him—'who possesses the hearts and souls of his servants, gives them an inward feeling of their own misery, and of his infinite mercy—unites himself to their spirit, replenishing it with humility and joy—with affiance and love—and renders

* See Ps. lxxiii. 1–20.   † Lavater.   ‡ Nisbet.

them incapable of any project or aim — but himself.'* Thus
is it well with them now. And how will it be to them at
death — to find it the gate of life? How in eternity — "to
be at home, and for ever with the Lord." (2 Cor. v. 8. 1
Thess. iv. 17),—to " behold" (Ps. xvii. 15. John, xvii. 24),
yea, even to share (Matt. xxv. 24–26) his glory — unclouded
— everlasting? (John, xvii. 22. Rev. iii. 21.)

But what is the record of *the wicked?* And here we must
include a large mass of character—who seem to halt, and
to occupy a neutral position between the two — not only the
ungodly and profane—not only the negative body, who live
only for the barren purpose of doing no harm; but the useful
member of society, decorous and upright, the lovely and
conscientious. For it is an awful and affecting truth, that
all these shades and modifications of character are stamped
with ungodliness in the sight of God, because without the
steady, commanding, practical principle—*the fear of God.*†
It may seem to be *well with him* in the esteem of his fellow-
men, and in the testimony of his blinded conscience; but,
wanting the one principle that connects him with God,
it *shall not be well*—(meiosis again)—' it shall be very ill'
with him, so long as he remains in his natural condition.
Even in his highest prosperity, he goes in and out under
the curse of God. He hath no other prospéct than to quit
with horror the world, which hath cheated and ruined him for
ever. (Job, xviii. 18. Prov. xiv. 32.) Or should he " have
no bands in his death"— the more overwhelmed will he
be at the last in eternal despair—in unanticipated woe.. All
this comes in the natural course. Nothing is more easy than
to ruin ourselves for ever. Only sit still, and do nothing,
and we perish in our own slumber. We are cast out as
" wicked," because " slothful, servants." (Matt. xxvi. 26–30.)

---

* *Thoughts,* xx.
† See Ps. xxxvi. 1. See the apostle's climax, Rom. iii. 18.

Only just "*neglect* the so great salvation;" and it becomes to us "the savour of death unto death." (Heb. ii. 3.)

Take then the sum and substance of the matter — the child of God at his worst — *it shall be well with him;* the servant of sin at his best — it shall *not be well with him.* Each lives for the present life under the blessing or curse of God. Each will reap the full harvest of their principles throughout eternity. Balance the whole, and who can for a moment doubt on which side lies the *well* — on which side the ill? The ill of the godly — whatever that may be — is but for a moment; and his *well* is for eternity. The contrast is dark beyond expression. The ungodly grasps at happiness, and embraces vanity. He cannot *prolong his days* at his will. Their *shadow* — in contrast with the true substance — without good — passeth away, and all his portion is dark despair — the cutting rebuke ringing in his ears — "Son, remember!" (Luke, xvi. 25.)

And observe — how decided is the verdict — *Surely I know.* This is no bare conjecture or probability. No truth in the Bible is more demonstrative. The firm conviction is wrought in the heart by the Spirit of God enabling us to rest confidently on the word. The promise of both worlds is assured to godliness. (1 Tim. iv. 8.) The experience of all the *God-fearing* confirms the testimony. Ask Marolle — the French confessor in his filthy dungeon — enduring all that man could heap upon him for the crushing of his confidence. Doubt might sometimes rise up like the locusts eating up the pleasant green things. (Exod. x. 15.) But on the main point he was ready. '*It is — and it shall be — well.* 'Eighty-and-six years' — was Polycarp's witness — 'have I served my Master, and he hath never wronged me.' How could he after all have turned his back upon him, who had never turned away from him? "I have fought the good fight" — is the voice of a yet nobler witness — "Henceforth the crown."

204 — EXPOSITION OF ECCLESIASTES.

(2 Tim. iv. 7, 8.) But not less decided is the judgment— *I know that it shall not be well.* The blessing and the curse stand upon the same firm rock—the word of God; not one jot or tittle of which has ever fallen to the ground. What then is my present state? Living for heaven—or for hell? O my God! for which? May the stamp upon me be "a brand plucked out of the fire!—a sinner saved by grace!"*

14. *There is a vanity that is done upon the earth, that there be just men, unto whom it happeneth according to the work of the wicked: again, that there be wicked men, to whom it happeneth according to the work of the righteous. I said, that this is also vanity. 15. Then I commended mirth, because a man hath no better thing under the sun, than to eat, and to drink, and to be merry; for that shall abide with him of his labour the days of his life, which God giveth him under the sun.*

We have another picture of *vanity* doubly marked. The All-wise and righteous Governor of the world never forgets the vitally-important distinction between *the righteous and the wicked.* But he is not pleased to make it the standard of his providential dispensation. (Chap. ix. 1, 2.) It often therefore *happeneth* as if *the just* were punished, and *the wicked* rewarded. *It happeneth,* not as if it fell out apart from the foreknowledge and providence of God; but in the ordinary course of the Divine Government. 'Nothing'—as Beza remarks—'is more repugnant to reason than this apparently strange distribution.' It would seem as if the righteous "had cleansed his heart in vain." (Ps. lxxiii. 13.) This may justly

* Zech. iii. 22, with Eph. ii. 8; 1 Cor. xv. 10. Dathè remarks upon these verses as 'a fine testimony to the certainty of a future life after death and judgment.'

be called a *vanity*—not as reflecting upon the government of God in permitting them; but because the instruments are the fruit of man's corruption, and the display is that of the utterly unsatisfactory state of earthly things. But—be it remembered—we only see the surface view. There are depths in Providence far beyond our vision. In his own time and way the Lord will bring perfect order out of seeming confusion, and astonish us with the manifestation of his glory.

After all, this is only *a vanity upon the earth.* ' In the other world good is given to the good, and evil to the evil.'* Here—though we know but little, yet enough to be quiet. Providences were not made only for man now, but for man in eternity. Meanwhile it is beautiful to mark how they fulfil, and thus confirm, Scripture; so that a wise observer is at once rich in experience, and established in the good ways of God.

' Say then—Christian sufferer—does thine heart rebel, to see *the wicked* prosper, and thyself in woe? Say, wouldst thou change? Is he better off than thou? Are his earthly blessings better than thy grace? Is not Jesus more than silver and gold to thee? Hast thou the *lesser* portion, because thou hast the Lord?'† Leave thyself with God, and be at peace. Let this living faith preserve thee from that brooding discontent, which seems to throw a cloud upon the goodness of thy most gracious God. (Chap. ii. 24; iii. 12; v. 18. 1 Tim. iv. 3–5.) Never suppose that the overflow of temporal enjoyments can form the chief good. Enjoy the gifts of God—whatever portion of them be allotted to thee, as the stream from the fountain of his special interest in thee. (Gen. xxxiii. 5.) This enjoyment can never be in unholy sensualism, or unrestrained indulgence — but with that

* Lavater.   † Mylne.

Christian mirth—cheered—as in the bright era of the
Church (Acts, ii. 46)—with the smile of Divine acceptance,
which makes "a continual feast."* Let this be our *abiding*
portion *all the days of our life*—every new day bringing a
fresh gift of God for his service and glory. Whatever we
may lose, the grand interest is secured.

16. *When I applied my heart to know wisdom, and to see the
business that is come upon the earth (for also there is that
neither day nor night seeth sleep with his eyes) ; 17. Then
I beheld all the work of God, that a man cannot find out
the work that is done under the sun, because, though a man
labour to seek it out, yet he shall not find it ; yea further,
though a wise man think to know it, yet shall he not be able
to find it.*

' Too much attention'—we are wisely reminded—' cannot be bestowed on that important—yet much-neglected
branch of learning—the knowledge of man's ignorance.'†
Here how deep and humbling is the picture! All the
efforts of diligence—earnest perseverance—intense *application of heart*—the laborious exercise of sleepless nights‡—
all fail to enlighten. A vast *terra incognita* lies beyond us.
The most profound inquirer can only stand upon the ocean's
shore, and cry.—"O the depth" of the arbitrariness?—no—

* Prov. xv. 15. ' He is not here commending Epicurean pleasure,
but he teaches, that when man cannot see or alter his own condition,
the best thing is to abstain from vain cares, and to content himself
with a quiet life, enjoying the good things of God.'—*Dathè.*

† *Detached Thoughts and Aphorisms*, from Abp. Whately's
Writings.

‡ Luther on this passage remarks, that he never gained anything,
except by the labour of *sleepless nights.* On the other hands an old
Commentator recommends, ' that our evening meditations should
rather be devotional than scholastical.' 'To beat our brains'—he
adds—' will leave it without fruit or rest.'—*Cotton.*

but " of the wisdom and knowledge of God. How un-searchable are his judgments, and his ways past finding out." (Rom. xi. 33.) Yet if all was brought down to our poor level—if revelation contained no mysteries—if it were stripped of everything supernatural—surely its credentials, as professing to come from God, would be very doubtful.* It is natural to expect—according to Butler's impregnable argument—that Revelation should have its difficulties, as well as Creation—*his* word thus corresponding with his works. Nor ought we 'to draw *down* or submit the mysteries of God to our reason, but contrariwise to raise and advance our reason to the Divine truth.'†

We open our Bibles. The doctrines instantly press upon us with difficulties. But to cavil is rebellion. If we reject one doctrine for its difficulties, we may as well reject another, standing as they all do upon the same testimony. The first lesson that Pythagoras taught was silence. The same lesson meets us in the Bible school, "Be still, and know that I am God." (Ps. xlvi. 10.) He makes no mistakes. But "he giveth not account of any of his matters." (Job, xxxiii. 13.) It is no more unnatural, that some of the doctrines of Revelation should overwhelm our understanding, than that the sun in full blaze should overpower our sight. Yet if the mind is shaken, the heart is upheld in energy. It is faith—not indolence. Exertion and diligence are in full activity.

Clearly Revelation was not proposed to indulge curiosity,

* See Job, xi. 7–10.

† Lord Bacon's *Advancement of Learning*, b. ii. c. vi. 2. 'The prerogative of God extendeth as well to the reason as to the will of man. So that as we are to obey his law, though we find a reluctation in our will, so we are to believe his words, though we find a reluctation in our reason. For if we believe only that which is agreeable to our sense, we give consent to the matter, not to the author, which is no more than we would do to a suspected and discredited witness.' —*Ib.* c. xxv. 1.

but to provide a remedy for man's blindness and misery. If it be viewed with a merely speculative eye, we marvel not, that it should stir up hard thoughts of God. But facts—if they do not convince, are yet sufficiently clear to silence, the gainsayer. That man is obviously treated—and ever has been treated since Adam's fall—as a creature under punishment—let who will dispute—none can deny. Does not this strongly prove a sure, though mysterious connexion with Adam's sin, charged upon his children to the end?

But to advert to one field of inquiry—*the business that is done upon the earth*. To obtain a clear and satisfying view of the whole framework of the Divine government—to search into the reason of the administration, and out of all the seeming incongruities to bring out one work of beauty, order, and completeness—all this is *labour* and travail. And after all the attempt is vain—*Man cannot find out the work. Labour and wisdom*—the two grand instruments of discovery—even in their combined exercise, both leave us in darkness. We can only pray for humility to believe, that whatever is done—however contrary to our apprehensions, is both wise and righteous. Secret it may be, but always holy, so that

> 'When reason fails
>   With all her powers,
> Then faith prevails
>   And love adores.'—*Watts.*

The mystery of perplexity is " a mystery of godliness."

The fact is—as Bp. Butler admirably states it—' Every secret that is disclosed—every discovery which is made—every new effect which is brought to view, serves to convince us of numberless more which remain concealed, and which we had before no suspicion of. There is no manner of absurdity in supposing a veil on purpose drawn over some scenes of infinite power, wisdom, and goodness, the sight of which might some way or other strike us too strongly; or that better ends are designed and served by their being concealed, than could be by their being exposed to our knowledge. The Almighty may cast "clouds and darkness round about him," for reasons and purposes of which we have not the least glimpse or conception.'* Light enough he has given to make faith rational, and to leave unbelief without excuse.

Are we then to refrain from searching into *the works of God?* So far from it—we are encouraged "to seek them out." (Ps. cxi. 2.) A spiritual understanding of the "loving-kindness of the Lord" will be to us an enriching harvest. (Ps. cvii. 43.) But how many a self-deluded victim has Satan reasoned into the bottomless pit! The pride of disputation is man's native corruption. Let *that* be restrained, and "light ariseth in the darkness." (Ps. cxii. 4.) Man's ignorance is to be traced to an understanding darkened by the fall. The remedy therefore, which restores from this awful calamity, will bring restored rays into the dark prison. The heart turned away from its proud reasonings—reason humbled to "the obedience of faith"—will bring a new atmosphere of light. "The entrance of thy words giveth light; it giveth understanding unto the simple." (Ps. cxix. 130.) 'Give me the Bible'—cried an eminent Christian—'and may the Lord give me faith to fix on it, or my head will grow giddy with amazement, confusion, and dread!'† Bright indeed and encouraging are the remarks of a thoughtful mind—'If we have not banished the Divine Spirit by slights and excesses; if we have fed his lamp in our hearts with prayer; if we have improved and strengthened our faculties by education and exercise, and then sit down to study the Bible with enquiring and teachable minds, we need not doubt of discovering its

* See his profound and interesting sermon on the Text. Comp. *Analogy*, Part ii. Chap. iv.

† *Memoirs of Mrs. Hawkes*, p. 381.

meaning; not indeed *purely*—for where find an intellect so colourless as never to tinge the light that falls upon it? *not wholly*—for how fathom the ocean of God's word? but with such accuracy, and to such a degree as shall suffice for the uses of our spiritual life.'* Take another testimony from a sound practical Christian—'I find that the benefit I receive from Scripture in a great measure depends upon myself. How often, in turning to it to clear up some historical sequence, or some obscure doctrine, to find material for imagination, or ground for hypothesis, I only get at the shell instead of the kernel! Or again—if in high-wrought times, a clearer insight be afforded, how prone are we to seek and improve and define it by our own strength, and so to bring human fictions, instead of Divine Truth, to light! *The mysteries of Holy Scriptures are revealed to us, only when we are seeking for nothing else, but for the way of reconciliation with God, and for help in our battle with selfishness and sin.*' Again, 'I learn more and more to discern the Divine wisdom, which has set limits to revelation. All that we need for our happiness is given us; and were the curtain lifted further from holy mysteries, man would be lost in hopeless bewilderment.'*

After all however, "secret things," as "belonging to the Lord our God," will remain "secret" still. But "the things that are revealed" will be the precious portion for "us and for our children"—for all the purposes of godly obedience.‡ As much light as is conducive to our welfare will be graciously vouchsafed. If the midday beams be withheld, let us thankfully walk in the twilight—improving diligently what is given—not murmuring at what is restrained. "Perfect day" would leave no room for the exercise of faith—the

* *Guesses at Truth.* First Series, p. 285.
† *Life of Perthes.* Chap. xxix. xxxvi.
‡ See Deut. xxix. 29.

discipline of the present dispensation—wisely appointed to humble us in the sense of ignorance, and to wean us from self-conceit in the exercise of confidence in God. In this spirit we shall be humble, patient, diligent, intelligent learners, sitting at the feet of our Divine Teacher; not disputing, or leaning unto our own understanding, but willing to be led in his own best way, on any ground, by any means that may seem good in his sight.

In fine—let it be remembered, that man's highest intellect can never receive one spiritual apprehension. ' Our endeavour therefore to be wise above what is written, must involve us in sin and perplexity, and can never lead to any satisfactory conclusions. But to believe and obey here will be a preparation for that world hereafter, where " we shall know even as also we are known." '*

CHAPTER IX.

1. *For all this I considered in my heart even to declare all this, that the righteous and the wise, and their works, are in the hand of God; no man knoweth either love or hatred by all that is before them. 2. All things come alike to all ; there is one event to the righteous and to the wicked ; to the good, and to the clean, and to the unclean ; to him that sacrificeth and to him that sacrificeth not ; as is the good, so is the sinner ; and he that sweareth, as he that feareth an oath.*

THE mysteries of Providence still pressed heavily upon Solomon's mind. Proud man would bring the God of heaven and

* Scott. 1 Cor. xiii. 12.

earth to his bar. His humble child is taught the infinite distance between the creature and God. He therefore bows before him, and hears the voice out of the cloud—"Be still, and know that I am God." (Ps. xlvi. 10.) He could not find out all *the work of God*. (Chap. viii. 17.) But his search brought out many valuable discoveries. The security of God's people was a bright and precious truth. He *considered in his heart to declare all* this, *that the righteous and the wise are in the hand of God.* Where could they be safer? Here is rest indeed. What more do we desire as the ground of our confidence, than this truth sealed and witnessed on the conscience. All his saints are *in thy hand?* (Deut. xxxiii. 3.) We are spared no trials however severe—no conflict however painful —no furnace however heated. But nothing touches our foundation. We are *in his hand.* We are "a crown and diadem." Gladly would the great enemy secure the prize. But we are *in the hand of the Lord.* (Isa. lxii. 3.) We are in the fold—exposed to peril. But the security is—"None shall pluck them out of *my hand*." (John, x. 28.)

Our *works* also are with God—remembered for good, and to be brought out before the assembled world "in that day, when he maketh up his jewels." (Mal. iii. 16, 17.)

And yet — notwithstanding this high privilege, the heart of God towards us—whether *it be love or hatred*—no *man knoweth by all that is before them.* All things come*

---

* Romish perversion insists from this declaration, that no one can know himself to be the object of Divine love. Melancthon (quoted by Bp. Patrick) calls it 'the interpretation of monks, who distorted the words of Solomon, and wreathed them to their own dotages.' The more pious expositors of this school—not absolutely denying the doctrine—declare it to be 'a deep and difficult dogma.' Lorin considers the Apostle's persuasion (Rom. viii. 38, 39) to be a special revelation to himself. But in truth the statement has no distinct reference to this point of controversy. Solomon only assures us, that no man can ground a personal confidence upon *all that*

alike to all.   There is one event to the righteous—*to the good*
—*to the clean*—*to him that sacrificeth*—to him that feareth
an *oath*—on the one side ; to the wicked—to the unclean
—to him *that sacrificeth not* — *to him that sweareth on the
other side.*   The same Providential dispensations belong to
both. If Abraham was rich, so was Haman. (Gen. xiii. 2.
Esth. v. 11.)   If Ahab was slain in battle, so was Josiah.
(1 Kings, xxii. 34. 2 Kings, xxiii. 29.)   The Lord's outward
dispensation proved therefore neither his *love nor his hatred.*
Therefore

> "Judge not the Lord by feeble sense."
>   *Olney Hymns.*

The inward work is the real demonstrative evidence.   A
larger portion of outward prosperity may be dealt out to the
wicked. (Ps. lxxiii. 2–12.) Yet where is the child of God who
would envy this lot, or who would change for it the lowest
experience of his Father's love ?

3. *This is an evil among all things that are done under the sun,
    that there is one event unto all ; yea, also the heart of the
    sons of men is full of evil ; and madness is in their heart
    while they live, and after that they go to the dead.*

Solomon is here continuing his subject.   He seems to
consider that in some view it is *an evil,* that *all things come*

is before them, since *all things come alike to all.*   The true Scriptural
doctrine remains firm—equally so the confidence grounded upon it.
" We have known and believed the love that God hath to us.   The
Spirit itself beareth witness with our spirit, that we are the children
of God." (1 John, iv. 16. Rom. viii. 15.) 'The very principal, and
indeed effectual effect of faith is that persuasion and trust,
whereby we *assuredly* believe the forgiveness of sins. The which
trust he that taketh away from faith, doth altogether weaken and
destroy it.'—*Serran.*

alike to all.   Not that he reflects upon this appointment of
God, as if it were *evil* in itself.   But it is *evil* in its consequence and abuse as it were of no account whether men were
righteous or wicked, since *there is one event to all.**   We cannot wonder at this perversion, when *the heart* is described to
be *evil—yea, full of evil*—evil habitual—deliberate—unmingled—from the fountain-head.   Stand before the mirror.
How hard to believe one's self so vile as is here pourtrayed !
And yet, when under the deep teaching of the Spirit of God,
how can one forbear the confession—" Behold ! I am vile."
(Job, xl. 4.) ' O Lord'—said the dying Thomas Scott—'abhor
me not, though I be most abhorrible.' There can be no
exaggeration or mistake.   It is our Maker—the Great
Searcher of the heart—he who alone knows it—it is he
that writes, and draws the picture.†   Nay, he gives a list
of the enormities—pouring out of the heart—defiling every
member of the body—every faculty of the soul.‡   Nor is
the picture confined to any particular age or nation.   It is
the *heart of the sons of men*—the history of every child of
man in his natural unconverted state.   Even under the highest
influence of morality—evil passions, as vile as the source
from whence they come—are only waiting the unrestrained
moment, ere the torrent flow out.   Nor are the ignorant
only in the list.   Men of the most acute sagacity—the most
profound wisdom—the largest grasp of mind—the most
honoured talent, are shut up in the same prison—the blinded
captives of sin !   Can there be a more humiliating picture of
man ?   This *fulness of evil* unrestrained rushes onward to
madness — be it remembered — responsible *madness* — the
will consenting to the sin—the heart loving it—the whole
course of it pursued to the end.   Let the sinner think a

----

* See Ps. lxxiii. 11–13.   † See Jer. xvii. 9, 10.
‡ See Matt. xv. 19.

moment. Is not every act of rebellion against God an act of *madness?* For "who hath hardened himself against God, and hath prospered?" Or "who hath resisted his will?" (Job, ix. 4. Rom. ix. 19.) Then look at man in his character, habits, and judgment. His choice of worldly in preference to heavenly things surely betrays the loss of the right exercise of his understanding. It is the maniac throwing away his gold, and preferring straws to pearls. You see man in miserable delusion—the unconscious dupe of an universal imposition.

Such is the dark view as Solomon saw it, and as every man—had he eyes to see—might see it in his own heart, or in the world around him. Shall we extend the view to the spiritual apprehensions of the Gospel—man's interest in it, and his perverted judgment of it? What is the sight before us? A world of sinners on the brink of ruin! Yet the greatest good—the great gift of God— that which covers us from all evil, and blesses us with all good—that which fits us to lead a Divine life on earth, and to die full of immortal hopes—this good is slighted— despised! Surely it is no libel, but plain solemn truth, to look at this sight, and cry—*Madness is in their hearts!*

And then again, to see this mass of our fellow-sinners, trifling with infinite evil—the everlasting wrath of God; while the wheels of night and day are fast hurrying them unprepared to "fall into his hands!" (Heb. x. 31.) Can this be the sight of rational beings? What else but *madness in their hearts* could thus drive them onward to self-destruction?

Sad, indeed, is the consciousness that this is no mental aberration, but a spiritual world within, where all is distorted and contradictory; and where the unhappy victims of the delusion are so depraved, that they cannot understand their own depravity. Such a world of evil! Did we but know it, could we trifle with sin? It is impossible for the sinner to be more dangerously *mad* than he is, except by growing into greater wickedness. What worse *madness* is human nature capable of?—fleeing from God—from mercy—from heaven —serving the devil—drudging in the world of vanity and sin —living under the curse of God, and on the brink of damnation.

And yet more awful is the thought, that, as regards the mass—*madness is in their hearts while they live.* They persist in this course to the end. Time will soon be a blank and shadow—Eternity a present reality, where the madmen will be brought to their senses in hopeless conviction. As sure as the Bible is true—this is true. *After that they go to the dead.*—Alas! not to the "blessed dead that die in the Lord." (Rev. xiv. 13.) What meetness has there been for that home? No home, therefore, can be for them in that state of bliss. How important is it to cherish deep spiritual sensibilities! This picture—could we behold it with the piercing eye of eternity—would be perhaps the sight every moment of our poor thoughtless fellow-sinners, pouring into the regions of dark despair, adding their miserable souls to the countless millions fixed for ever—in the world of "weeping and gnashing of teeth." (Matt. xxii. 11.) Awful beyond thought or conception is the immortality of hell. What a wondrous power of preventing mercy, and of Omnipotent grace must there be in the Gospel—that can hide a sinner from such hopeless ruin, and bring him out into light, liberty, and salvation! Whatever points to the Redeemer brings this sovereign remedy to view.

4. *For to him that is joined to all the living there is hope; for a living dog is better than a dead lion.* 5. *For the living know that they shall die; but the dead know not anything; neither have they any more a reward; for the memory of them is forgotten.* 6. *Also their love, and their*

hatred, and their envy, is now perished; neither have they any more a portion in any thing that is done under the sun.

Solomon had before taken an opposite view. He " had praised the dead which were already dead, more than the living, which were yet alive."* Here however he praises the high advantage of life above death. Awful indeed is it to see the state of the living—their *hearts full of evil*—even to *madness.*. But while there is life—while we are *joined to all the living, there is hope.* Living on the land of hope, the very possibility of escaping the dark despairing home of the impenitent dead, is an unspeakable blessing. One almost seems to realize the awful scene of these dark regions.† And comparing the meanest thing with the noblest dead, we are ready to take up the Proverb—*A living dog is better than a dead lion.*‡

Another ground for this preference is that *the living know that they shall die.* Hence therefore the time and opportunity —perhaps also the desire—to make preparation. There is time to fix our interest in heaven—to live upon the real substantials of godliness—to look upon this world's glare with sober dignity, as utterly beneath " the high calling of God in Christ Jesus." All of this world is passing away. The glory and great end of life is that life, which makes it " gain to die." (Phil. i. 21.) Its possession is but for a moment—'only an annuity for life; not a portion for eternity.'§

On the other hand, *the dead know not anything.* They

---

* See Chap. iv. 2, 3.　　　　　† See Isa. xiv. 9–12.

‡ The dog is often spoken of as the meanest of creation (Matt. xv. 26. Phil. iii. 2)—the lion as the noblest of beasts. (Prov. xxx. 30.)

§ Henry.

have no further knowledge of anything here on earth.* They have no further *reward* of their worldly labour. *The memory of them* is soon *forgotten. The love, hatred, and envy,* which they bare to others, and others to them, *is now perished*—so far as connected with this world. Whatever might have been their *portion* on earth, they have it no longer.

This is the world—all that it can give. This is the substance of those who have their "portion—their good things in their lifetime." (Ps. xvii. 14. Luke, xvi. 25.) What is it to thee—child of God!—but a very bubble? What is it as compared with thy rich reversion—"begotten as thou art to an inheritance incorruptible, undefiled, and that fadeth not away?" (1 Pet. i. 3, 4.) And yet to see men of large and comprehensive minds—living as if there was no God to whom they are accountable—no heaven or hell to receive them for ever—or as if these states were painted shadows, instead of Divine realities! This surely is besotted blindness. Can it be anything but wilful wickedness, that centres the heart in alienation from God—in darkness and in death?

7. *Go thy way, eat thy bread with joy, and drink thy wine with a merry heart; for God now accepteth thy works.* 8. *Let thy garments be always white, and let thy head lack no ointment.* 9. *Live joyfully with the wife whom thou lovest all the days of the life of thy vanity, which he hath given thee under the sun, all the days of thy vanity: for what is thy portion in this life, and in thy labour which thou takest under the sun?*

Some striking pictures of vanity have been before us.

---

* This Bp. Hall produces as an argument against invocation of saints, 'the ground of which is their notice of our earthly condition and special devotions.'—*Old Religion*, chap. x. sect. ii.

Here is God's bright remedy. *Go thy way.* Enjoy your mercies while you have them. The charge of melancholy is a libel upon religion. The man that is an heir to "a lively hope, anchored within the veil" (1 Pet. i. 3. Heb. vi. 19) —what ground has he for melancholy? Why—we find him "greatly rejoicing," even in the midst of "heaviness." (1 Pet. i. 6.) A sinner has no right—a Christian—supported by Divine strength, favour, and consolation, has no reason—to complain. His treasure includes the promise of all that he wants, in deep sense of his own unworthiness, and of his Father's undeserved love.

Eat thy bread and drink thy wine with a merry heart. Temporal blessings are doubly sweet, as coming from him. He is exalted to bestow—we are invited to receive—them. All is our special portion. We are not only the heirs of heaven, but we are new-born to "inherit the earth." (Ps. xxxvii. 11. Matt. v. 5.) He has the clearest confidence for the heaven above, who has that heaven now in his own soul.

Thus indeed we have the largest—because the sanctified —enjoyment of earthly blessings. We have them in connexion with the grand mystery of mercy— *God now accepteth our work.* Bright indeed is the sunbeam of Divine favour. The way is now opened—friendship with his fallen creatures, who had no right to expect anything but eternal banishment from his presence. The blood of the sacrifice has made the consecrated pathway. Through this medium all his thoughts are peaceful to us. The true means *now* to enjoy the creature is to find this *acceptance* with God. Doubt not his fatherly heart. Expect nothing from him but good. Expect no good from any other quarter.

Solomon's directions are for a joyous religion. We must not indeed forget the "time to mourn" (chap. iii. 4) nor the moderation needed in our times of rejoicing (1 Cor. vii. 30), nor the profit of seasons of humiliation and restraint. (Dan.

x. 2, 3.) Yet we should remember our obligation to shine
—to exhibit our *white garments* of praise,* and use the
fragrant *ointment* (John, xii. 3. Cant. i. 3), as the customary
mark of festive occasions. Nor should this be the rule for
particular times, or peculiar circumstances. *Let thy garments
be always white*—a rule in the true spirit of the precept, which
involves both our duty and our privilege—" Rejoice evermore." (1 Thess. v. 16.) In our deepest sorrow our ground
for rejoicing is the same. It is indeed too rare to find a real
Christian—much more rare to find a joyful one. And yet a
gloomy professor is a sad sight; neither the Church nor the
Gospel has sympathy with him. He is gloomy, not because
he has too much religion, but too little. Glad indeed should
we be to bring him out of his dark shadow—to bring a sunbeam upon his brooding spirit. Let him think of the
glorious work of the Divine Mediator—giving to his
afflicted ones " beauty for ashes, the oil of joy for mourning,
the garment of praise for the spirit of heaviness." (Isa. lxi. 3.)
Do we really believe the Gospel to be " glad tidings of great
joy?" (Luke, ii. 10.) Then surely we belie this professed
belief by "hanging our heads like a bulrush" (Isa. lviii. 5)
and shewing the marks of an inveterate melancholy? Is
there no danger, lest an unthankful spirit should wither our
present blessings? Is it not well to take account from day
to day of the mercies—sovereign and undeserved—flowing
in upon us? Ill does it become us to appear before our
Father with a wrinkled brow, instead of acknowledging his
just claim to our affectionate, dutiful, unreserved, delighting
confidence.

Solomon could not have laid down *his last* rule of happiness without a poignant pang, in the recollection of his own
awful violation of it—*Live joyfully with the wife whom thou
lovest*—a single—undivided love—so contrary to the un-

---

* See Esth. viii. 15. And comp. Rev. iii. 4, 5, 18; xix. 8.

restrained lust, which had been his appetite and indulgence.*
Here is indeed a special freeness of delight and liberty of
love—yet under the godly restraint of honour and sobriety.
(Gen. xxvi. 8. Prov. v. 19.)

This rule gives no sanction to the state of celibacy, as a
higher level of Christian perfection†—contrary to our
Maker's express declaration—" It is not good that the man
should be alone" (Gen. ii. 18) and not less opposed to
" marriage"—as declared to be not only lawful and blameless,
but " *honourable* in all men." (Heb. xiii. 4.)

The difference between conjugal and adulterous love, is
—that in the one a man *may live joyfully*—sweetly enjoying
his life—the other belongs to one, whose " feet go down to
to death; her steps take hold on hell." (Prov. v. 5.) The
godly union of souls in mutual forbearance with each other's
infirmities, and mutual stimulating each other's graces—this
surely is 'a fragment of true happiness that has survived the
fall.' ‡ As one remarks—who had tasted this sweet cup
with the most refined enjoyment—' Conjugal happiness lives
in the depths of the heart, even amid the sorrows and trials
of life. Indeed it is by these only the more deeply rooted,
as I know by my own experience, thank God.' §

* See 1 Kings, xi. 1–3.

† Bp. Taylor strikes the balance in his own beautiful style, pre-
ponderating on the opposite side.—*See his Sermon on the Marriage
Ring*, Part ii.

‡ Mylne.

§ Letter of Caroline Perthes to her married daughter. In an
after letter this admirable woman writes with a Christian balance
—'Your mutual love can be a means of happiness and blessing, only
as it increases your love to God. And can you not imagine, that to
turn directly to God, and love him without the intervention of any
human medium, may be far, far better ? . . . I believe that every
young woman acts wisely, when she turns her affections to God,
instead of looking about her with yearning and anxiety for an earthly
object. This latter is a melancholy state of mind, which withers
and dries up the heart, and annihilates all happiness.'—*Life of
Perthes*, chap. xxiii.

And well will the man acknowledge this gift *which God hath given him* (Prov. xix. 14), *under the sun*—to be, if not his best—yet his temporal portion—his staff—support —earthly rest. 'Child of God—*Christ's glory*, dignity, and office is to love his bride—the Church. *Thy glory* is to imitate thy Lord.'*

And yet how wisely are we reminded—twice for our deeper impression—that these days of enjoyment are *the days of the life of our vanity*—"few and evil" at best. (Gen. xlvii. 9.) As *to the present vanity* most valuable is the advice —'Cling to one another in your grief. Let neither conceal it from the other. Do not try to calm one another down, but rather let your sorrow flow out into a common stream. It will then be changed into a quiet happiness, and will unite you more intimately than mere prosperity ever could have done. Cling to one another, I say. Community of love changes the profoundest grief into a blessing from God.'† *As to the future*, the recollection comes to us. Sooner or later—one or other will be in desolate loneliness. Here then we may listen to the voice of one who speaks from the mouth of God—"This I say, brethren—the time is short; it remaineth, that those that have wives be as though they had none." (1 Cor. vii. 29.) 'All those things that now please us shall pass from us, or we from them; those things that concern the other life are permanent as the numbers of eternity. And although at the resurrection there shall be no relation of husband and wife, and no marriage shall be celebrated but the marriage of the Lamb; yet then shall be remembered how men and women passed through this state, which is a type of that; and from this sacramental union all holy pairs shall pass to the spiritual and eternal, where love shall be their portion, and joys shall

---

* Mylne.
† *Life of Perthes*, chap. xxxii.

crown their heads, and they shall lie in the bosom of Jesus, and in the heart of God, to eternal ages.' *

10. *Whatsoever thy hand findeth to do, do it with thy might ; for there is no work, nor device, nor knowledge, nor wisdom in the grave, whither thou goest.*

Conjugal and social affections are our warranted indulgence ; but not so as that we should be given up to them. We have now a rule, to stimulate the glow of vital energy. There are works to be done—difficulties to be overcome—talents to be traded with—the whole *might* to be engaged. And in truth—' man's wisdom in this dying world consists in cheerfully using present comforts, and diligently attending to present duties.' † Every moment brings its own responsibility. And the rule for the discharge of this responsibility is—*Whatsoever thine hand findeth to do, do it with thy might.* Obviously some limitation is implied. 'What we are admonished thus to do must be in its nature lawful and right. *The hand may find to do* what God has forbidden. But this, instead of being *done with might,* must not be done at all.' ‡ That which occasion calls for (Judg. ix. 33, M.R.), in the path of duty and of Providence, is the thing *to be done.* The active exercise of the *hands* as the instrument of the work, will bring a fruitful result.

This direction finds its place in the Apostolical code— "Not slothful in business" (Rom. xii. 11)—*Do it with thy might.* Sir M. Hales's advice is full of weight—' The crumbs and fragments of time should be furnished with their suitable employments. It is precious ; and therefore let none of it be lost.' Again—' Remember to observe in-

* Bp. Taylor's *Marriage Ring.* Finis.
† Scott.   ‡ Wardlaw.

dustry and diligence; not only as civil means to acquire a
competency for yourself and your family, but also as an act
of obedience to his command and ordinance; by means
whereof you make it become in a manner spiritualized into
an act of religion.' *

How ready is this obedience, when the object is near the
heart! What energy it gives to that effort, which is so needful
for success. For indeed 'nothing of worth or weight can
be achieved with half a mind, with a faint heart, with a lame
endeavour.' † Would Stephenson have accomplished his
locomotive triumph with a powerful opposition thwarting
every step of his progress—if he had not *done it with his
might*? Every man must have an object of pursuit to keep
him in healthful exercise. The dreaming privilege of doing
nothing will soon melt away into real misery. ' Let others
take the riches'—said Melancthon—'Give me the work.'

But the main sphere for this important and invaluable
rule is the work for eternity—the " working out of our own
salvation." (Phil. ii. 12.) The purchase price binds us to
the work under the most constraining obligation. (1 Cor. vi.
20.) We cease to be our own, from the first moment that we
are bound to him. And here—in his work—is need of our
might—all our *might*—*might* flowing from the fountain of
might. There is no illusion of great things to be done at some
distant future. It is the present energy—the moment's work
—the instant sacrifice—the whole-hearted service—the first
of the day—the first part all the day. Whoever found Satan
asleep in his work? 'It is lawful'—the proverb reminds
us—'to be taught even by an enemy.' ‡ His *might* is
always put out to work. So let it be with me. Let my *might*
be thrown into every prayer. Let every effort of faith—every

---

* *On Redemption of Time.*
† Dr. Barrow's *Sermon on Industry.*
‡ ' Fas est et ab hoste doceri.'

exercise of perseverance be at work. As a godly Puritan expresses his ' good wish that *what my hand findeth to do—I may do it with all my might :* that I may be of the number of those that spend themselves with labour, and not of those who waste in rust and laziness. Lord! let me rather wear out in the work, than consume (like a garment laid by with moths) for want of use.' *

Ought not this verse to be our daily text—written in our inward parts—before us in our first waking hour— ' What have I to do to-day? What duty—what work of love?—what talent to be employed? What service does my Lord call me to do for him ?'—" Lord! what wilt thou have me to do ?" (Acts, ix. 6.) The more vigorous the exercise, the more strength. Every step supplies the strength. " The way of the Lord is strength to the upright"—and how is it communicated ? " They that wait upon the Lord shall renew their strength." (Prov. x. 29. Isa. xl. 29–31.)

But look at our Great Exemplar—How fine the exhibition of determination for the work—" I must work the works of him that sent me while it is day." Here was *doing with* his *might*—the motive also was the same— " The night cometh, when no man can work." (John, ix. 4.) *There is no work, nor device, nor knowledge, nor wisdom, in the grave, whither thou goest.* Here the highest glory of earth concludes. Thou art travelling to the end. Every moment brings thee nearer. And when come to the *grave,* there is *no work* there. We cannot do our undone duties there. All power is withered and gone. There is no *device* there. All scheming is gone. No way of escape can be planned. *No knowledge* is there of any means of help. *No wisdom* — spiritual or intellectual — nothing that distinguishes man made in the image of God from " the beasts that perish." A melancholy picture of man — arrived

* Swinnock's *Christian Man's Calling,* Part I. Chap. xxvi. Finis.

at "the house appointed for all living!" (Job, xxx. 23.)
And what—if he shall have trifled away his "twelve hours
of the day" (John, xi. 9)—if his light shall have gone out
—if his work shall have been found undone—if the night
shall have overtaken him, while amusing himself with the
fool's word—*To-morrow!* If religion is no business now,
what will it be in the dying hour? One day may be worth
years. Wasted hours will find us out at last. A little
neglect will be an eternal loss. Oh, the dreadful gain of
winning the world by the loss of heaven! There will be
but one wail throughout eternity, condemning self—justify-
ing God—" O my soul, thou hast destroyed thyself." (Hos.
xiii. 9.) For our great work we have only one little life,
which with all its precious privileges and solemn responsibilities is passing—Oh! how quickly—away!

> Make haste, O man, to do
>   Whatever must be done;
> Thou hast no time to lose in sloth,
>   Thy day will soon be gone.
>   Make haste, O man, to live!
>
> Up then with speed, and work;
>   Fling ease and self away:
> This is no time for thee to sleep;
>   Up, watch, and work, and pray,
>   Make haste, O man, to live.
>
> Make haste, O man, to live;
>   Thy Time is almost o'er;
> O sleep not, dream not, but arise;
>   The Judge is at the door.
>   Make haste, O man, to live.
>   *Bonar's Hymns of Faith and Hope,* p. 262.

11. *I returned, and saw under the sun, that the race is not to
the swift, nor the battle to the strong, neither yet bread to
the wise, nor yet riches to men of understanding, nor yet*

*favour to men of skill; but time and chance happeneth to
them all.*

Solomon is now *returning* to another view of the matter,
which caused him perplexity. If he would have us "work
out" our object *with might,* it must be "with fear and
trembling." (Philip. ii. 12.) Persons of feeble and un-
decided habits may lose many valuable opportunities of doing
good. On such let the rule be closely applied—"*Whatsoever thy hand findeth to do, do it with thy might.*" Others
of a more sanguine temperament never dream of any issue
but success. They need a balance on the other side—
humility—self-distrust. Let them be here reminded, that
the best means, and the most powerful agency, will not
ensure success; and that, when they have done the work,
they must commit the event to God.

It is natural indeed to believe, that the race would *be to
the swift,* and *the battle to the strong ;* that prudent *wisdom*
would obtain a competent provision, and courtly *skill* would
be the way to favour. But it is not always so. The racer
may make an incautious step. 'The fortune of war' (so
called) may take an unfavourable turn. Men of wisdom
continue to be poor, and gifted with no very successful
favour. Oh! Christian—do not you find it hard to possess gifts, and not to rest in them?—to have riches, and not
to trust in them?—to have wisdom and skill, and not to
glory in them?—to exercise simple dependence upon God,
as if we had and were nothing? Far is he from discouraging the use of means. He would only direct us in the use
of them not to "sacrifice to our net." (Hab. i. 16.)

There is, indeed, an adaptation of these means to the
end, and a tendency to work the proposed end. But with
all men's practised and persevering efforts, the issue is with
God—*Time and chance happeneth unto them all.* Not that

there is anything fortuitous or unforeseen, but something
that we cannot see—some opportunity of *time*—favourable
or unfavourable—which balances against seeming probabili-
ties—some occurrence* which Providence casts in the way,
which determines success with a decisive effect upon our
lot in life. We see not the direction, and therefore we cannot clearly judge. But all things fall into the place infallibly ordained by God. And if it is casual to us, it is
counsel to him—a train of causes appointed to " work the
counsel of his own will " (Eph. i. 11)—the under-working
of that hand which made the worlds. And this wise and
holy hand directs the most apparently fortuitous events to
the accomplishment of his own most righteous will.† Shall
we then claim to know the secrecies of his Providence ?
No—rather let us lie before him in silent unreserved submission, and leave to him the free liberty to guide and
govern us in his own way. We are sure to come out clear
from all our perplexity, if our eye be steadily fixed upon
him. But none of this doubtfulness belongs to the ways of
God. There is no uncertainty in the Christian race. (1 Cor.
ix. 26.) *The battle* is for the strong in the strength of the
Lord. " The meat that endureth" is reserved to the " labourer." (John, vi. 27.) If fools go away with the world,
we envy them not. The *man of understanding* grasps an un-
searchable treasure. *The favour* of God is found, when
heavenly *skill* knows where to seek it. A sure covenant dis-
penses spiritual blessings. Providence uncertain to us pro-
miscuously bestows the earthly portion.

12. *For man also knoweth not his time ; as the fishes that are*
    taken in an evil net, and as the birds that are caught in the

* The proper meaning of the word chance. So translated
1 Kings, v. 4.
† See 1 Kings, xxii. 34. Esth. vi. 1–11.

snare ; so are the sons of men snared in an evil time, when it falleth suddenly upon them.

Time and chance happen to all alike, and where they are least expected. *For man knoweth not his time.* (Chap. viii. 7.) This is true alike of success or failure, either of which depends—not upon man's effort, but upon God's supreme will. The illustrations limit the reference to the ungodly, and shew the ignorance of the *time* to be man's ruin for eternity—*as the fishes taken in an evil net, or the birds caught in a snare.* Can we wonder at the yearning of the faithful minister—following precious souls even to the very gates of perdition—if haply he might rescue here and there one from this unutterable ruin ? Solemn indeed to us all is the warning of the coming day, that *" as a snare* shall it come on all them that dwell on the face of the whole earth." (Luke, xxi. 35.) Each of us has our *time. Evil will that time* be, if *it falls suddenly upon us;* if it finds us slumbering on the brink of eternity ; trifling with its infinitely momentous concern ; making the world our portion—our refuge—our rest. (Luke, xii. 19, 20.) But will it be *an evil time* to those that are watching—waiting—serving their Lord in the joyous expectation of his coming, and of being with him for ever ? (Ib. vv. 35–43.) Blessed Lord ! " Hasten thy coming in thy time."

13. *This wisdom have I seen also under the sun, and it seemed great unto me.* 14. *There was a little city, and few men within it ; and there came a great king against it, and besieged it, and built great bulwarks against it.* 15. *Now there was found in it a poor wise man ; and he by his wisdom delivered the city ; yet no man remembered that same poor man.* 16. *Then said I, Wisdom is better than strength ; nevertheless the poor man's wisdom is despised, and his words are not heard.*

This incident—illustrating the power of *wisdom*—passed
under Solomon's own eye. *He saw it under the sun.* And
though others might have passed it by, *it seemed great
unto him*—perhaps the more so, as being overclouded with
poverty. Here was *a Great King* against a little city—a
besieging army *building great bulwarks against it,* when there
were but *few men within it.* The danger appeared to be imminent, and the destruction certain. Yet at the moment of
extremity *one poor wise man by his wisdom delivered the city.*
We might have expected the highest rewards for *this poor
wise man.* Yet we are told, that *no man remembered him.*
When he had wrought *the deliverance,* no man looked after
him. He sunk into forgetfulness. His *wisdom was despised,
and his words were not heard.*

Such is the story*—What is the application to ourselves, that which makes it practical truth? Learn to estimate men by their *wisdom* and godliness, not by their outward show. Value *wisdom* as the gift of God. The more
we feel our need of the gift, the more stimulating must be
our earnest pleading for the continued supply—The wise
man learned from this history that it was *better than strength,*
inasmuch as *one poor wise man* in the city shewed himself
stronger than a large army without. And most encouraging is it to see great results from apparently feeble
means, which the world know nothing of, and which, if
they did know, they would only despise.

Learn also to prepare for disappointment. Work for the
best interests of your fellow-creatures; but not for their ap-
probation or reward. Let not their praise be our motive.

---

* A very similar story is recorded in the history of David,
where a woman's wisdom was the deliverance of the city. (2 Sam.
xx. 14-22.) Classical history gives the record of Archimedes, saving
the city of Syracuse from the whole force of the Romans, by sinking
their ships in the harbour by his machines upon the walls.

Many may obtain what they did not deserve; or what
justly belonged to us, as Americus stole the laurel from
Columbus. But there is no ground to be disheartened by
failure. If we miss the worldly favour, and seem to be forgotten, the time is at hand, when " the honour that cometh
from God only" will be found to be the substantial and un-
fading reward.

We have a plain proof here of the vicissitudes of Providence just adverted to (Ver. 11) — We see how that the
battle was not to the strong, nor bread to the wise, nor
riches to the man of understanding—The man was *poor*
with all his *wisdom*, and little in *favour* with all *his skill*.
His words were *not remembered*. Well would it be for us,
if this were the only instance of forgetfulness. But the
thought of the Great *Deliverer* flashes across one's mind—
and with it the remembrance of daring and most guilty
forgetfulness, the slow remembrance of ungrateful hearts.
How many are living, as if there had been no deliverance
wrought—or no need of deliverance! May memory be filled
with the deepest sense of infinite obligation to Him, who
well deserves the name of *the Deliverer*, "even Jesus, which
delivered us from the wrath to come!" (1 Thess. i. 10.)

17. *The words of the wise men are heard in quiet, more than
the cry of him that ruleth among fools.* 18. *Wisdom is
better than weapons of war; but one sinner destroyeth
much good.*

'A very remarkable verse'—Dr. Chalmers observes—'in
these days of mobocracy!'* There seems however to be upon
the surface some apparent inconsistency. *The words of the*
wise man had just been spoken of as slighted, and *not remembered.* Here however considerable weight is ascribed to

* *Scripture Readings.*

them. Though the case of the foregoing verse is of frequent occurrence, yet exceptions may be found. *The words
of the wise,* spoken *in quiet* and unobtrusiveness, may be little
thought of at the time, and yet may command attention,
when circumstances bring them out. Often will they
drown the senseless clamour of him *that ruleth among fools.*
Noisy popularity indeed has its influence for a moment. But
the real and solid good are *the words that are heard in quiet.*
Popular oratory in the pulpit may stimulate excitement. But
it needs much unction and humility to give it practical influence. We are directed to behold our Lord's ministry, as
words *heard in quiet* — " Behold my servant!—he shall not
strive or cry; neither shall any man hear his voice in the
streets." (Matt. xii. 18, 19.) Yet this implies no heartless-
ness, but the " doctrine" dropping as "the rain upon the
mown grass"—upon hearts made ready to receive its Divine
influence. (Deut. xxxii. 2. Ps. lxxii. 6.)

The contrast drawn from the history of *the wise man* is
vivid. Not only is *wisdom better than strength*, but *better
than weapons of war—strength* made ready, and armed for
the exigency.* And yet if we see that one *wise man,*
though poor and unhonoured, can *do much good;* sad indeed
is the conviction forced upon us from the contrary side. *One*

---

* 'We see that 'knowledge is power;' and we constantly repeat
the saying, as if Bacon had been the first who had remarked the
strength of skill. But six-and-twenty centuries before the days of
Lord Verulam, King Solomon had said—" A wise man is strong.
Wisdom is better than strength. Wisdom is better than weapons of
war." Perhaps it is owing to the imperfect sympathies that exist
between theologians and philosophers, that such scriptural sayings
have received so little justice. And hence it has come to pass, that
many a maxim has got a fresh circulation, and has made a little fortune of renown for its author, which is often a medal fresh minted
from Bible money—the gold of Moses or Solomon used up again
with the image and superscription of Bacon, or Pascal ,or Benjamin
Franklin.'—*Hamilton's Ecclesiastes,* Lect. xvi.

sinner destroyeth much good. This is the picture on all sides
—*in a kingdom*—the black mark upon Jeroboam the son of
Nebat, *who made Israel to sin* (1 Kings, xxii. 52.)   *Trace the
evil in the different circles of contagion*—" Evil communications
corrupt good manners" (1 Cor. xv. 33)—a moral and spiritual
pestilence! Witness the infidel poisoning the unwary by the
plausibility of his evil—the Sabbath-breaker's evil example
—the enticing influence of the pleasure-loving worldling.
Look at the Church—the careless, unenlightened, or heretical, minister—the inconsistent professor—as the "little
leaven, leavening the whole lump" (1 Cor. v. 6)—" the
root of bitterness springing up, and troubling, and *thereby
many defiled.*" (Heb. xii. 15.)   *In the family,* how awful
the spreading corruption of parental example—the taint
communicated from this source! When will its deadly influence cease to be felt? In a vast multitude of cases, alas!
it flows on to eternity.

And who of us is freed from the responsibility of spreading this plague? How many have yet further communicated
the contagion received from us!—how many has it confirmed
in the ways of ungodliness! And too often how fruitless
have been the persevering efforts to melt away the evil!
Bitter, indeed, were the tears, which Mr. Cecil shed over his
unavailing efforts to reclaim those, whom he had been too
successful in bringing into the infidel snare. Yet when
tears are fruitless, there is blood to cleanse. And here let
the contrite sinner lie, where " the fountain is opened for sin"
(Zech. xiii. 1) and where acceptance is ready for the sinner
in all its fulness of blessing.

CHAPTER X.

1. *Dead flies cause the ointment of the apothecary to send forth a stinking savour : so doth a little folly him that is in reputation for wisdom and honour.**

The accident here referred to might often happen. Where *flies* and winged insects of all kinds abounded, one or more falling in might spoil the *apothecary's ointment.* Solomon drew many of his illustrations from common life. And his quick discernment made a ready application of the incident to set out and enforce a moral principle. The lesson which he draws from it is—that as the *dead fly,* though only a little creature, gives an *ill-savour* to the most costly *ointment ;* so even a small measure of *folly* mars a fair *reputation for wisdom and honour.* He had just before mentioned the awful fact, that " *one sinner* destroyeth much good." The Apostle—as we have seen—makes a similar statement of the wide-spreading plague even of a small measure of evil. " *A little* leaven leaveneth the whole lump." (1 Cor. v. 6.)

But it is not only the shame of gross sins that injures purity. *A little folly* is enough to produce immense mischief. The unguarded moment—the hasty word—the irritable temper—the rudeness of manner—the occasional slip—the *supposed* harmless eccentricities—all tend to spoil the fragrance of *the ointment.* The minor morals of the Christian code require strict attention. Take care that the Christian life is wholly Christianized in outward points. The neglect of

* The verb is singular and the nominative plural, *i. e.* any one of *the dead flies.* The note of comparison is also wanting—a frequent omission. See Ps. cxxv. 2; Prov. xi. 22; Jer. xvii. 11. There is also an ellipsis of the word in the last clause, which is to be repeated out of the former member of the sentence—*causeth to send forth,* &c.

serving the Lord in little things excites revolt. The smallest extremities of the system—no less than its more important parts—should be kept sacred for God. Let every corner of the field be cultivated for him. It is not enough that we be "sincere." We must be "without offence—the sons of God without rebuke"—thinking of things that are "lovely and of good report"—as well as the things that "are honest, just, and true." Thus we shall "shine as lights in the world, holding forth the word of life." (Phil. i. 10; ii. 15, 16; iv. 8.) The practical influence of truth is the strongest evidence of its reality. If the standard be only preached, it may be considered impracticable. Yet where it is manifestly and substantially attained, who can doubt that it is attainable?

But the illustration leads us to ask—how did the *fly* come into *the ointment?* Was there no lack of proper care in *the apothecary?* Had the box been carefully closed, the injury might have been avoided. And does not this speak to ourselves? Is it not when prayer and diligence are neglected, that little inconsistencies are allowed, such as almost imperceptibly destroy the savour of holiness? How important is it to walk uprightly with God, and just in our own appointed sphere to lay ourselves out unreservedly in his service! The *dead flies* will trouble us to the end. But a watchful self-discipline will be a cover to us. The moral atmosphere will be more clear. The intellectual character will be elevated and imbued with Christian taste and sobriety. Yet who does not know, that self-government is the most difficult of all governments?

Often then let the prayer rise upward—"Teach me good judgment and knowledge." (Ps. cxix. 66.) The man of prayer will be in the large receipt of all needful wisdom and grace. His walk will be like "the Sun of Righteousness," carrying such "healing in his wings" as to make

his very presence the harbinger of joy.'*   Liberty will be
connected with a subdued will.   There will be a rule—or at
least an attempt to rule—over the ruling power of our own
spirit.   The heart bowing to the self-denying principles of
the Bible will realize a mystery of heavenly joy.†

"Blessed is he that watcheth, and keepeth his garments,
lest he walk naked, and they see his shame." (Rev. xvi. 15.)

2. *A wise man's heart is in his right hand; but a fool's heart
    is at his left.   3. Yea also, when he that is a fool walketh
    by the way, his wisdom faileth him, and he saith to every
    one, that he is a fool.*

This is a proverbial rather than a literal maxim.   We
have had it in substance before.   "The wise man's eyes are
in his head; but the fool walketh in darkness." (Chap.
ii. 14.)   Here it contrasts the *wise man's* ready prudence and
circumspection with the *fool's* rashness and want of thoughtfulness.   *The right hand* is more ready for exercise than *the
left,* and therefore illustrates the better advantage, which the
wise man makes of his resources.   He has his principles, as
Mr. Newton somewhere remarks—'at his fingers' ends.'
The *heart* evidently stands for all the faculties ‡—'the centre
of affection—the seat of knowledge—the source of purpose
and emotion—the very soul of the spiritual life.' §

For want, however, of sound discipline we lose the power
of mastering the mind.   Frivolous minds continue frivolous
to the end of the chapter; amusing themselves with listless
vacuity, and creating for themselves fictions of fancy, yielding no solid advantage.   Intellectual power—sometimes of

* Hamilton's *Ecclesiastes,* Lect. xv.
† See Isa. lxiv. 5.   ‡ Geier.
§ Mylne.   It is the same word, that is rendered in the next verse
—*wisdom.*

a high order—is wasted in this desultory occupation, without issuing in any one practical result.

There are various exercises on opposite sides, which shew the great need of *the heart* being in its right place. As an excellent Christian writer remarks (and the value of his sentiments will apologize for their length), ' There is a servility of mind, which leaves it the slave of mere authority, without forming opinions for itself by personal enquiry. And there is a rude and reckless affectation of mental independence, or liberty of thinking, which leads a man to despise authority, to aim at striking out for himself a system, distinguished from the received opinions of those around him—led, it may be, by a love of singularity, or the vanity of appearing wiser than his neighbour, or perhaps by the condition of his moral feelings, to argue himself into the disbelief of what he wishes not to be true. From all such distortions of the understanding a regulated mental discipline tends to preserve us. It induces us to approach every subject with a sincere and humble desire for truth; to give its due influence to authority, to give its proper weight to every kind of evidence, without partial views, or imperfect examinations; and to direct the whole powers—not to favour, establish, or overturn particular opinions, but honestly and anxiously to discover what is truth.'*

A thorough keeping of the heart with God is our best security ; living upon truths, not upon notions ; seeking— not variety for our taste, but grace for our souls ; substituting the spiritual for the sensuous ; connecting excited feelings with pure simple doctrines. If we have found the satisfying sweetness of our doctrine, we shall not readily give it up. But if we do, it is a fearful peril ; if our Bible is degraded to a common-place book, we shall lose the keen appetite

* Dr. Abercrombie's *Essays and Tracts.* The Cultivation and Discipline of the Mind. Addressed to the Young, pp. 36, 37.

for its contents.   The dread of error will be less felt, and
with it will fade away the love of truth.

But to come to daily life.   *The right hand* marks the
dexterous skill of application.*   Scriptural examples abound.
Jacob's careful approach to Esau (Gen. xxxiii. 13–23)—
Jethro's wise counsel to Moses (Exod. xviii. 17–24)—
Abigail's prudent restraint of the murderous impulse (1 Sam.
xxv. 20–35)—Paul's skilful diversion of the mob from their
purpose (Acts, xxiii. 6)—all shewed *the heart to be at the
right hand*.   This active energy is most important in the
Christian life, when our ever-ready enemy is always on the
watch to take us by surprise, and when the habit of instant
prayer is our only effectual cover.

But *the fool*—where is he?   *Left-handed* in his work,
everything is in the wrong place.   *His heart* is not in his
work, and therefore it does not help him.   Not a step does
he take *by the way* without a painful exposure of his *folly*.
He ' goes about his business as awkwardly as a man whose
right hand was tied behind, and he had only his *left hand* to
help him.' †   He needs not tell every one *that he is a fool*.
His conduct leaves no doubt upon the matter.   Nor does
this arise from the defect of natural wisdom; but from the
want of perception of the value of spiritual wisdom, and the
want of heart to apply for it, where it is always "liberally
given." (Jam. i. 5.)   Hence he stumbles in the plainest
path.   He is always behind his time.   He sees things too
late.   His whole course is blundering, and shewing ' the
ridiculous licentiousness of the tongue,' ‡ he becomes the
object of pity and contempt.

It is true however that this judgment upon *the wise man*

* The word anglicized — dexterous—from the Latin *dexter* —
right hand.
    † Bp. Reynolds.
    ‡ Bp. Butler *On the Government of the Tongue.*

and the fool is often formed upon most mistaken premises.
The man—wise in the estimation of the world—is often
proved to be the most foolish of men. For—as an old commentator remarks—'who can be more foolish than he, who
turns away from Christ the Author of our salvation—who
prefers transitory to eternal things—who denies the expectation of the future life—or who hopes to obtain it in the
course of folly.'* Surely—whatever be his reputation
among his fellow-creatures for *wisdom*, his *heart* must be that
of *the fool at his left hand*. We hear him boasting of his
freedom from his old fetters. We see him hurrying from one
opinion to another. But all is conceit, rank in selfishness
and pride. God's balances are far more sure, and just; and
to be "weighed, and found wanting" here—will be unutterable and eternal ruin.

4. *If the spirit of the ruler rise up against thee, leave not thy place; for yielding pacifieth great offences.*

'Virtue'—we have been well reminded—'consists in
earnestly setting one's self to the performance of every
duty.'† Here loyalty is inculcated; and that "not only to
the good and gentle, but also to the froward." (1 Pet. ii. 18.)
This rule has been given before.‡ The faithful adviser may be
constrained to give unpalatable counsel; and the *spirit of the
ruler* may *rise up against* him. Still let him not hastily *leave
his place*. Jonathan indeed under this heavy provocation
left his place, probably only for a time (1 Sam. xx. 34,
42); but, generally speaking, the rule of patience is wisdom.
George Herbert's words are worthy of attention—

> 'Be calm in arguing; for fierceness makes
> Error a fault, and truth discourtesy.'—*Church Porch.*

* Lavater.
† Abp. Whately's *Lessons on Morals*, xiv. § 6.
‡ See chap. viii. 3.

This is good sense, and Christian patience rarely to be found.
Surely the subject, like the soldier, should hold *the place*
assigned to him, though it may cost him much trial. Let
him not throw up his commission; but rather restrain all im-
patient or disloyal thoughts. Indeed 'retiring upon dis-
pleasure'—Lord Bacon remarks—' is of all courses the un-
fittest; for a man leaveth things at worst, and depriveth
himself of means to make them better.'* Extremities may
indeed justify the retirement.† But the ordinary path is
quiet suffering in faith, in the full consolation of a present
defending God.‡

' The charm of *yielding* is worthy of being specially noted.'§
The power over the spirit is a far higher glory than an
earthly triumph. A victory over ourselves is more glorious
than a victory over others. (Prov. xvi. 32.) The vehement
impulse seems to shew, that we think more of ourselves
than of our cause. Yet this *yielding* must never arise from
cowardice, from a mean-spirited fear of losing the favour of
man. Where conscience is concerned, the true-hearted man
must at once *leave his place*, whatever be the consequence.
In an upright course fear not the face of man: not forgetting
man. Yet where conscience is not concerned, nothing is to be
gained by the display of an unbending spirit. ' Anger
irritates and inflames the wound; meekness mollifies,
cleanses, and heals it. Resentful pride adds fury to the
storm. A mild demeanour changes it into a calm. By the
pouring on of oil we may smooth the wave, which we should
lash and rebuke in vain.‖ Let " the elect of God " ever

* *Advancement of Learning*, book ii. xxiii. 5.

† David fleeing from Saul, 1 Sam. xix. 10. Even Christ from
Herod, Matt. xiv. 13. See also the rule, Ib. x. 23.

‡ See Isa. li. 12, 13 ; 1 Pet. iv. 19.

§ Dr. Chalmers's *Scripture Readings.* Comp. Prov. xxv. 15.

‖ Wardlaw. ' The weak reed, by bending in a rough wind,
receiveth no hurt; when the sturdy oak is torn up by the roots.'—
Trapp *in loco*.

" put on " their garments—so adorning to their profession. (Col. iii. 12–15.) What need there is of the continued power of the Divine work to maintain the full display of Christian grace ! Let us take up the prayer of our godly poet—

> Lord, mend, or rather make, us. *One* creation
> Will not suffice our turn ;
> Except thou make us daily, we shall spurn
> Our own salvation.—*Herbert.*

5. *There is an evil which I have seen under the sun, as an error, which proceedeth from the ruler. 6. Folly is set in great dignity ; and the rich sit in a low place. 7. I have seen servants upon horses, and princes walking as servants upon the earth.*

Solomon follows up his exhortation to loyalty by noticing a common occasion of disloyalty which he had *seen*—*misgovernment.* He had often alluded to this disorder as a national evil;* specially when men have been raised, or have risen, to an high elevation. " The brother of low degree may rejoice in that he is exalted." (Jam. i. 9.) It may be—as in Joseph's case—for an enlarged sphere of usefulness.† The Great Ruler " takes the poor out of the dust, that He may set him with the princes of his people." (Ps. cxiii. 7, 8.) The records of all ages—particularly of our own—shew men raised from the people to the highest honour in the state. *The evil* here noted is the misplacing of men—*folly set in great dignity*—' men by indignities coming to dignities.'‡

* See Prov. xix. 10 ; xxvi. 1 ; xxviii. 12, 28 ; xxx. 21, 22.

† Ps. cv. 17–22, and David, Ib. lxxviii. 70–72.

‡ Bacon's *Essays*, xi. ' Ahab'—it has been well observed—' displays in clear lines the irreparable mischief which can be done to society by a character intrinsically insignificant, when external circumstances have exalted it into a situation among the public agents of the world.'—Archdeacon Evans's *Scripture Biography*, iii. 158.

This is an error which proceedeth from the ruler. The responsibility lies at his door to fix the fittest men in the places which most need them; "doing nothing" either "by partiality" or by prejudice. And a matter of much evil and grief is the capricious advancement of despicable upstarts—power placed in unworthy hands—great interests entrusted to men of low life, who have neither will nor wisdom rightly to discharge their trust. While these minions—the creatures of the *rulers'* own will—are advanced,* *the rich* in knowledge and large capacities† — well qualified for high offices—are *sitting in low places.* A similar sight—*servants on horses,‡ and princes walking as servants on the earth* to do them honour (Esth. vi. 8, 9) Solomon elsewhere describes, as "one of the evils which the earth cannot bear." §

If order is heaven's first law, whatever infringes this law presents a distorted view of the Divine economy. If servants rule, and masters serve—if subjects dictate, and kings bend before them, it is the power of man's will—not of God's ordinance. Hooker's dying comfort was to meditate on ' the blessed obedience and order of angels, without which peace could not be in heaven. And oh'—he added—' that it might be so on earth !' ‖ If we then rule, let it be so as to give no pretext for discontent or revolt. If we be in a subordinate position, let it be to fulfil the responsibilities of our position, without seeking to "come up higher."

The evil is greatly increased, when the high stations of the Church are bestowed upon unworthy men, passing by men of God, sound in doctrine, and upright in heart. But

---

* Such as by our Edward II. Comp. Prov. xxviii. 3 ; Esth. iii. 1.

† Evidently opposed to *folly.* See also Ps. xlv. 12.

‡ A mark of honour—Ezek. xxiii. 23. Jer. xvii. 25. The latter text marks a National honour—let Britain mark it well—connected with the National keeping of the Sabbath. (Vv. 21–25.) The custom is continued to the present day. See Harmer.

§ See Prov. xxx. 21, 22.   ‖ See Izaak Walton's *Life.*

as Lord Bacon quotes the proverb—' A place sheweth the man ; and it sheweth some to the better, and some to the worse.'* It is hard to say how a man will behave himself in his high responsibility, till he has been tried. None but those who are divinely-furnished can stand the trial, and glorify God in it.

Such is this world—a mere pageant—a " fashion that passeth away," with all its pomp, and glory, and cheat. Lord ! let me be ever content with my appointed lot, never aspiring to any higher name or reputation. How little exaltation could I safely bear with such a corrupt and worldly heart ! What a mercy is it to be kept upon humble ground, not climbing the pinnacle, where the head so soon turns giddy, and where special watchfulness is needed; because the greater the height, the greater the fall. Never, Lord, let me seek great things for myself, " when thou hast said—Seek them not." (Jer. xlv. 5.)

8. *He that diggeth a pit shall fall into it ; and whoso breaketh a hedge, a serpent shall bite him. 9. Whoso removeth stones shall be hurt therewith ; and he that cleaveth wood shall be endangered thereby.*

These four pithy illustrations obviously point to one and the same end. Evil shall fall upon the heads of its own authors. *He that diggeth the pit may fall into* it himself.† As the *breaking* of an old *hedge* might hazard *the serpent's bite;*‡ so the attempt to root up ancient fences of government may be an undoing project.§ The *removal of stones* from a building may bring them upon our head. Even the *cleaving*

* *Essay* xi. *ut supra.*
† See Job, v. 13. Ps. vii. 15, 16 ; ix. 15 ; cxli. 10. Prov. xi. 5, 6 ; xxvi. 27 ; xxviii. 10. Examples of Haman (Esth. vii. 10), Daniel's enemies (Dan. vi. 24). ‡ See Amos, v. 19.
§ See 2 Sam. xviii. 14. 1 Kings, i. 5 ; ii. 25.

of wood may be a work of personal *danger*.* 'Let there be neither a secret conspiracy against the established order of things,
nor a violent inroad on its fences and landmarks : else there
may be a recoil on the perpetrators themselves ; just as the
renders and pullers down of things material are in danger of
being hurt therewith.'† It is far more easy to blame than to
mend; to pull down the house, than to build it up again.
And yet such is the power of self-delusion, that if the mysterious finger could shew the handwriting upon the wall—onward men will go — so natural and easy is the downward path !

10. *If the iron be blunt, and he do not whet the edge, then must he
put forth more strength ; but wisdom is profitable to direct.*

Whatever be the object of the man in *cleaving the wood,*
he cannot work effectively with *blunted* tools. If, therefore,
he does not whet his hatchet's edge, he must *put forth more
strength;* yet only to belabour the tree with heavy, but in-
effectual blows. Thus unskilful and indolent workmen often
increase their difficulties by the want of hearty exertion. In
working for God, our materials are rough. Feeble, indeed,
are our efforts to *cleave* the knotty *wood*. The stubborn will
resists, and there is no apparent result.

But is it not the secret of this bluntness, that we have
not whetted the edge, that prayer has been let down — that
faith has been in slumbering exercise — that the lust of the
world has been indulged — and heavenly prospects clouded ?
Yet we must not cast away the enfeebled weapon. *Let the
edge be whetted.* Substitute a religion of sustained energy
for a religion of complaints. We are fighting for a " kingdom that suffereth violence." The crown is hard to get, and
harder still to keep. But " the violent "—those who have

---

* See Deut. xix. 5.

† Dr. Chalmers' *Scripture Readings.*

whetted their edge and put forth more strength—they "take it by force." (Matt. xi. 12.)   So far as faith is in real exercise —it must and will prevail.

> 'Fight, though it may cost thy life :
>   Storm the Kingdom, but prevail ;
> Let not Satan's fiercest strife
>   Make thee, warrior, faint or quail.
>
> 'Art thou faithful ? then oppose
>   Sin and wrong with all thy might ;
> Careless how the tempest blows,
>   Only care to win the fight.'*

But, after all, the grand cause of failure is, that we do not go *straight* to God for the strength of Omnipotence to be "made perfect in our weakness." (2 Cor. xii. 9.)   There having gone and *whetted the edge*—now to your work. They that have a little strength, shall have more.   "He giveth power to the faint, and to them that have no might, he increaseth strength." (Isa. xl. 29.)   Ours is not a fitful work—of strong, but temporary, excitement.   The thought that it is God's work—done for God—done on earth, as it cannot be done in heaven—this puts energy into every effort.   It is not the work of the scholar or the theologian, but of the practical servant of God.   It is not the work of natural power, but of Christian confidence.   'When'—as godly Bp. Latimer declares—'I am in a settled assurance about the state of my soul, methinks then I am as bold as a lion.   But when I am eclipsed in my comforts, I am of so fearful a spirit, that I could run into a very mouse-hole.'   Here is the true *whetting of the edge.*   The secret of our strength is the recollection of our standing as a child accepted.   To hold on in advance only a single step is victory.   We think not of the hardness of the fight, but of Him who is

* *Lyra Germanica.*   Septuagesima Sunday.

ever with us—ever sufficient for us. One promise of His grace is more powerful to hold us up, than all the assaults of hell to throw us down.

There will indeed be perplexities to the end. But *wisdom* —" the wisdom that is from above"—*is profitable to direct.* It puts us in the right way of working. It sets before us the best objects, and the most fitting occasions. The want of this practical *wisdom* has hindered much good, and induced much injury to the great end. Children have been trained in gloom, rather than in brightness. Amiable people have been revolted from the Gospel by well-meaning but unsuited faithfulness. Imprudence—perhaps only a single instance —has excited a prejudice, very hard to melt away. And therefore for consistency and usefulness in our sphere of duty, what so important as to take the precious promise as the polar star of our course?—" If any of you lack wisdom, let him ask of God, that giveth to all men liberally, and upbraideth not; and it shall be given him." (Jam. i. 5.)

11. *Surely the serpent will bite without enchantment, and a babbler is no better.*

Scripture elsewhere alludes to man's power in *enchanting the serpent.* But *without enchantment surely the serpent will bite.* It is his nature. (verse 8.) *The babbler is no better.** It is as much his nature to *babble,* and quite as dangerous, as for *the serpent to bite.* He is all tongue. And well indeed is this " tongue described as an unruly evil, full of deadly poison!" (Jam. iii. 8.)

The evil here more distinctly in view is breach of con-

---

* 'A babbler is nothing better than a serpent, who stings without provocation.' Luther's Version.—See Beza. The marginal reading—' *Master of the tongue*'—supposes the proud independence of all restraint. See Ps. xii. 4.

fidence. So baneful is its influence—that it is hardly safe to "trust in a friend, or to put confidence in a guide." Nay—it may sometimes be wise to "keep the door of our mouth from her that lieth in our bosom." (Mic. vii. 5.) 'The dismantling and rending of the robe from the privacies of human intercourse' cannot be justified. 'He that entrusts a secret to a friend, goes thither as to a sanctuary; and to violate the rites of that is sacrilege and profanation of friend-ship.'* Follow in 'its course a secret thus let loose. One tells it to another. Thus it goes from mouth to mouth—from ear to ear; depositing in many hearts what never should be known; gathering as it flies untold excess of scandal. If "itching ears" are bad (2 Tim. iv. 3); itching lips are worse—more hurtful in the end.'† Learn to prize the friend who can keep a secret as an inestimable jewel. To resist the charm of telling the secret unadvisedly—is an honourable mark—" shewing all good fidelity in all things." (Tit. ii. 10.)

The evil of this *babbling* involves all the fruits of pure selfishness — tossing about our neighbour's name — the dearest part of him—as the veriest bauble. And how naturally do we slide into this sin—ere we are aware of it! Everywhere it goes with us—at home and abroad—in large or small society—in common intercourse of the day. The tongue flowing without restraint, becomes " the fountain sending forth bitter waters." If it be the prerogative of man to *enchant the serpent,* much more is it the Omnipotence of God to "bridle the tongue." " *No man*"—it is emphati-cally stated—" can tame it." (Jam. iii. 8.) The sins of the tongue are deeply marked in the word of God, as matter for discipline, humiliation, and prayer. Oh, for that careful, tender sensibility, that makes a conscience of a word—of a

* Bp. Taylor's *Sermon on the Good and Evil Tongue.*
† Mylne.

ook." No sins tend more to banish the Divine Comforter from our houses and from our hearts. What proof can there be of grace in the heart, if there be not a bridle on the tongue? *

12. *The words of a wise man's mouth are gracious* (Heb. Grace) *; but the lips of a fool will swallow him up.* 13. *The beginning of the words of his mouth is foolishness ; and the end of his talk is mischievous madness.* 14. *A fool also is full of words : a man cannot tell what shall be ; and what shall be after him, who can tell him?* 15. *The labour of the foolish wearieth every one of them ; because he knoweth not how to go to the city.*

Again we have the contrast drawn out between wisdom and folly—between that which cometh from God, and the flowing stream of our corrupt nature. The tongue—as Bp. Taylor describes it in his graphic colouring—' is a fountain both of bitter waters and of pleasant. It sends forth blessing and cursing. It praises God, and rails at men. It is some-times set on fire, and then it puts whole cities in combustion. It is unruly, and no more to be restrained than the breath of a tempest. It is volatile and fugitive. Reason should go before it ; and when it does not, repentance comes after it. It was intended for an organ of the Divine praises ; but the devil often plays upon it, and then it sounds like a screech-owl, or the groans of death. Sorrow and shame, folly and repentance, are the notes and formidable accents of that discord.' †

How valuable then is the art of enchanting our tongues ; bringing them under wholesome discipline, so that they may

* See Jam. i. 26.   † *Sermon on the Tongue.*

pacify and instruct, instead of bringing the serpent's sting! And truly heavenly wisdom pervades the entire and new man, as folly pervades every faculty of the old man. *The words* therefore *of the wise man's mouth are gracious—grace* in the very essence. Thus was it with our Divine Master. The enraptured Prophet could not restrain his song—" Thou art fairer than the children of men : *grace* is poured into thy lips." (Ps. xlv. 2.) And when this Incarnate Wisdom was manifested—can we marvel, that they wondered "at the *gracious* words, which proceeded out of his mouth?" (Luke, iv. 22.)

Solomon elsewhere draws the same picture of the godly tongue—" The tongue of the just is as choice silver. The lips of the righteous feed many. The tongue of the wise useth knowledge aright. The heart of the wise teacheth his mouth, and addeth learning to his lips." * And "how forcible are these right and *gracious words !*" (Job, vi. 25.) Did they not melt the iron heart of Esau ? (Gen. xxxiii. 1–16.) Did they not recall the rash purpose of David to a considerate restraint ? (1 Sam. xxv. 22–35.)

Take, again, a modern example from the annals of our Church History. What did Luther owe to *the gracious words* of his friend Staupitz, bringing him out of bondage! ' In order to be filled with the love of that which is good, you must first be filled with the love of God. If you wish to be really converted, do not follow these mortifications and penances. Love him who has first loved you.' These words —the Historian adds—' penetrated the heart of Luther. Guided by this new light, he consulted the Scriptures. He looked to all the passages, which speak of repentance and conversion—words, which were no longer dreaded, but became the sweetest refreshment. Those passages of Scripture, which once alarmed him, seemed now—he says—to run to

* Prov. x. 20, 21 ; xv. 2 ; xvi. 23. Comp. Ps. xxxvii. 30.

him from all sides, to smile, to spring up, and play around him.' *

There is indeed a power in godliness beyond man's wisdom. *Grace* is often mightier than intellect. The man 'whose " conversation is seasoned with this *grace*" will be ready with his " answer" against many an acute disputant on the arena of scepticism.† Considering his tongue as a talent to be used for his Master's glory, and having his heart as a treasury filled with the things of God—his *gracious words* will be full of power. Few can listen, without being wiser and better.

Here is wisdom in its solid influence. Now mark the contrast of *folly*. *The lips of the fool swallow up himself*. Adonijah's self-willed proclamation was to his own ruin. (1 Kings, i. 5 ; ii. 25.) Rehoboam's foolishness—giving grievous instead of *gracious words* to his people—made " his own tongue to fall upon himself." (Ib. xii. 1–19. Comp. Ps. lxiv. 8.) Wisdom guides the nearest way to our own security. (Prov. x. 9.)—Folly the surest road to our own ruin. Look at *the lips of the fool* filled with scorn against his Maker— his scoffing contempt alike of his mercy and his judgments —are not these the words of *folly* in the path of ruin ? (Ps. ii. 1–4.) And will not the justly merited destruction at the great day of retribution fearfully—irrevocably—*swallow him up?* (Jude, 14, 15.)

Nor are *the fool's lips* only a curse to himself. They become a pest to all around him—from beginning to end. The beginning of his *words is foolishness*. But he goes from bad to worse—often as if he was worked up to a phrenzy. If his oracular voice does not command attention, he is all on fire—all is a blaze and smoke—till his anger becomes a sort of *mischievous madness*. Thus this combustible talker spreads mischief wherever he goes—in his family—in society,

* D'Aubigné's *History of the German Reformation.*
† See Col. iv. 6.

stirring round about him " envy and strife, confusion, and every evil work."

The next distinctive feature in the portrait of *the fool* is his torrent of words—*full of words*—Many words but few ideas—a Babel system of confusion—mere word-rubbish. He talks from first to last in the circle of folly—talking and talking on at random, determining to have the last word, although at the end it is the same as at the beginning— such common-place truisms, that no man can *tell what shall be*—what shall come next; and so loose and incoherent, *that what shall be after him who can tell him?*

In fact, it is generally found, that those who have the most discourse have the least knowledge. Words are too often the substitute for thinking, rather than the medium of thought. In the use of them men think they know their own wisdom. But how few comparatively know their own foolishness ! *The fool* passing from his words to his daily business—his *labour wearies every one* connected with him. Impertinently busy, without any object ; yet so extreme is his ignorance upon the most ordinary matters—such a total want of common sense—that it is as *if he knew not* the plainest track—*how to go to the city,* close at hand. We wonder not that man should be *wearied* with his intercourse, yielding as it does no profitable result. Thus 'men, who neglect to employ Christ for " eye-salve, that they might see" (Rev. iii. 18) things of greatest concernment for his glory, and for the salvation of their own souls, are often, for their so doing, left to miscarry in their most common affairs.'* Man's wisdom becomes his foolishness, if he is content to live without dependence upon his God.

We do not often see this portrait of *the fool* fully drawn out. Yet we are frequently conversant with persons gifted

* Nisbet.

with great volubility of speech, combined with perfect shallow-
ness of understanding ; and who, if they were strongly excited,
would pour forth the overflowing foolishness here described.
Indeed the fountain principle is in us all from the beginning.
"Foolishness is bound up in the heart of the child" (Prov.
xxii. 15) ; and unless it give place to the Omnipotence of
the gracious principle, its enfeebling and perverting influence
will fully proclaim itself.   The man who neglects Divine
Teaching, will be a fool to the end of his days in heavenly
wisdom, with all the fearful responsibility of wilful folly.

16. *Woe to thee, O land, when thy King is a child, and thy
    princes eat in the morning.   17. Blessed art thou, O land,
    when thy King is the son of nobles, and thy princes eat in
    due season, for strength and not for drunkenness.*

Solomon's code of morals comes out with greater point
and brightness, the more it is examined.   This book of
Ecclesiastes is truly a hand-book of morals, for all ranks and
classes of society.   And not among the least important is the
place, which Solomon gives to the great and noble of the earth.
Kings and rulers like himself, far from being exempted by
their rank from the common laws of men, are strongly warned
against sins, which might have seemed to belong only to
the lowest and most degraded of their people.   In point of
fact—the higher the rank, the more aggravated the sin.
And that of intemperance, here reproved, is not only ruinous
to the *prince*, but brings a curse upon the nation.*

Solomon had learned naturally to connect the personal
character of the Monarch with the prosperity of the land.
A child in years—as Josiah, and others—may be a national
blessing.†   But when *the king "was a child* in understand-

* See 1 Kings, xvi. 9, 10 ; xx. 16-21.
† 2 Chron. xxxiv. 1-3.   Cartwright, writing in Elizabeth's days,

ing," (as was his own son in the maturity of age)*—then
woe unto thee, O land. (Isa. iii. 4.) The character and habits
of *the princes* were generally after the example of the Sovereign. A corrupt king (like our Charles II.) brings up a
corrupt court. If he were indulging his ease and pleasure,
they would probably plunge into the same gulf (Hos. vii.
3–5), giving up *the morning*—the prime of the day—to
appetite; rather than appropriating it, as they were bound
to do, to the public service.†

In contrast with the *woe* of a childish monarch, is the
blessing of a *king—the son of nobles*. And as before, it was
the child, not in years, but in qualities; so he now speaks
of *a king—noble*—not in blood, but in wisdom and godliness. For 'this is the true nobility, when piety, wisdom,
righteousness, and the fear of God, do adorn the royal blood,
and render persons truly illustrious. Nobility of blood,
without nobility of virtue and holiness, addeth nothing to
a governor at all.' ‡ The completeness of the blessing is,
when the king reigneth in righteousness, and *the princes*—
following his example—" rule in judgment." (Isa. xxxii. 1.)
The contrast is marked in well-disciplined exercise. They
did not eat *in the morning* in unrestrained indulgence—
but *in due season*—in moderation, *for strength,* and *not for*

adds to the list 'Edward VI. in our memory'—but with this signi-
ficant reserve—'so long as he was guided by his own judgment and
will.'

　　* See 2 Chron. xii. 13.

　　† See Jer. xxi. 12. 'The breakfast of the Orientals usually con-
sisted of the simplest eatables. Hence to *feast* in the morning was a
proof of intemperance, as well as neglect of duty.'—Holden. *See
Pictorial Bible.*

　　‡ Bp. Reynolds. 'As a son of death or perdition is one devoted
thereunto ; so *a son of nobles* is one *nobly* seasoned with principles
of honour and government.'—*Ib.* 'So a son of Belial—a son ex-
tremely wicked—in the superlative degree.'

drunkenness—" making provision for the flesh"—to satisfy
the wants—not " to fulfil the lusts thereof." (Rom. xiii. 14.)
This habit of self-control was emphatically commended to
rulers with some experience of its need and value—" It is
not for *kings,* O Lemuel, it is not for *kings* to drink wine,
nor *for princes* strong drink ; lest they drink, and forget the
law, and pervert the judgment of any of the afflicted."
(Prov. xxxi. 4, 5.) When this royal temperance is based
upon Christian principles of government, may we not truly
say—*Blessed art thou, O land?*

Look at our own land—our vast increasing empire—
joining colony to colony—like "house to house, and field
to field"—her fleets riding the acknowledged lords of
every sea—mistress of half the islands in the globe—what
if our rulers would grasp their weighty responsibility of
'planting the colonies of Christ—instead of those of Mammon?'—when we should thus see her crowned with the
honour of her God, should we not then take up the delighting voice—*Blessed art thou, O land?* Surely we would
respond to the utterance of a well-thinking mind—' O that
statesmen would consider what a glorious privilege they
enjoy, when they are allowed to become the fathers of a
new people!'* The more elevated our station—the wider
our sphere—the more *felt* our influence will be—whether
for good, or for evil.

18. *By much slothfulness the building decayeth ; and through
idleness of the hand the house slippeth through.*

Luxury and intemperance give ready occasion to *much
slothfulness.* They are naturally linked together—" The
drunkard and the *glutton* shall come to poverty, and *drowsi-*

* *Guesses at Truth.* First Series.

ness shall clothe a man with rags." (Prov. xxiii. 21.)   The
ruler and *princes*, given up to sensual indulgence, will slumber in the affairs of the state.   The commonwealth therefore will be like *the building decaying* for want of proper
support—*the house slipping through*—not weather-proof—
for *the idle* want of exertion to keep it in repair.   The house
must be kept up.   The damage—small at first—increases
rapidly by neglect.   The yawning sluggard drags out his
daily excuse—'It is but a brick is gone.   A few hours will
make no great difference'—till by daily procrastination the
injury is beyond repair, and *the decaying* tenement *slippeth
through*.   The less the pains required at first, the more in-
excusable the delay.   A little care at the beginning would
have saved *the decay*.   'To-morrow'—says the proverb—
'comes never.   And the same tempter, who leads you to
put off doing what is right to "a more convenient season," will be as ready to suggest an excuse to-morrow as
to-day.'*

Want of family discipline issues in the same result.
When evils, apparently trifling, are allowed, the tendency to
decay becomes more and more visible.   Indeed everywhere
the neglect of present effort hastens on the ruinous crisis.
Public institutions and laws—however permanent they may
seem to be—need continual and active review in order to
their amendment.   Otherwise abuses creep in, like moss on
the old building, or a gap in the wall, in the first instance
scarcely discoverable, but gradually widening with threatening prospect.

There is also an intellectual *slothfulness* much to be resisted, unless we would allow the palsy of every faculty.
'It is only this that induces so many to take for granted
the opinions of others.'†   As another powerful writer well

* Abp. Whately's *Lessons on Morals*, v. § 7 ; xix. § 1.
† Coleridge's *Lecture on Shakspeare and Milton*.   Sect. i. p. 5.

remarks—'An aversion to doubt—a dislike to have the judgment kept in suspense—combined with indolence in investigation, induces the great mass of mankind to *make up their minds* on a variety of points, not one of which they have been enabled thoroughly to examine.' *

But the subject invites a closer probing. The pursuit of truth in the *first* place marks the whole-hearted Christian —*in the second place* the slothful professor. '*Idleness*'—as Dr. Barrow observes—'is indeed the nursery of sins, which as naturally grow up therein, as weeds in a neglected field.' †
Idleness of hands is often connected with worldliness of heart. If there be any niche left in the heart for the setting up of the idol, the whole work *decays*. There will be fighting without victory, complaint without prayer—" the hands hanging down, and the knees feeble." Nothing so paralyzing to Christian energy as this hopeless despondency.

While we study the awful catalogue of sins of commission,‡ let us not forget that the sins of omission are equally guilty.§ We learn to do evil, by doing nothing. We satisfy ourselves in irreligious habits with the delusion, that we have done no harm. But is it really no harm to have trifled away all opportunities of doing good ? the " talent laid up in the napkin" (Luke, xix. 20) of *idleness*—duties neglected —times of usefulness frittered away—and gone—never to be recalled ?

' Indeed the very nature and essence of virtue doth consist in the most difficult and painful exercises of soul; in the extirpating rooted prejudices and notions from our understanding ; in bending a stiff will, and rectifying crooked inclinations ; in overruling a rebellious temper ; in curbing eager and importunate appetites ; in taming wild passions;

---

* *Detached Thoughts*, from Abp. Whately's Writings, p. 31.
† *Sermon on Industry*.
‡ See Gal. v. 19–21.   § See Jam. iv. 17.

in withstanding violent temptations; in surmounting many
difficulties, and sustaining many troubles; in struggling with
various unruly lusts within, and encountering many stout
enemies abroad, which assault our reason, and "war against
our soul." In such exercises its very being lieth. Its
birth, its growth, its subsistence, dependeth on them; so
that from any discontinuance or remission of them, it would
soon *decay*, languish away, and perish.' *

How painful, therefore, it is to° remark this deadly *slothfulness* pervading every part of the system! A soft and
delicate life gives force to temptation, which might easily be
subdued by one effort of "hardness." An indolent or desultory man can never be a "vessel unto honour" in the
Church of God. In the experience of the inner man what
danger is there of being satisfied with a certain measure of
attainment—something short of the very best of Christ-
ianity! And yet if we are satisfied even with much, without
prayer for more, does it not stir up the question whether
we have any at all? Truly "grey hairs are here and there
upon us; yet we know it not." (Hos. vii. 9.) Never expect
spiritual wealth, while indulging carnal sloth.

It is an awakening thought, that the living principle of
Christian diligence may be palsied in the midst of much outward exercise—that external energy and inward sloth may
be found in the same person at one and the same time—
that *much slothfulness* is the highroad to apostasy†—the
stepping-stone to many and fearful sins. Well is it, when
God stirs up conviction by giving us an errand to the throne
of grace—conscience urging to go *at once*. Oh! whatever
insensibility, or feebleness may belong to prayer, let it never
be given up. Still pray on—still cry. There can be no
reason for despair. Be determined to seek the blessing, till

* Barrow, *ut suprà*.   † See Heb. v. 11–14, with vi. 1–6.

you are really made partaker of it.   Let nothing supplant it
in your heart, or outweigh it in your judgment.   Desire is
only good, as it quickens to exertion.*   Turn every opportunity to account.   Perseverance is the main test of principle.   We have not finished our responsibility, even when
the house is built.   There will be the continual care to watch
against its *slipping through*.   The first labour in God's work
is only the starting-point.   Vigour must be in constant exercise, till the crown is won — till labour is exchanged for
eternal rest.

> In what the world calls weakness lurks
>   The very strength of evil ;
> Full mightily it helps the works
>   Of our great foe the Devil.
>   Awake, my soul, awake ;
>   Thy refuge quickly take
> With Him, th' Almighty, who can save.
>   One look from Christ thy Lord
>   Can sever ev'ry cord,
> That binds thee now — a wretched slave.
>   *Lyra Germanica*, 12th Sunday after Trinity.

19. *A feast is made for laughter, and wine maketh merry ;
but money answereth all things.*

Many are the resources of *laughter and merriment*.   But
money brings a wider range of influence.   It *answereth* not
only the pleasure, the *feasting and wine*, but *all things*, which
the craving appetite of man can desire.   In itself it is a
blessing, contributing largely to our temporal comfort.   If
we despise it, we must be content to live without many of
the ordinary indulgences of life.

And yet this universal empire of *money* involves many

* See Prov. xxi. 25.

limitations. It cannot give health, happiness, or immortality. It cannot provide the principles of moral excellence. It cannot give peace of conscience, or furnish a ransom for the soul.* Yet with all these reserves as an instrument of commerce, *it answereth all things*. The man who has it, wants nothing that this world can give.† It supplies a thousand advantages—not only the necessaries, but the conveniences, indulgences, and embellishments of life. It is the price and measure of *all things*. The worldling with his full chest fancies a sort of Deity in it—resources inexhaustible.

The real sphere of the usefulness of *money* is the object and use of it—when we hold it as stewards—when the two great ends are combined in one—the glory of God, and the good of our fellow-creatures.

How grand is the object!—how widely extended is its sphere of usefulness—when expended in the spread of the Gospel—the schemes of Christian education, and all the methods of social improvement, which are stirring up, and exciting such general interest! The more good will be done, when we take the most delight in doing it. But how dangerous—yea—how fatal is the profession, when it is suffered to usurp God's place in the heart! The larger the mass, the more grace is needed to preserve from its deadly temptation. Nothing can set out its great power more strongly than our Lord's solemn declaration—"How hardly shall they that have riches enter into the kingdom of God!" (Mark, x. 22.)

But fearful indeed is the responsibility of money, when spent only upon *the feast for laughter and wine*. For of them, "whose god is their belly, and who mind earthly

* See Ps. xlix. 7–9.

† Lorin gives various classical allusions to this vast influence and resource of money.—*In loco.* Also on v. 20.

things"—it is emphatically declared—"whose end is destruction." (Philip. iii. 19.) Their present state is the insensibility of "death."* Their future prospect is death in all its infinite and everlasting horrors.† O my God, let me find my *feast* in thy love—in the privileged joy of thy salvation. Let me find in thee—in the fountain of life—a portion, that shall *answer all things—answer* all my spiritual wants, with abundant and eternal supply. (Ps. xvi. 5.)

20. *Curse not the king; no—not in thy thought, and curse not the rich in thy bed-chamber; for a bird in the air shall carry the voice, and that which hath wings shall tell the matter.*

Some of Solomon's words—as Lord Bacon observes—'have more of the eagle than others.'‡ But taking them as instructions for life, their minuteness of practical detail shews a singular acuteness of observation of the highest practical value. He had adverted to rulers—bad and good. He now speaks to subjects. The veto here given evidently refers to the *woe* of misguided rule. This evil naturally excites revolt. Yet if it be our duty to protest, we must not forget the respect due to their office, apart from their personal character. The Mosaic code forbade to *curse the Ruler* of the people "even by evil *speaking*." (Comp. Exod. xxii. 28, with Acts, xxiii. 5.) The rule here goes deeper, and chains even *the thought*.

The allusion to *the rich* clearly refers to the ignoble *princes of the land*. Here, again, we are forbidden to "speak evil of dignities." (2 Pet. ii. 10.) 'God's government is so peculiarly of God, that he will have it supported for the

---

* See Rom. viii. 6; 1 Tim. v. 6.   † See Luke, xvi. 19–24.
‡ *Advancement of Learning*, Book II. xxiii. 5.

benefit of mankind.'* Treason will " be proclaimed upon the house-tops." Elisha's case was miraculous. But God may work in the ordinary course of his Providence. (Comp. 2 Kings, vi. 11, 12, with Esth. ii. 21–23.) Nay, rather than this secret wickedness should be undiscovered, he might make *the bird of the air to carry the voice.* The matter will come to light—how—no one knows. Even *the bed-chamber* may be made to speak. "The stone shall cry out of the wall; and the beam out of the timber shall answer it." (Hab. ii. 11.) †

The advice, therefore, here given seems to be that of caution against speaking lightly of the faults of rulers. Think not that you should do it with impunity. Kings and nobles—especially in despotic governments—supply the need of just laws by spies, who do their work too surely to admit of escape, reporting to their sovereign expressions, that may be the ground of treasonable accusation.‡ If the thought that the eye and the ear of God were always open to our most secret thoughts, we should often be kept from speaking what, if discovered, might bring us into trouble.

A modern writer gives a graphical application of this proverb—'It is dangerous to speak, where secrecy is required. The thought is thine own, while you keep it to yourself;

* Dr. A. Clark, *in loco.* 'The worse and the more malignant the world is, the more studious and laborious Solomon teacheth us to be in doing our duty—particularly in *honouring the magistracy,* because it is a Divine ordinance, and the better part of the world, by which God manages all things under the sun.' Luther *in loco.*

† This, as well as the bird, is a proverbial hyperbole. Many similar instances are given in Scripture—ascribing senses and feeling to inanimate matter. See Hos. ii. 21. Luke, xix. 40.

‡ Cromwell was brought to the scaffold by this cruel artifice. See Froude's *History of England,* vol. iii. 490–494; also Burnet's *History of Reformation,* Part i., book iii. Fuller's *Church History,* Book v., Sect. 5. The proverb—'that the king has many ears, and many eyes,' had reference to this mean system of espionage.

but *once* the cage is opened, and *the bird* let loose, who knows how far its flight may bear it ? At first you think of tying it by the foot. You tell your secret to a *single* friend. He tells it to another, who mentions it to *a chosen few.* The cord is loosened ; then it is slipped ; your bird will no more roost in secrecy. Then learn to keep your secret to yourself. It is snug to know *the bird* is in the cage, securely fastened. And though it flutter against the bars, desiring its liberty, still keep it close. No harm it will do while there. What mischief it might do if let loose, you know not. If you think evil of a man, what need to mention it ? His faults are known to thee. But why repeat them ? Who has a right to ask it ? God suffered thee to know these, that thou mightest *pray* for him, and not to harm him and others by spreading his dishonour. Pray for him, if you will, the more the better. Think what God's grace may do for him. Such *thoughts* are safe. But if you harbour thoughts against *the man,* and not against *the sin,* most probably the thought will out, and injure you.'*

And then, if *the thought* of disloyalty against *the king* be forbidden, much more against the Great King. He does not want *a bird of the air to carry the voice.* " I know the things that come into your mind—every one of them." (Ezek. xi. 5.) All is heard and noted down with infallible clearness and certainty. Learn then the lesson to " kiss the Son" (Ps. ii. 12) with reverential affection. And say not —" We will not have this man to reign over us." (Luke, xix. 14.) How powerless the *curse* against a fellow-creature ! God may in a moment interpose and nullify it. How much more powerless the *curse* of our *thought* against him ! But oh ! his *curse* against us—the hand-writing upon the wall—the harbinger of unspeakable eternal ruin !

* Mylne.

CHAPTER XI.

1. *Cast thy bread upon the waters* (face of the waters, M. R.)
   for thou shalt find it after many days.

PRECEPT and promise are linked together. Faith in the
promise gives life to the precept. There may and will be
much trial in the work of God. But there can be no disappointment. "All the promises of God"—those of the
Old, no less than of the New Testament—"are in Christ
Jesus yea, and in him are Amen." (2 Cor. i. 20.) Divine
faithfulness is therefore their security. The labour wrought
out—the seed sown—will assuredly bring its own harvest.

The figure here is that of *bread,* or rather *bread-corn**
cast upon the face of the waters ; apparently wasted and
perished, yet *found after many days.* It might be asked—
' Of what use can it be to *cast* it away ? And how vain the
hope of finding it again !' It might seem to be the business
of a senseless fool—a waste and unwarranted destruction of
the "precious seed." The inundation of the Nile illustrates the figure. The time for sowing the seed, is just
when the waters are going down, leaving a loamy bed, in
which the seed apparently lost is deposited, and produces a
most luxuriant harvest.

An encouraging—constraining motive for Christian
bountifulness ! Did we spend our whole earthly substance
in this course, it would be put out to the best security—
"lent unto the Lord." (Prov. xix. 17.) "Good measure,
pressed down and shaken together, and running over, shall
men give into your bosom. God is not unrighteous to

* So translated Isa. xxviii. 28.

forget your work, and labour of love, which ye have shewn
towards his Name, in that ye have ministered to the saints,
and do minister." (Luke, vi. 38; Heb. vi. 10.) 'Sow the
seed-corn without any hope of harvest. Do good to them,
on whom you even think your benefaction is thrown away.'*
Nothing is lost that is done for God. If it for the time
seem to be lost, *thou shalt find it after many days*—it may
be—not till the days of eternity—"thou shalt be recom-
pensed at the resurrection of the just." (Luke, xiv. 24.)

But how few believe this, or act as if they believed!
Often we hear of many impoverished by extravagance—few
indeed by liberality. Unless the tide of Christian beneficence rises higher than we are used to see it, a scanty or
withered harvest seems to be our only prospect.

But surely the subject admits of a more extensive application. See how it furnishes to the Minister of God a valuable rule and encouragement. "The sower goes forth to
sow" "the precious bread-corn—the bread of life." (Matt.
xiii. 3; Mark, iv. 14.) Much of his toil seems to be in
vain. Much disappointment arises from the world—often
more from the Church. The soil is uncongenial—the prospect of harvest precarious. But "blessed are ye that sow
beside all waters." (Isa. xxxii. 20.) The promise is sure
—*Thou shalt find it after many days*. He looks around.
He "sees not his signs." It is as if his "prayers would
return into his own bosom." (Ps. lxxiv. 9; xxxv. 13.) But
the promise is sure—"My word shall not return unto me
void." (Isa. lv. 10.) It may be that some wanderer may
have been brought back to the fold by the recollection of
his teaching, even after his voice was silent in the grave.
It may be that the seed has been re-sown again and again
from one heart to another, and that some whom he had

* Bp. Lowth's *Lectures on Hebrew Poetry*, lect. x.

never known in the flesh may welcome him " at the presence of the Lord at his coming as his glory and joy."
(1 Thess. ii. 19, 20.) " He that reapeth receiveth wages,
and gathereth fruit unto life eternal; that both he that
soweth, and he that reapeth, may rejoice together." *

Thus also in respect to the after influence of instruction.
The present sight seems as if the seed *cast upon the waters*
had perished. How scanty the present practical influence
from the instruction of the young ! But the promise is
above all uncertainty. *Thou shalt find it*—not the corn, but
the harvest. The scoffing world understand it not. " To
what purpose"—they cry—" is this waste"—of money—
time—pains ? But wait a while. God's time is best—
many days. The season of confirmation—some moment of
temptation—the hour of affliction—one or other of these
seasons stirs smothered conviction to life and reality. Go on
then. Use the means. Generations unborn may reap the
fruit. (Gal. vi. 9.)

Once more—mark the trials of the Christian life. Outward circumstances are discouraging, as if the seed *cast
upon the waters* had perished upon the wide waste—hindrances from the world without, and Satan within. But
sow thy seed—whatever be the discouragements. Though

---

* John, iv. 36. We transcribe an interesting record of Missionary faith from the journal of one of our Indian labourers—' I
have thought much on Ecclesiastes, xi. 1. Holy, prayerful, and
devoted men, have spent their short Missionary lives in these
districts; and no outward marks remain *according to man's eye*
and thinking. But yet we are assured, that their " labour should
not be in vain in the Lord." Who then can tell the works of God,
while India—this strong-hold of Satan—is travailing with its pre-
dicted Christian population ? We must work and wait on the Lord
in faith, *for the bread which we cast upon the waters will* assuredly
*be found after many days.'—Journal of Rev. A. Frost, Church
Missionary at Nasik, India. Church Missionary Record,* Dec.
1856.

prayer seems as if it died on your lips, continue in it.
Though thou haltest in the weary conflict—hold on. *Thou
shalt find it.* "They that sow in tears shall reap in joy.
He that goeth forth and weepeth, bearing precious seed,
shalt *doubtless*"—mark the word—"come again with
rejoicing, bringing his sheaves with him." (Ps. cxxvi. 5, 6.)

The *many days* between seed-time and harvest are days
of special anxiety—hoping seeming impossibilities—believing paradoxes. But the promise is God's own living truth;
and it will be found not the less sure for the delay. And when
waiting days have done their work, humbling us in entire
dependence upon God, and ripening us for the harvest of
blessing in due season—*in God's good time* (the constantly
recurring expression from Mr. Scott's death-bed.)   "We
shall reap, if we faint not. The vision is yet for an appointed time; but at the end it shall speak, and not lie;
though it tarry, wait for it, because it will surely come;
it will not tarry." (Gal. vi. 9. Hab. ii. 3.)

2. *Give a portion to seven, and to eight, for thou knowest not
what evil shall be upon the earth.*

Here Solomon adds another motive to beneficence. Every
day is an opportunity. How long it may last, who can tell?
"As we have opportunity, let us do good" (Gal. vi. 10)—
large-hearted, and open-handed, '*giving*—not a pittance, but
a portion'*—not giving it to one or two—or even *to seven*—
as if we might stop there—but *also to eight* †—the torrent
flowing on, "as God hath prospered us." (1 Cor. xvi. 2.)
The allusion may be to the Jewish custom of distributing
portions on festive occasions.‡   If the custom be passed

* Cotton and Henry.
† Definite for indefinite. See Mic. v. 5.
‡ See 1 Sam. i. 4, 5. Neh. viii. 10–17. Esth. ix. 22. Comp. Gen.
xliii. 34.

away, let the spirit remain. Our motives are more constraining. Let our hearts be more enlarged. The grand
example pours forth a constraining influence. Forwardness,
sincerity, self-denying devotedness—all flow from the experimental "knowledge of the Saviour's grace." * *That* display
is at once our pattern, our standard, and our principle.

Cheerful liberality is the burden of the rule : digging
open the several springs of usefulness which, having once
begun to flow, will spread into streams. 'Spring up, O
well'—will every true Israelite sing.† The higher we rise to
our standard, the brighter our atmosphere, the more fruitful
our course of practical habits. The likeness of our Divine
Master will be the unmistakeable stamp of our profession.

But a strange reason is given for this energy of love.
Thou knowest not what evil shall be upon the earth. 'Therefore'—says the selfist—'I may want my money for myself.
Times may alter. An evil day may be at hand. I must be
prudent, and restrain. It is best to save while I can.
"Why should I take of my bread and my flesh, and give
to I know not who?"' (1 Sam. xxv. 11.) 'Therefore'—says
the noble-minded, trusting servant of God—'I will improve
my stewardship while I have it. Like my Great Master, "I
will work the works of him that sent me while it is day."'
(John, ix. 4.) Thus the covetous worldling uses as the only
excuse for hoarding the very circumstance, which Solomon
produces as a motive to liberality. The one applies it as an
hindrance to godliness—the other as an incentive to it.
There is no danger of becoming poor by our charity. The
God of Heaven is the Surety for the poor. Mr. Scott gives
his valuable testimony—the result of well-tried experience.
'*There is no risk in expending money in an urgent case, and
from good motives. A penurious prudence, springing from*

* See 2 Cor. viii. 1–9.
† See Mather's *Essays to do Good.* Num. xxi. 17.

weak faith, is impolicy as well as sin.' 'It is wise'—as Bp.
Reynolds reminds us—'to do God's work in God's time.'
And his time is the present time—perhaps the only time
that may be given. Large-heartedness is after all true
Christian prudence. "There is that scattereth, and yet
increaseth; and there is that withholdeth more than is meet;
but it tendeth to poverty. He hath dispersed—he hath
given to the poor—his *portion to seven, and also to eight.*"
What is the issue? Is he the poorer for his bounty? "His
righteousness endureth for ever: his house shall be exalted
with honour." (Prov. xiii. 24. Ps. cxii. 9.) Oh! for the un-
selfish spirit, that finds the truest happiness in ministering
to the wants and sorrows of our fellow-sinners; and whose
experience puts a fresh seal to the Divine Tradition—"It is
more blessed to give than to receive." (Acts, xx. 35.)

'And if a portion of your worldly substance be required for
the purpose of imparting the bread of life to famishing millions,
will you withhold it? "Honour the Lord with your substance." (Prov. iii. 9.) Let the pleading voice of the whole
heathen world be heard. Let the claims of "the seed of
Abraham, God's friend" (Isa. xli. 8), awake the grateful sensibilities of your heart, and open your hands to liberality.
Seek not after apologies for refusal. Cover not a grudging
disposition by plausible objections. Let not conscience be
bribed and cajoled by avarice. Put not to the credit of
prudence and principle what belongs to the account of hard-

---

* *Life*, chap. viii. The Italics are the biographer's, justly point-
ing special attention to the testimony. Grainger mentions an application to the wealthy members of a congregation to increase their
Minister's income. The answers were as follows : 1. 'The more I
give, the less I have.' 2. 'I see the fore-end of my life, but I see not
my latter; I may come to want that which I now give.' 3. 'Our
minister is old, and past preaching; let his son, if he would, give to
preaching.' 4. 'I know how to bestow my money better.' Selfishness never wants excuses.

hearted selfishness, and the " love of this present world."
Give a portion to seven, and also to eight. *

3. *If the clouds be full of rain, they empty themselves upon the
earth; and if the tree fall towards the south, or towards
the north, in the place where the tree falleth, there it shall
be.*

Solomon abounds in happy illustrations.† Here he
pictures the sun exhaling its watery vapours from the earth,
not to retain, but to discharge them, that they may break
as clouds 'big with blessings' upon the earth again. And is
not the man of God *the cloud full of rain*—blessed, as a child
of Abraham, that he may be made "a blessing?" (Gen. xii. 2.)
The blessing will not be lost. There is good security for the
return of well-principled benevolence. Where it has been
dispensed, there let it be looked for : there it will be found,
here or hereafter—just as *the tree*—*in the place where it falleth*
—*whether towards the south or towards the north*—*there it
shall be.*

Let me ask then—what blessing am I bringing to my
fellow-creatures—in the family—in the Church—in the
world ? Does my profession attract and recommend my
principles ? Are those around me enriched by my gifts and
graces ? Are they benefited by my prayers and good service ?
The power to do good flows from the willingness to do it.
The very breathing of the heart is the principle of love. Let
me not wait for the call of importunity; but hasten at once
into the sphere of practical work. Splendid services are not
always required ; but acts of kindness to the weakest and
meanest of his people, worked out in the true spirit of love
to himself. (Matt. xxv. 40.)

* Wardlaw.   † Mercer.

May not the accommodation of Solomon's figure place it vividly before our eyes—how short our time of work may be—how soon—"*now*" even the "axe may be laid to the root of the tree" (Matt. iii. 10) and our state unchangeably fixed for eternity? *Where the tree falleth, there shall it be.* Death changes, purifies nothing. Inexpressibly solemn will be the sentence pronounced—" He that is unjust, let him be unjust still ; and he that is filthy, let him be filthy still ; and he that is righteous, let him be righteous still ; and he that is holy, let him be holy still." (Rev. xxii. 11.)

4. *He that observeth the wind, shall not sow ; and he that regardeth the clouds, shall not reap.*

Solomon still seems to have in his eye the dispensing of charity. And he is led to remark how trifling hindrances damp its glow, and restrain its exercise. The man who is constantly *observing the wind,* and thinking how every gust will blow away his seed, *will never sow.* Nor will he, who in feebleness of purpose *regards the clouds, ever reap.* Just so —little objections of doubt as to the fitness of objects, under the feigned name of prudence, occupy the mind, and the season of opportunity passes away. So much for the literal figure. Lord Bacon gives a more general application, and remarks upon it, that there is no greater impediment of action, than an over-curious *observance* of time and season. He adds, ' A man must make his opportunity, as oft as find it.' †

But this expressive figure describes a large class of Christian professors of the same " doubtful mind" (Luke, xii. 29) forming pretences against the present season of doing

* *Advancement of Learning*, Book ii. C. xxiii.

good, and putting off duty to a more fitting time. This is
the man, who would not sow in *wind or rain,* lest his seed
should be blown away, and his harvest lost. Whereas by
yielding to present discouragements, he never does his business to good purpose, and really loses his harvest. " The
sluggard will not plow by reason of the cold ; therefore shall
he beg in harvest, and have nothing." (Prov. xx. 4.) Mark
the present call to duty—the opportunity of good now put
into our hands ; not letting future contingencies in the hand
of God frame an excuse for delay of service.

In our wider sphere of Christian responsibilities take the
same warning. A measure of discouragement will always be
connected with present duties. A plausible excuse for delay
will never be wanting. To-morrow will be more favourable
—the storm will be over, and our business will be done with
less hazard. So says the trifler in his own delusion. But in
fact the weather is not in fault. There is a want of spring
in the heart—a want of decided purpose for God. He
flatters himself that there will be a better and less hazardous
time than now—the threatening storm will have blown over
—and he will be more free for the whole-hearted service.
But the real mountain is within—"the evil heart of unbelief—the hardening deceitfulness of sin." (Heb. iii. 12, 13.)
The faithless, sluggish heart is under the power of the great
enemy, beclouding his path, palsying his strength, raising
mountains of difficulties in the way. Activity of mind,
promptness of habit, determination of purpose--let all be
brought into exercise under the overcoming power of a living
faith. It is a great work of self-possession to rise above
present discouragement—not to magnify every trifling difficulty, or to start objections against present duty. This is
only " the slothful man" planting " his hedge of thorns" or
crying out in cowardly fear—" There is a lion in the way—
a lion in the streets." (Prov. xv. 19 ; xxii. 13.)

This well-regulated habit will bring a deep and vital influence for good over our whole character. The trifling discouragements of the *winds and the clouds* are the appointed
trials of faith. And when does our God honour faith, till he
has first tried it? Or when does he fail to honour it, either
in the trial or out of it?* How little should we have known
of the power of faith, the privilege of prayer, the preciousness
of the promises, the faithfulness and sympathy of the
Saviour, if difficulties had not shewn to us our weakness, and
made the Gospel a Divine reality to our souls! The victory
over the lesser difficulties strengthens us in conflict with the
greater. The 'triumph will be complete, and the crown
glorious.

Still an halting spirit quenches the glow of Christian
energy. Feeble effort ensures defeat. One prompt, practical
exercise is worth an hour's deliberation. Do not despise the
smallest success. Five minutes' prayer for this object may be
worth a world. Our present happiness — so far as we realize
it — consists in an intelligent and affectionate preference of
God — solemnly — deliberately choosing him, in opposition to
everything that is constantly drawing us from him. There
is no indecision here. Trifling discouragements have now no
weight. They are cast upon God — not that they may be
removed, but that enduring perseverance may be vouchsafed
under them. *Wind and clouds* no more hinder work. ' *When
God calls — when grace moves — when the heart feels — when
Christ is nigh* — there may be then risks and difficulties, both
wind and *clouds;* yet that is the time for sowing, and that
the time of reaping; that is " the accepted time, and that the
day of salvation." ' †

5. *As thou knowest not what is the way of the spirit, nor how*

* See 1 Pet. ii. 7.
† *Sermon.* By Rev. Josiah Bateman, p. 237.

the bones do grow in the womb of her that is with child ;
even so thou knowest not the works of God, who maketh all.

Another humbling and valuable recollection of human
ignorance! Man prides himself upon what he knows, or
fancies he knows—the extent of his knowledge. Much
more reason has he to be humbled for the far wider extent of
his ignorance. He does not see the harvest from the distribution of his charity. But his ignorance does not disprove
the fact. How little does he know of the things before his
eyes! How ignorant are we of our own being! So "fearfully and wonderfully made!" so "curiously wrought!"
(Ps. cxxxix. 12–14.) The attempt to comprehend one's
self conquers our understanding. Anatomical experiments
may bring out some facts. Questions may be asked. But
they can only be answered by the confession of our ignorance
—*the way of the spirit,* or the human soul—how it is formed
—whence it comes—whether by the immediate creation of
God—how it is conveyed into and animates the body—the
formation of the body itself—*how the bones* (without which
we should only creep as worms) are jointed and *grow in the
womb*—the union of the soul with the body—of the imma-
terial spirit with the gross corporeal substance—in all this
the soul is a mystery to itself. *We know not the way.*

If, then, we cannot know him in his ordinary works of
nature—in his works near at home—much less *can we know
the works of God, who maketh all.* Truly he "doeth great
things and unsearchable; marvellous things without numbers." (Job, v. 9.) 'Our wisdom is but as a drop in the
bucket—yea, but a drop in the ocean. Can our drop compare with his ocean? A bucket shall as soon take in the
ocean, as man the wisdom of God.'*

And ought not this sense of ignorance to furnish a con-

* Caryl *on Job,* xxviii. 14.

vincing reply to many things that are called objections to
Revelation? When tempted to pry—'On such subjects'
—said a serious thinker—'I have no confidence in reason. I
trust only in faith; and as far as we ought to enquire, I
have no guide but Revelation.' * We should indeed be prepared in this *Terra Incognita* to expect difficulties; nor
should we forget our own nature, by insisting upon a view
of things to our beclouded reason wholly free from difficulty.
If we have not complete evidence *according to our measure*,
should we not be thankful for any measure that may be
vouchsafed; instead of rejecting the guidance of the lesser
light, because it was not the sun itself? † *Knowledge of God's
works* is valuable, just so far as it is connected with a sense
of our own ignorance, and an earnest application for Divine
Teaching and practical obedience. We have been well reminded—'To dare to believe less, or to pretend to understand more, than God has expressly revealed, is equally profane presumption. We should study to be wise—not *above*
Scripture, but *in* Scripture; not in the things which God
has *concealed*, but what he has revealed.' ‡

6. *In the morning sow thy seed; and in the evening withhold
not thine hand; for thou knowest not whether shall prosper,
either this or that; or whether they both shall be alike
good.*

The seed sown upon the prepared soil promises a rich
harvest. "Sow to yourselves"—saith the prophet—"in
righteousness; reap in mercy." (Hos. x. 12.) *The morning
and evening* work mark the diligence—" instant in season—
out of season." (2 Tim. iv. 2.) The active exercise of

* Sir Humphry Davy's Collected Works, vol. ix. p. 381.
† See Bp. Butler's *Sermon on Human Ignorance.*
‡ *Detached Thoughts* from Abp. Whately's Writings, p. 60.

charity seems to be the lesson primarily inculcated.* For ' deeds of charity are the seeds of the harvest of eternal life.'† The uncertainty as to particular results—*whether this or that* —instead of bringing doubts and difficulties, quickens to diligence. The *morning and evening* imply also the continu-ousness of the exercise. Charity is too often a fitful impulse, rather than the daily habit. It must not be confined to alms-giving, which is the mere external work. But let it be with it, or without it—in every way. Lose no time—no oppor-tunity. A wide field lies before us. Do the Lord's work in *the morning of life; and in the evening withhold not thy hand.* It may be given you to be weary of life—not of well-doing—nor of life, so far as it may be filled up to the end with fruitful godliness. Leave the result of your work in the hands of your gracious God. " In due season we shall reap, if we faint not." There is no uncertainty as to the end in the work of God. (Gal. vi. 9.) The question is not whether *any* shall prosper—but what the measure — *whether this or that—or whether both shall be alike good.* " To him that soweth righteousness shall be a sure reward." (Prov. xi. 18.)

But the Scriptural figure seems to point to a more de-finite application. " The sower soweth the word." (Mark, iv. 18.) When ? *In the morning* of life. The value of the seed sown in the hearts of the young is beyond all calcula-tion. If the type or character of the young be ignorance, it is not absolute hardness—the fruit of nature indeed, but not of nature hardened by habit. Let them know what the world is—a mere bauble—or worse ; what the hope of the Gospel is—full of joy and immortality ; what are their wants—what their resources. With all the heedlessness of youth—its volatility and self-will : in many a case the listlessness will be roused—the vacant look brightened into

* Comp. 2 Cor. ix. 6–10.   † Diodati.

intelligence—the stubbornness disciplined by conviction.
There is, indeed, a world of sorrow and temptation before
them. But a new and bright colouring is given to their
prospect. Provision is made for the roughness of the road.
A Friend is engaged on their side—A Guide, Guard, and
Father, who will never leave nor forsake.

Nor let this work be confined to the *morning*. Let
vigour of perseverance hold on to *the evening*. Shut out
despondency—the extinguisher of faith. The cases of long
standing in hardness may soften. The freeness of the Gospel
is Omnipotent love. And many a high thought and proud
imagination have given way to its attractive power. We do
not forget that this cheering prospect is connected—not
with the mechanism of the means, but with the unction
and blessing from above. And yet does not hope rise to
certainty in the exercise of faith, diligence, patience, and
prayer ? We do not presume to determine *whether shall
prosper — either this or that*—what word of instruction may
work the Divine purpose. But we know, that as the natural
harvest is not lost, though a portion of the crop may perish ;
so the promise of the spiritual harvest is linked with the
use of the means, sealed in the covenant of God, and can
never disappoint. The sovereignty of God reserves the
means and times to himself. But his faithfulness secures
the substance of his promise to the obedience and diligence
of faith—and oh ! the joy of harvest—will it not abundantly compensate for the toil ?

7. *Truly light is sweet ; and a pleasant thing it is to the eyes
to behold the sun. 8. But if a man live many years, and
rejoice in them all ; yet let him remember the days of
darkness ; for they shall be many. All that cometh is
vanity.*

Solomon, drawing to the close of his discourse, brings

us nearer to eternity, and presses closely the matter of preparation for it. Present comfort is indeed admitted: *Truly light is sweet : and a pleasant thing it is to the eyes to behold the sun.* His rising is the most magnificent spectacle in the creation. His course — how it enlightens — warms — fertilizes — beautifies—blesses—filling the air with songs, and the gardens with foliage, fruit, and fragrance ! Thus to enjoy *the light of the sun*—our present earthly comfort—is *sweet* to those whose hearts centre in earth : how much more to those, who by Solomon's rules have obtained wisdom to be delivered from the vanity and vexation so deeply connected with the best of this world's blessings.

When we see the insect enjoying the bright *sun* — expanding its wings, and spending his little day in fluttering from flower to flower, who does not enjoy its pleasures ? Who would cloud or shorten them, by reminding it that its happy life would soon pass away—that the winter with *its days of darkness* must come — and perhaps ere its arrival, some premature cold or rain may end its existence. The present is its all. And therefore we gladly say of it—' Let it sip the sweet, and revel in the light and warmth ; for to-morrow it dies.' And if man had no future—if the present were *his* all—we should say too of him—' Let him enjoy the good things of life—Let him crown himself with rose-buds, before they be withered*—Let him eat and drink ; for to-morrow he dies.' (1 Cor. xv. 32.)

And thus it is ; while the sun shines upon the earthly horizon, *the evil days* are put to a distance. We can scarcely admit the possibility of a change of scene. We exclude the prospect of *dark days* as an unwelcome intruder. The young revel in their pleasure—in the gay enjoyment, as if it would never end. But oh ! the folly—the presumption of creatures born for an eternal existence—and to whom the

* See *Wisdom of Solomon*, ii. 8.

present life is but the preparation-time for a never-ending
one, and to whom death is but the door of eternity—so
wilfully shutting their eyes to this near approach—determining to live for this life only, and to let eternity take
its chance !

But whatever be the *sweetness* of the present prosperity
—*though we live many years,* and—comparatively speaking
—*rejoice in them all ;* yet remember—what is beyond !
Days of darkness—many—how *many !* how *dark !* To the
man of God, indeed, all is *light,* whatever his outward *days*
may be. " Light is sown for the righteous, and springeth
up out of darkness." (Ps. xcvii. 10 ; cxii. 4.) A better *sun*
than that in the earthly firmament "rises upon him—with
healing in his wings." (Mal. iv. 2.) But the case here supposed—at least mainly so—is one, who finds all " his good
things" here,* and looks for nothing beyond—who has never
put forth one hearty effort upon his soul's salvation—scarcely
spent a solemn thought upon it—prepared only to live—not
to die. *Days of darkness*—at least towards the close of life
—(Chap. xii. 1)—must be calculated upon—the bloom of
health blasted by disease—the seeds of some incurable
malady shooting up—worldly disappointments corroding the
mind—nature gradually sinking under the weight of years
—the natural power to enjoy gone—(Job, x. 21, 22)—
the fatal stroke of death upon some object of the tenderest
affection. And without the consolations of the Bible, how
many and dark will their days be !—as the darkness of the
grave !—(Job, x. 21, 22)—the banishment from light !—
from the presence and favour of God !—(Ps. xlix. 19 ; 2
Thess. i. 9)—the " outer darkness—the blackness of darkness for ever !" (Matt. xxii. 13 ; Jude, 13.) The *sweetness
of the light—the pleasantness of the sun*—for a moment—
how short a moment—what a miserable compensation for

* Luke, xvi. 25. Comp. xii. 18–20; Job, xxi. 7–13.

the after *darkness !* The poverty of the choicest earthly pleasures as a centre of rest, when all is *dark* beyond—*many days*—never ending ! " Woe unto you that are rich; for ye have received your consolation ! Woe unto you that are full, for ye shall hunger. Woe unto you that laugh now, for ye shall mourn and weep." (Luke, vi. 21, 23, 24, 25.) Soon will the despised portion of God's people shine forth in all the glories of eternity. " Then shall the righteous shine forth as the sun in the kingdom of their Father." (Matt. xiii. 47.) Empty in contrast with it is the best of earth's treasures—" O my soul, thou hast said unto the Lord, Thou art my God.—All my springs are in Thee." (Ps. xvi. 2 ; lxxxvii. 7.)—*All that cometh* from any source beside Thee—*is vanity.*

9. *Rejoice, O young man, in thy youth ; and let thy heart cheer thee in the day of thy youth ; and walk in the way of thy heart, and in the sight of thine eyes : but know that for all these things God will call thee into judgment.* 10. *Therefore remove sorrow from thy heart, and put away evil from thy flesh : for childhood and youth is vanity.*

It is not natural for the *young man* to think of *the many days of darkness.* His spirits are buoyant. His senses are full of glow. His imagination is warm with the bright colouring of opening life. There is indeed a becoming grace in the liveliness of youth. And most readily would we shew him all the over-flowing pleasures, which the Bible fully allows, and which the last *judgment* will not condemn. And, indeed, we cannot doubt, but the exhortation to *joy and cheerfulness* would be most cordially welcome, if Solomon's meaning did not speak too clearly in the opposite direction —giving an apparent license, only to ground upon it a most solemn admonition.

Obviously, therefore, the wise man is referring to excessive indulgence. The pleasures of sin—not of godliness, are described by the *walk after the way of our heart—and the sight of our eyes.** Here are the ' baits, with which Satan tricketh up all his temptations, when he layeth wait for our souls.' † And *for all these things*—we are warned—*God will bring us into judgment.*

If, then, unlawful gratification be the subject, the exhortation to *rejoice and be cheerful* in it cannot be intended—but emphatically the very contrary. It is in truth the language —not unusual in Scripture‡—of deep—solemn—cutting irony; not pouring oil upon the flame, but restraining the vehement excitement of the passion struggling for indulgence. When argument, exhortation—and pleading have been tried—and tried in vain, the shaft of irony sometimes becomes a weapon of effective conviction. ' Thoughtless *young man*—thou art determined to *rejoice in thy youth.* Thou hast no idea of *cheering thine heart,* but in carnal enjoyments. Go on in thy course. Indulge thine appetite. Gratify all thy passions. Throw contempt upon the warnings of conscience, and the authority of the Bible. But count the cost—think at what a risk—*know thou*—the day of jollity will not last for ever—you may have your pleasure to-day—but the day of reckoning is at hand. *For all these things God will call thee into judgment.'*

Fearful, indeed, must be the peril to the *young man* from persisting in his own way, when to a man of God—perhaps young in years, but matured in grace—the warning was deemed to be needful—" Flee youthful lusts." (2 Tim. ii. 22.) The poison is suited to every diversity of taste. *The*

* See Num. xv. 39. Deut. xxix. 19. Jer. vii. 24.

† Bp. Sanderson's *Sermon on Eccl.* vii. 1.

‡ See 1 Kings, xviii. 27 ; xxii. 15. Ez. xxviii. 3, 4. Matt. xxvi. 44, 45. Comp. also from the mouth of God, Gen. iii. 22.

young man, ere ever he is aware, becomes in this atmosphere the "companion of fools." And whether these fools be unprincipled, licentious, ungodly scoffers; or degraded — unblushing infidels — all have the same object in view — the destruction of their devoted victim.

The fact is, that *the young man* too often has no idea what temptation is. He realizes no need of any special warning. He fancies himself well able to be his own keeper. He has never allowed the thought, that none but God is capable of knowing what he is, if he be left to himself. Let him take his Bible, and learn by it what he has yet to learn — the knowledge of himself. He will then realize something more distinctly awakening of the infinite peril of staying one moment on Satan's ground, while conscience is speaking to him — that sin is much more easily resisted at the beginning than in the progress — that his true prosperity begins at the moment, when he engages his heart to God — that sin and happiness can never be identified — that pleasure for a moment only — there may be in the ways of sin — but happiness can never be. The man who is only half-hearted for God, may soon become a man fully on Satan's side — and where can be his happiness? Compromising with the world, he is trifling with his highest interests — he is grasping at two shadows — the world and a worldly religion. Between these shadows — he loses the substance — loses heaven — loses his own soul. Most accurately is *the young man's* course described as *the way of his own heart.* Hence all the wandering — all the misery. Wisely did a Christian mother write on this point : — ' As self-will is the root of all sin and misery ; so whatever cherishes this in children ensures their after-wretchedness and irreligion ; whatever checks and mortifies it, promotes their future happiness and piety. This is still more evident, if we further consider, that religion is nothing else than the

doing the will of God, and not our own : that the one
grand impediment to our temporal and eternal happiness
being this self-will, no indulgence of it can be trivial, no
denial unprofitable.   Heaven or hell depends upon this ;
so that the parent, who studies to subdue it in his child,
works together with God in the renewing and saving a soul ;
the parent who indulges it does the devil's work ; makes
religion impracticable, and salvation unattainable.'*

While, indeed, man "turneth every man to his own way,"
(Isa. liii. 6,) the honey of indulgence passes away, but the
sting remains behind.   Whether it be physical or intellectual
happiness, if it be sought as an end, there must be vanity.
The unwelcome thought forces itself, notwithstanding all
the smothering of conviction.   *Judgment to come.*—This is
no dream, or " cunningly devised fable "—no terrific picture
—no theory for vain sophistry to explain away.   Guilt fore-
bodes it.   Conscience confirms it.   The Bible declares it.
It will be a personal matter.   God will *call thee* to judgment.
The extent will be universal.   *For all these things*—for all
the sins and vanities of *thy youth*—for all those things,
which are now so grateful to our senses—for all our time,
talents — opportunities — their use or abuse.†   Actions
forgotten by ourselves will rise up with all their freshness.
Even where traces had been worn out, our past history will
be read again—the manifestation of all hearts—of all the
secrets of all hearts.   Willing or unwilling, we must stand
before the great white throne (Rev. xx. 11, 12) alone in the
midst of the countless throng—no evasion—no escape—
no shelter—(Ib. vi. 15—17)—no advocate—no change—
the curse of God—the entrance into an eternity of woes.

What, then, is the present—the only—way of escape ?
Separate thyself from sin, ere sin bind thee to hell.   *Remove*

* Letter of Mrs. Wesley to her Son, the Rev. John Wesley. See
Dr. A. Clarke's *Life of the Wesleys.*   † See chap. xii. 14.

sorrow and evil from thee. They are both linked together.*
Evil brings *sorrow* both to body and soul. Let there be an
instant tearing away from besetting indulgences. *Childhood
is vanity*—because it has so little power for good—*youth*—
because such active power for evil. The world passeth away,
and the lust thereof. (1 John, ii. 17.) ' *Youth* is but as the
aurora, or early morning of a day—quickly gone, from
thence to noon, and from noon to night. Therefore care
should be taken to spend it in such a manner, as that we
may have an abiding fruit and pleasure, which will not
vanish with the years, which were consumed in the pursuance
of it.'† *Childhood* is indeed *vanity,* because children are
often trifling in serious things, and serious in trifles. *Youth
is vanity,* because so often preferring *vanity* to godliness—
eager in delusive expectations. Who does not yearn over
their best interests, and long to sweep away their false hopes,
and their delusive charms ? The heart turned from its own
way, and turned to God, brings the substance of happiness,
instead of the shadow—the reality, instead of the name.
Youth devoted to sin is the saddest — *youth* consecrated to God
is the brightest—object in a world of darkness and sorrow.

CHAPTER XII.

1. *Remember now thy Creator in the days of thy youth, while
the evil days come not, nor the years draw nigh, when thou
shalt say, I have no pleasure in them.*

THIS earnest and affectionate exhortation continues the preceding chapter. Solomon had warned *the young man* by

---

* See Prov. xiv. 13 ; v. 11, 12.   † Bp. Reynolds.

emphatic irony against those passions and pleasures, to which his slippery age is most addicted. Now for the grand object set before him—*thy Creator*. For he who created the universe is the Creator of man—not only of the first man, but of all men, whose birth—however natural—was only wrought by his Omnipotent and Sovereign influence. For not only did he "form the spirit in man" (Zech. xii. 1), but his body also—so fearfully and wonderfully made (Ps. cxxxix. 14–16). It is he, and no other, who is here presented before us—*the Creator*—the Almighty—the only wise—the chief good—in whose name we were baptized (Matt. xxviii. 19) —to whose service we are consecrated. For if we be of him, should not we be for him ? Do not we owe our service to him, from whom we have received our being ? If he has made us—much more if he has new-made us—what a weight of obligation ! We cannot resist it. Each Person in the Sacred Trinity equally claims our interest and our service.*

This *remembrance of God*—though our paramount duty —is far from being our nature and habit. What says conscience ? Is not forgetfulness of God our course—keeping him out of mind—like the heathen—" not liking to retain God in our knowledge ?" (Rom. i. 28.) Alas ! do we not naturally make every effort to shrink from him ? The heart too plainly witnesses to this revolt. ' Any opinion which tends to keep out of sight the living and loving God—whether it substitute for him an idol, or an occult agency, or a formal creed—can

* The best critics insist upon *Creators* as being the strict and accurate rendering—a plural appellation of God—intimating a plurality of persons in the Godhead. The same construction, Gen. i. 26. Job, xxxv. 10. Ps. cxlix. 2. Isa. liv. 5. Witsius remarks, that 'although we are all created by the one power and action of one God, and so have only one Creator ; yet there are more Divine Persons to whom creative power and action is ascribed.'—*On Eccl.* xii. 1–7. *Misc. Sacra*, vol. ii. vi. See the work ascribed to the Father, Gen. i. 1 ; the Son, John, i. 3 ; the Spirit, Job, xxvi. 13. Ps. civ. 30.

be nothing else than a portentous shadow projected from the selfish darkness of the unregenerate heart.' * Our concern is with the God of the Bible. To worship any other is to deify the creature of our own imagination.

The *remembrance of our Creator* is in connexion with every godly exercise. Does a day ever pass in the wilful neglect of the Bible without serious loss ? Do we not suffer seriously in our own souls by giving too little time—too little heart—to secret prayer ? Wherever God can be found, let us be in the act and energy of seeking him. 'Acknow-ledge'—as one says—'his *Word,* by consulting it—his *Providence,* by observing it—his *Wisdom,* by admiring it—his *Sovereignty,* by acquiescing in it—his *Faithfulness,* by relying on it—his *Kindness,* by being thankful for it.' †

Who of us will doubt the claim, which God makes upon us for constant *remembrance?* It is the duty bound upon all men—every age—every time. The whole of our time is not our own but God's.‡ And lest there should be only a moment in our life subtracted from his claim—the exhort-ation directs—" Be thou in the fear of the Lord *all the day long.*" (Prov. xxiii. 17. Also Ps. xvi. 8.) Yet there is one season of special application—*the days of thy youth.* Here, however, the great enemy meets us with the ungodly adage— ' *Youth* for pleasure—age for business—old age for religion.' ' Let the devil have the prime, and God the dregs. Time enough to think of religion when we are old—when we can serve the world no longer. Now is the time for pleasure —to see as much of life as we can. Religion will come

* A. H. Hallam—quoted in Dr. Tweedie's *Lights and Shadows in the Life of Faith*—an interesting volume. Edinburgh.

† Witsius brings quotations from some of the more enlightened heathen philosophers (*e. g.* the Emperor Antoninus—' the Solomon of the Romans ') bearing—alas! in the shadow only—upon this exhortation.—*Miscell. Sacra,* vol. ii. *Exerc.* vi. vii. &c.

‡ See Ps. lxxiv. 16.

in course.' Frightful delusion! the delusion of him who
"is a liar, and the father of it.". (John, viii. 44.)

Who then shall have the present *now* — the only sure part
of life? If any man can shew a better title to *youth* than
God, let him bring it. Meanwhile the call is: Let manna
be gathered early in the day. Let *youth's* days be choice
days—choosing days. Oh! what a mercy—when the two
masters are claiming our service—to be enabled to make the
choice—not as the slave of sin—but the happy child of God
—the youthful witness for his name! This is the bright
star in the dark night of a miserable world. What minister
would not delight in a galaxy of these stars in his spiritual
horizon?

Do we want any argument to enforce the present *remembrance of our Creator?* Think of the *evil days* at hand—
not necessarily days of moral—but of painful—evil without
natural *pleasure;* and, as one remarks—'If thou wilt
have God to pity and help thee in *evil days,* thou must
serve him in thy good days.'* Old age, with all its train
and retinue of weakness and infirmities, will come. But if it
bends thy back, do not keep thine iniquities to *break it.* Since
the days of old age will be *evil days,* lay up as many graces
as thou canst to sweeten it—as many comforts as thou canst
to strengthen thine heart against the evils of it. Gather in
summer against such a winter as this (Prov. x. 5), that old
age may not be to thee an *evil* age, but as it was to Abraham
"a good old age"† as respects the natural evils. "I am
this day"—says one, speaking from painful experience of
these *pleasureless* days—"fourscore years old, and can I discern between good and evil? Can thy servant taste what I
eat, and what I drink? Can I hear any more of singing men
and singing women?" (2 Sam. xix. 35.)

---

* Bp. Reynolds.   † Ib.

Such *days* will come, and when they come without God, *evil* indeed they are—days of painful weariness, and dark foreboding. 'I am determined'—said a worn-out man of pleasure—'to kill time in the speediest way I can, now that it is become my greatest enemy.'* Is it not then the part of the prudent man—"foreseeing the evil"—to provide against it —to have a staff to lean upon, that will bear his whole weight; when "the earthly house of this tabernacle is dissolving, to know that he has a building of God—an house not made with hands—eternal in the heavens?" (2 Cor. v. 1.) The time then before the *evil* days come—which may draw out to years—is the time for God—*for the remembrance of our Creator.* Every day is lost that is not spent for him. Let not the deceiver cheat us out of all time, by cheating us of the present time. 'Believe me, my dear son'—writes a Christian mother† lately alluded to—'old age is the worst time we can choose to mend either our lives or our fortunes. If the foundations of solid piety are not laid betimes in sound principles and virtuous dispositions; and if we neglect, while strength and vigour last, to lay up something ere the infirmities of old age overtake us—it is an hundred to one odds, that we shall die both poor and wicked.'

Early principle inwrought in the inner man is therefore the line of temporal—(so this mother in Israel lays down)— no less than of spiritual prosperity. As to the latter—in the *evil* days when we shall say, 'I have no natural *pleasure*,'— God's pleasures will still remain—full—fresh—heavenly— abiding. There will indeed be no *dark and evil* days. "My flesh and my heart faileth; but God is the strength of my heart, and my portion for ever." (Ps. lxxiii. 26.)

---

* Lord Chesterfield in pp. 5, 6.

      'Oh, the dark days of vanity! while here
        How tasteless! and how terrible when gone!'—YOUNG.

† Mrs. Wesley, *ut supra.*

What better can we do, than take those exquisite words from Charles Wesley's dying lips?—

> 'In age and feebleness extreme,
> Who shall a helpless worm redeem?
> Jesus: my only hope thou art;
> Strength of my failing flesh and heart.
> O let me catch a smile from thee,
> And drop into eternity.'

2. *While the sun, or the light, or the moon, or the stars, be not darkened, nor the clouds return after the rain.*

These *evil days* are yet further described—a mental gloom, as if—like Job—we were going " mourning without *the sun*" (Job, xxx. 29), or as if the lesser luminaries were eclipsed, as in the Apostle's voyage, " when neither *sun, nor stars,* in many days appeared; and all hope that we should be saved was taken away." (Acts, xxvii. 20.) Another feature of the desolation—not " the shining," but *the clouds return-ing—after the rain*—a tempestuous sky—one cloud follow-ing another—one evil treading upon another—the end of one trouble —the beginning of another.

Such is the general picture of old age—in its gradual weak-ness of nature—decaying of sense—weakness of physical energy. One cannot wonder that the heathen philosopher— knowing nothing of its divine alleviations—should describe it as ' a load that lies heavier than Mount Ætna.'* Cheerless indeed it is without religion—earthly comforts withering like the plants in the desert—nothing to supply their place— leaving one world, with no hope or joy for another. And is this time of darkness the season to begin the service of God, which asks for man's energy in his best estate?

---

* ' Onus se Ætnâ gravius dicant sustinere.'—*Cicero de Senectute.*

Let us look then—What resources have we to meet this last stage of life? 'No sun can dispel *the clouds* and sorrows of old age, but Christ, who is the Sun of Righteousness.'* They roll along the stormy sky. Let every intermission of the trouble bring in solemn—active preparation for the last great storm—storing the heart with such *remembrance of our Creator,* as may be a stay, when all is sinking around us. The presence of the chief good will sweep away threatening evil. "The hoary head, if found in the way of righteousness," is indeed "a crown of glory." (Prov. xvi. 31.)

3. *In the day, when the keepers of the house shall tremble; and the strong men shall bow themselves, and the grinders cease, because they are few; and those that look out of their windows be darkened. 4. And the door shall be shut in the streets, when the sound of the grinding is low; and he shall rise up at the voice of the bird; and all the daughters of music shall be brought low. 5. Also, when they shall be afraid of that which is high; and fears shall be in the way; and the almond-tree shall flourish; and the grasshopper shall be a burden, and desire shall fail; because man goeth to his long home; and the mourners go about the streets. 6. Or ever the silver cord be loosed, or the golden bowl be broken, or the pitcher be broken at the fountain, or the wheel broken at the cistern.*

The last verse is a prelude to this elegant and figurative picture of old age. Criticism has wasted much useless ingenuity in its explanation. The more common interpretation—apart from one or two doubtful points—is mainly satisfactory. Solomon had before given a general view. He now enters into particulars—the succession of pains and discomfort, which usually belong to this period of life. Such a

* Bp. Reynolds.

picture of infirmity! sometimes sinking almost to the level of mere animal existence. Yet upon this feeble stay are often borne the vast concerns of eternity. That which ought to be filling the most vigorous energy of life is delayed to the last stage of an enfeebled habit!

The figure is that of a house—" the house of clay"— the "earthly house of this tabernacle" (Job, iv. 19. 2 Cor. v. 1)—its gradual dissolution—every part in decay—hastening to ruin. *The keepers of the house* evidently represent the hands and arms hanging down in tremulous weakness "in age"—the time when our " strength faileth."* *The strong men bowing* picture the legs and thighs—before so robust— now beginning to bend under a burden hitherto carried with vigour. (Isa. xxxv. 3.) In *the grinders,* we see the teeth performing the millstone work for our food, cutting the meat, and breaking it into small pieces, preparing it for the digestion and turning it into nourishment. Yet even here, when *the grinders are few,* the masticating labour makes the meals a daily drudgery. Still more grievous is the trial, when *they that look out of the windows are darkened*—a very common affliction—when the eyes looking through the socket are dim, so that they cannot see, or see only indistinctly.† The prospect is a blot—all is mist and shadow—all pleasures of reading are more and more fading. To supply this failure— even the kindly effort of public reading is defeated by the dulness of hearing. *The doors are shut in the streets.* The opening for the mutual intercourse is barred up—and though unnatural effort may partially *open the door,* yet it is a poor compensation for the easy-flowing pleasures of younger and brighter days. The door of speech as well as of hearing is shut up. *The sound of the grinding is low.* The loss of the

* See Ps. lxxi. 9. Also Zech. viii. 4.

† See Gen. xxvii. 1. Comp. xlviii. 10. 1 Sam. iii. 2. 1 Kings, xiv. 4. Contrast Deut. xxxiv. 7. Josh. xiv. 10, 11.

teeth affects the speech.* The impaired organ sounding *low* deprives social life of half its charms. Early wakefulness is another trial. Sleep is no longer 'tired nature's sweet restorer.'† *He rises up at the noise of the bird*—not " going forth to his work and to his labour" (Ps. civ. 23), but in feeble weariness. *All the daughters of music shall be brought low*. The lungs—the voice—the ear—the organs employed in the production or enjoyment of it *shall be brought low*—as in the case of Barzillai—utterly incapable of performing their functions. 'By these defects we are instructed in the days of our youth, to open all the doors of our heart, to let Christ in; that in old age he may be with us, and when our appetite faileth, he may sup with us (Rev. iii. 20); and when our sleep faileth, he may give us rest; and when all other delights are worn out, a good conscience may be a continual feast, and may " give songs in the night." '‡

The picture proceeds—marking the feebleness of the feet. *They shall be afraid of that which is high.* Every ascent— which in earlier days they had bounded with youthful elasticity—becomes a trouble. They have lost their enterprize. *The fears* of stumbling in the way are a matter of apprehension. " The hoary head" is *like an almond-tree*—covered with its snow-white blossoms.§ So extreme is the feebleness, that —proverbially speaking—*the grasshopper*—even in its lightest hop, *is a burden*. *The desire faileth*—even for the world of pleasure—in which Solomon had attempted to find or to

---

* See the connexion in the fine description of Leviathan. Job, xli. 14.

† Young.   ‡ Bp. Reynolds.

§ 'The almond-tree is here a resemblance of an " hoary head ;" yet with this difference. 1. The almond-tree flourisheth in the spring ; "the hoary head " in the winter of our age. 2. The tree flourisheth before fruit ; but the head flourisheth after it. And yet it may indeed be said, that " the hoary head " is the flourishing of the old man in the spring of another world of immortality.'—*Cotton*.

make a centre of rest. (Chap. ii.)   "The world passeth
away, and the lust thereof" (1 John, iii. 17)—all is passed
away with the glowing warmth, or the vigour of maturity.
How quickly does old age sweep away the comfort in them !
A dream ! a dream !   Alas ! such a dream as will bring to
the *now* deluded sleeper—the voice of cutting eternal consciousness—" Son, remember ! " (Luke, xvi. 25.) And what
does this affecting picture prove?—man is close to the end
of his journey.   "The earthly house of tabernacle" is falling
to pieces.   The inhabitant is on the brink of *his long home.**
And *the mourners go about the streets.*   The Jewish custom
of public or hired *mourners* was probably referred to—a
mercenary, because unnatural sorrow—a burden indeed to
our secrecies and sympathies.   Thus did they honour Josiah,
who so well deserved honour from his people.†   With us the
picture is but too familiar; yet still it is the profitable
picture *in the streets* of a world of sorrow.   ' Since the grave
is our *longest* home, let our greatest fare be to have that a
home of rest and of hope unto us.' ‡

The imagery of the next verse—beautiful as it is—presents some difficulties in the interpretation.   It evidently
describes the *loosing* of the inexplicable bond of union between the body and soul.   Hitherto we have seen the gradual
wasting.   We have now come to the final struggle—the
extinction of the vital principle.   The figure appears to be
that of drawing water from the well.   Here is the *cord*
(called *silver,* and the *bowl—gold* for preciousness)—*the
bowl* or bucket—*the pitcher and a wheel.*   As, when these
are broken, we can draw water no more ; so when the vital
parts are decayed, there is no hope to draw life into *the cistern*

* See Job, vii. 9, 10.
† 2 Chron. xxxv. 25.   Comp. Jer. ix. 17. Matt. ix. 23.
‡ Bp. Reynolds.

of the body. Here then is the moment of death.* *Then shall the dust return* —

Such are the *evil and dark days*—the days of feebleness and trouble—the last stage of mortality—man sinking under the infirmities of dissolving nature. "Their very strength is labour and sorrow." (Ps. xc. 10.) To advert again to an instance before alluded to—'I used to think'—said Sir W. Scott, in his last desolate hours—'a slight illness was a luxurious thing . . . It is different in the latter stages. The old post-chaise gets more shattered at every turn. Windows will not pull up. Doors refuse to open; or, being opened, will not shut again. There is some new subject of complaint every moment. Your sicknesses come thicker and thicker . . . . The recollection of youth, health, and uninterrupted power of activity, neither improved nor enjoyed, is a poor stream of comfort. Death hath closed the long dark avenue upon loves and friendships; and I look at them, as through the grated door of a burial-place, filled with monuments of those who were once dear to me, with no insincere wish, that it may open for me at no distant period, provided such be the will of God.'

Can we then too soon provide against these *evil days*— *or ever*—the last days come upon us in darkness? Is it time to begin the service of God, when we have scarcely power to serve ourselves?† Have we a heart to give—a heart glowing with the first love—with the freshness of the

---

* Bp. Reynolds and Scott agree with this exposition; Dr. Wardlaw elaborately describes the anatomy of the picture. But Mr. Holden considers it to be 'the sole intention of the writer to describe the cessation of those animal functions which are observable to every beholder.' He remarks, that medical knowledge, from the want of the practice of dissection among the Greeks, could not have shown the effect of age on the human constitution with anatomical accuracy. —*In loco*, and *Preliminary Dissertation*, sect. v.

† Bp. Patrick.

morning dew? Oh! let it be given to Him, who claims it as
the purchase of his blood — as his inalienable property — an
acceptable sacrifice for his service.   He loveth — not only "a
cheerful," but an early "giver."   He gives himself — an
unspeakable portion! — to them who give themselves to him.
If ever the cord be loosed, bind the exhortation upon thy
heart.   Remember *now — thy Creator* — in thy best days —
the days of thy youth.   Many have *remembered* too late —
none too soon.   It is the work of the whole man — of the
whole life.

We have spoken of the darkness and infirmities of old
age, as if it were a mass of infirmity.   We must not forget,
however, that it is often a season of cheerful serenity.   The
treatise of the heathen philosopher is read with lively,
and not unprofitable, interest.*   Physical energy often
melts down into sources of quiet and enduring happiness.
The silver cord is loosed so gently and so gradually, that
little strain is felt.   But more or less of this infirmity is felt
in the ordinary course of life.   And the wise man naturally
gives the general course, rather than the exceptional cases.

Abundant above all thought is the compensation, when
the *youthful remembrance* has been heartily cultivated.   The
God *remembered in youth* will be the Friend of old age.   The
prayer of one, who had grown old in this *remembrance,* is a
confidence that can never be disappointed — " O God, thou
hast taught me from *my youth;* and hitherto have I declared
thy wondrous works.   Now also, when I am old and grey-
headed, O God, forsake me not." (Ps. lxxi. 17, 18.)   And is
not this promise the sure ground of confidence — the unfailing answer to prayer?   "Even to your old age I am he;
and to hoar hairs will I carry you; I have made, and I will
bear; even I will carry, and will deliver you." (Isa. xlv. 3, 4.)

---

* Cicero *De Senectute* — the person of Cato described in what
Witsius stamps, *aureo libello.*

What was the good old age of Abraham,* Simeon, and those
like-minded with him? It was the sun breaking through
the dark cloud—the entrance into eternal rest. And for
ourselves in the same spirit—' When one sight after another
fades away from your darkened eyes, look much more to
Jesus. For if he be your joy, your hope, your life; the
faster you are clothed with the snows of age, the sooner will
you renew your youth in the realms of immortality.'† As
an eminent dying Christian observed, ' The golden chain,
which binds the believer's heart to heaven, is waxing stronger.
Its links are growing more firm and massive. All the powers
of hell will not prevail to break them.'‡

7. *Then shall the dust return to the earth as it was; and the spirit shall return unto God who gave it.*

Here is the end of our earthly history—all the vessels
broken up—man in the stillness of death. A deep and
solemn sorrow to those left behind! Who can forbear the
pang of inexpressible tenderness, even when life had long
been burdensome, and exhausted age worn out in weariness?
Old age we may never see—nor the *dark and evil days,*
which are the harbinger of it. But whether or not—here is
the winding up of all. Death is here. But what is it after
death?—what when the last breath—the last pulsation shall
have gently died away? The two parts—body and soul—
that unite to form that wondrous workmanship—man, are
now separated. All connexion with earth is passed. Each
finds his *long home.* Both are linked with eternity.

The home of the body is whence it first came. "The
Lord God formed man of the dust of the ground." (Gen. ii. 7.)

---

* See Gen. xv. 15; xxv. 8.   Comp. 1 Chron. xxix. 28. Job, v. 26.
† Hamilton, *Lect.* xix.   ‡ *Memoir of Rev. W. H. Hewitson.*

Poor, mean material! Yet till sin came into the world, it was immortality. Sin brought the sentence of death—"Dust thou art; and unto dust shalt thou return." (Gen. iii. 19.) This sentence stands in full force. "Thou takest away their breath, they die, and *return to their dust. His breath goeth forth*; he returneth to his earth." (Ps. civ. 29; cxlvi. 4.)

Yet it *returns to the earth*—not to waste—not to be scattered and lost. There will be a reunion—for happiness or for misery — and that for eternity. Meanwhile how precious the thought, in committing our beloved ones to the earth, that every particle of the redeemed *dust* is under charge — in safe keeping — under faithful guardianship! Not an atom of it can perish. Hear the acknowledgment of the charge—"This is the Father's will which hath sent me, that of all which he hath given me I should lose nothing, but should raise it up again at the last day!" * How can this be? The Omnipotence of the Redeemer † answers every objection of reason, and subdues it to the reverence and simplicity of faith. It must be so, because he hath told it, and pledged it. When he comes, he will give account of his charge. Every atom will be brought out united to his transfigured glory; death nor hell can never make void the interest in "our adoption"—to wit—"the" complete "redemption of the body." (Rom. viii. 23; Comp. Isa. xxv. 8.) But *the spirit*, who can tell what it is, and what is its destiny? *God gave it*, when he "breathed into his nostrils the breath of life, and man became a living soul." (Gen. ii. 7; Comp. Job, xxxiii. 4.) This is the Divine testimony: 'The body indeed is the gift of God—but not the breath of God. It is not such an immediate gift of God as the soul is. When the body of man was made at first, God took the dust

---

* John, vi. 40—not none, but *nothing*.   † See Phil. iii. 21.

of the earth, and formed his body out of it. But when he gave him a soul, he breathed that from himself. It was an immediate effect of God's power, not dealing with, nor working upon any pre-existing matter. *The spirit* or soul of man is purely of God—solely of God.' *

What then is the end of all? Each part of man *returns* to his original source—his body *to the earth as it was; the spirit*—to God of whom it is, and *who gave it.* And where now is *the spirit* found? In unconscious slumber of the grave? Far from it. It *returns to God*—home whence it came—to "the Father of spirits," who claims it for himself.† The body sleeps as the earnest of awaking again. But the soul is in conscious immortality. The God of Moses was the God of the Patriarchs long departed. But we are emphatically told, that he is "not the God of the dead, but of the living; for all live to him." (Luke, xx. 37, 38.) ' " This day shalt thou be with me in Paradise" (Ib. xxiii. 43), said our Lord to the malefactor, who was dying at his side. And in what state there? Senseless and lifeless? No: alive to its glories; transported with its blessedness. And when Paul thought of being " absent from the body," what did he connect with this absence? What did he look upon as its immediate and necessary consequence? He knew that he should be "found with the Lord." ' ‡ (2 Cor. v. 6-8.)

In this sure confidence of waking consciousness did the Divine Saviour yield his *returning spirit* into his Father's hands. (Luke, xxiii. 46.) In the same confidence did he receive the spirit of his first martyr falling asleep in him. (Acts, vii. 59, 60.) There had indeed been a mist upon eternity. But the rays were bright enough to shine in the cloudy sky, and as here, to cheer the darker dispensation with

* Caryl on Job, xxxiii. 4.
† See Ezek. xviii. 4. Comp. Num. xvi. 22. Heb. xii. 9.
‡ Bradley's *Sermons*, vol. iii. p. 246.

joyous light.   The life to come was not, therefore, an unconscious world, not a world of sleep, nor the promises of it
a golden dream.   As the philosopher, adverting to the dark
clouds seen at early dawn, fringed with gold by the sun,
remarks—' They may serve as an image of the hopes of immortality derived from Revelation.   For we are sure, from the
light reflected on those clouds, that the lands below us are
in the brightest sunshine.' *

Yet the spirit's homeward *return* is for no indifferent end.
It was sent here to glorify God.   It *returns to God* to give
an account of the great end proposed.   The *return to* God is
not always " the blessed hope." (Tit. ii. 13.)   It conducted
the rich man to the immortality of torment.   It brought
Lazarus into Abraham's bosom. (Luke, xvi. 22–25.)   Oh!
let Reader and Writer ponder it with solemn anxiety.—Where
will my *return homeward to my God* fix me for eternity—
among the lost to share their despairing wail, or among the
redeemed to tune my golden harp to their triumphal songs ?
" There is but a step between us and death." (1 Sam. xx. 3.)
This step—this great step—this step of transition from time
into eternity—Oh! let it not be taken without a God—a
Guide—a Saviour.   If life has been thrown away in wasteful
folly—how awful the guilt—how imminent the danger—of
throwing away eternity with it !   " Turn ye, turn ye," is the
voice of your pleading God.   " Why will ye die ? " (Ezek.
xxxiii. 11.)

8. *Vanity of vanities, saith the Preacher, all is vanity.*

The Preacher (so he calls himself three times in these
verses) has now concluded his subject.   He had begun with
this statement as his text. (Chap. i. 2.)   The whole book
may be considered as the material and substance of his

* Sir Humphry Davy's *Consolations in Travel.*

sermon, worked out with a large variety of illustrations and proofs. He is now shutting up his discourse; and how can he do it so impressively, as by leaving his text as his last word of demonstration? He 'took an inventory of the world, and all the best things in it. He cast up the account; and the sum total is *vanity*.'* He had now brought us to the universal terminus; and now looking back — what is the prospect before him and around him but one mass of *vanity?* If this world be indeed our all, what is it? The veil of fascinating delusion is torn from us. The emptiness of all earthly pleasures—we cannot deny it. It is the complaint of bitter disappointment — *all is vanity.* Where is the ground for satisfaction? Take away the home and confidence for eternity—all is poor indeed—not only illusion, but tasteless to the last degree. Oh! let the cry be—'Put me not off with such trifles.' Let me not wrap my heart in these wretched objects of *vanity.* The Christian can find no interest here, simply because his great objects connected with eternity fill up every vacuum with solid satisfaction. And what at the end? If nothing else, we can lift up our head in the dying hour with gladness—" I know whom I have believed." (2 Tim. i. 12.)

But is *the Preacher's* sermon only fitting for the gay and thoughtless? Is it only for those whose best and most glowing affections are centred in the world, and whose stamp of character is—" lovers of pleasure more than lovers of God?" (Ib. iii. 4.) Let the most eminent saint of God look to it. Let him carefully search the heart, and see whether the world is not loved in its hidden secrecies more than is good for his soul. Let him see, whether it is not the real danger—the world living in us—not we in the world. Oh! do we not all need deeper apprehensions of its vanity even at its best show, and brighter enjoyment of the

* Bp. Horne.

substantial portion contrasted with it ? It surely was not without just cause and reason that the beloved Apostle was directed to warn—not the ungodly and dissipated—but the "little children—the young men"—nay even "the fathers" in the Church. "Love not the world, nor the things that are in the world." What ! they who had known their "sins to be forgiven"—who had "overcome the wicked one"—nay—who have been maturing in the knowledge of God and his Christ—do they need the warning ? Who in the Church that knows his own heart, but will bear testimony to the need, in deep and humbling conviction ? For have we not each a world of our own—an inner as well as an outer world, entwining itself in a countless variety of ways with our tenderest heart-strings ? Surely we have advanced only a step—if indeed so much—in the course of non-conformity, when we have turned away from the out-ward show, or when we have failed to see upon our own world the stamp— *Vanity of vanities—all is vanity.* Shall we not then value the prayerful application of this book of Scripture to our hearts ? For how graphic is the representation of "all that is in the world"—with the clear mark, that it "is not of the Father, but is of the world"—with the manifest proof before our eyes—that it "passeth away, and the lust thereof"—and with the bright contrast of the Christian's substance for eternity—"He that doeth the will of God abideth for ever !" (1 John, ii. 12–17.)

The Christian substance is indeed a fine contrast with vanity —the real with the unreal.—'The more I exaggerate'— writes the saintly Martyn—' these ideal joys, the more do I treasure up subjects of woe. O what vanity has God written upon all things under the sun ! Adored be the never-failing mercy of God ! He has made my happiness to depend— not on the uncertain connexions of this life, but upon his

* *Life,* chap. v. *Journal,* Oct. 1806.

own most blessed self—*a portion that never faileth.* ' My God '—exclaimed the holy Baxter—breathing after this soul-satisfying portion—' in thee I expect my true felicity and content. To know thee, and love thee, and delight in thee, must be my blessedness, or I must have none. The little tastes of this sweetness which my thirsty soul hath had, do tell me that there is no other real joy. He dreameth, who doth not live to thee. Oh ! let me have no other portion, no reason—no love—no life—but what is devoted to thee, employed on thee, and for thee here, and shall be perfected in thee—the only perfect, final object for evermore.' *

9. *And, moreover, because the Preacher was wise, he still taught the people knowledge ; yea, he gave good heed, and sought out, and set in order many proverbs.*

Ere *the Preacher* shuts up, he adds a few words concerning himself, calculated to give weight and authority to his sentence. His *wisdom* was the special gift of God (1 Kings, iii. 5–12)—a special talent for his people. How could he forbear the diligent use of it, as the only reparation he could make to them for the sad misuse of it, when for a time "the light that was in him was darkness," and we had been left to mourn— "how great is that darkness ?" (Matt. vi. 23.) Now, therefore, the more *wise* he was, the more ready was he *still*—to the end—*to teach the people knowledge*. Physical science in all its diversified branches might have formed the matter of his *teaching.*† But this was not his object—certainly not his main object—though to the eyes of many doubtless it would have been the more desirable one. That which attracted the Royal stranger's interest was " his wisdom concerning the name of the Lord"‡ —the

---

* *Reasons of Christian Religion,* chap. xii.
† See 1 Kings, iv. 29–33.   ‡ Ib. x. 1.

knowledge and service of God. To this he applied himself under Divine Inspiration with unwearied energy. He was not negligent in exercising the wisdom already attained. Never did he indolently rest in the discoveries of those who had gone before him. Nor did he write at random, but he took pains in laborious study—*giving good heed, and seeking out* all that was true and profitable. One exercise seemed specially to have interested him—*setting in order many proverbs.* And here, probably, was the completion of that book (with the exception of chap. xxv.–xxxi.)—such a storehouse of practical wisdom—so deep in the knowledge of the heart—so accurate in the observation of human life —"the Proverbs of Solomon—the son of David—King of Israel."*

Thus, indeed, ministers must be men of store (Matt. xiii. 52), and men of distributive activity, if they would "make full proof of their ministry." (2 Tim. iv. 5.) When their exercises are (as an old writer expresses it) 'not the children of their brain, but the travail of their soul,'† God puts honour upon such faithful and diligent workmen, and will let none of their words fall to the ground. Whatever be our station in the Church—Oh ! let it not be forgotten—that—to be fitted for mutual helpfulness, there must be a " rich indwelling treasure of the word of Christ." (Col. iii. 16.) Have we not discovered how largely we enrich ourselves, in the very exercise of distributing our treasure to the Church ? ' As the widow's oil increased, not in the vessel, but by pouring out—and as the barley-bread in the gospel multiplied, not in the whole loaf, but by breaking and distributing —and as the grain bringeth increase, not when it lieth on a heap in the garner, but by scattering upon the land ; so are these spiritual graces best improved, not by keeping them

* Prov. i. 1. See Scott's *Preface to Proverbs.*
† Swinnock's *Good Wish about the Calling of a Minister.*

together, but by distributing them abroad. The talent gathereth nothing in the napkin, unless it be rust and canker ; but travelling in the bank, beside the good it doth as it passeth to and fro, it ever returneth home *with* increase.'*

10. *The Preacher sought to find out acceptable words : and that which was written was upright — even words of truth.*

Here was his wisdom — seeking to *find out acceptable words !* Think of the great moment belonging to them— of the great care to *seek and find them out*—like the pearls in the ocean. They were not men-pleasing words — not flattering words of vanity, but such as find an easy access to the heart—" pleasing our neighbour for his good unto edification." (Rom. xv. 2.) The most considerate human wisdom can never make the humbling truth of God *acceptable* to the natural heart.* Yet crude and revolting statements may add needlessly and hurtfully to the offence. Mr. Cecil wisely remarked—' It is a foolish project to avoid *giving offence.* But it is our duty to avoid giving *unnecessary offence.*† Good taste should be connected with good things ; and the word is not *less faithfully* spoken, because it is *" more fitly* spoken." (Prov. xv. 23 ; xxv. 11.) To *seek to be acceptable*—is by no means inconsistent with faithfulness. Christian consideration directs us carefully to distribute unpalatable truth in all the sweetness of per-suasion and sympathy. We have the Preacher's warrant for this. Look but at the very outside—the shell of the letter—and we must grant that *the Preacher* hath found out pleasant words. 'The nine first chapters of Proverbs are a

* Bp. Sanderson's *Sermon on* 1 Cor. xii. 7.
† See 1 Cor. ii. 14. Comp. Isa. xxx. 10.
‡ See his *Remains*—a rich storehouse of practical wisdom.

fine specimen of this wise teaching —such love combined with Divine authority and ministerial faithfulness ! In doctrine let us shew uncorruptness — in mode accept-ableness ; like our Heavenly Master, regarding—not so much what we are able to speak, but what our people are able to hear.'*

But here lies the grand responsibility—that the suavity of the mode be never without the boldness of the matter. Let the Preacher be sure that his *acceptable words*—whether *written* or spoken—are *upright*†—*even words of truth.* Great indeed is the danger of adulterating the Gospel in the well-intentioned attempt to commend it more widely. A self-deceiving delusion indeed !—to deprive it of its saving power. And happy, indeed, is it for ministers to have the humble "rejoicing testimony of their consciences"—"We are not as many, which corrupt the word of God ; but as of sincerity ; but as of God, in the sight of God speak we in Christ. By manifestation of the truth, commending ourselves to every man's conscience in the sight of God." (2 Cor. ii. 17 ; iv. 2).

But let us look to it in our familiar Christian intercourse. Oh ! we have great need of unceasing godly exercise. Be sure that *the words of truth*—not of man's wisdom—are the weapons for conviction. Beware lest Christian accommoda-tion descend to rational contrivance. Zeal for the souls of our fellow-men must be " according to knowledge," holy simplicity, and *uprightness*—not colouring but *truth*—not disputing, but leaving upon the conscience the plain tes-timony. To live near to God, while we are walking before men, is a Divine reality. Hence flows the power to deal out *words of delight* (marg.)—in singleness of aim and object. Think of the power and weight of a kind word, as one of

---

* Author's *Christian Ministry*, Part iv. chap. vi. sect. ii.
† See Prov. viii. 8.

old — a Great Master of these words — could testify — " Even
as I please all men in all things — not seeking mine own
profit, but the profit of many, that they may be saved."
(1 Cor. x. 33.)

11. *The words of the wise are as goads, and as nails fastened
by the masters of assemblies, which are given from one
shepherd.*

What are these *words of the wise?* They are no light
words. They cannot be the maxims of human wisdom,
because — unlike these multifarious tossings — they *are
given from One* Source. This Source is He, ' on whom all
of us ought to depend and stay — the Everlasting Son of
God — the Church's Chief and Supreme *Shepherd.'* * They
must therefore be his words — ' Hereby then is marked the
Divine Inspiration of the Holy Scriptures delivered by Inspiration unto the penmen thereof for the use of the Church
— the Spirit of God being in those that wrote them.' † They
are his words, and they come from him. They are not
therefore only *partly* Inspired — and therefore only *partly*
the word of God. But it is *the Shepherd* breathing his own
mind into the mind of his several penmen ; thus preserving
the Revelation contained therein from all possibility of error ;
— and bringing out for our repose an unfaltering testimony
and an infallible appeal.

Though *the Masters,* through whom the word is *given,*
are many, the authority is *the One Shepherd.* The Prophets
— Apostles — Preachers — Ministers of all ages — of all
degrees — are separated as *the Masters of assemblies* directing the service, and stirring up the affections of the *assemblies,*
and upholding the visible glory of the Great Head and King

* Serran and Diodati.   † Bp. Reynolds.

in his Church. And how striking is the sight — each of these *Masters* receiving his Authority from the *One Shepherd* — all acting by his Authority — all, serving in dependence upon his promised grace and blessing.*

Solomon illustrates the power of *the words of the wise* by *goads* — so needful to urge on the sluggish oxen in their forward pace — turning neither to the right hand nor to the left. And who of us does not need the *goad?* Slumbering as we are in cold formality — hearing the word, as if we heard it not — what a mercy is it to feel the piercing point of *the goad,*† experimentally to know the " Scripture as profitable for reproof" (2 Tim. iii. 16) — awakening — alarming — stirring up the cry of anxious distress, " What shall we do?" (Acts, ii. 37.) Is it not fearful to be under the power of the word, and yet to continue so insensible? as if *the goad* just touched the skin, and did not penetrate the heart?

The nails also form the Shepherd's furniture to *fasten* his tent to the ground, and to make the sheepfold thoroughly secure, not less are they needed by us. If the smart of *the*

---

* There is some difficulty in the translation of the words — *Masters of assemblies.* Our own version has warranted authority. But we may advert to Holden's translation — *The Masters of Collections* (an Hebraism for collectors), those who collected and set in order *the words of the wise* — the sayings of men Divinely inspired, *given from One* Source. See Prov. xxv. 1. This gives some idea of the mode, in which the sacred canon was gradually formed. Whitaker gives a curious discussion with the Jesuit — who produced the text in proof of the Pope's authority in matters of faith, as 'the Priest of the New Testament.' — *Disputations on Scripture,* pp. 422, 423. See also Lorin, *in loco.*

† ' This ' — as an annotator on Bp. Lowth remarks — ' is one of the geminate proverbs (or those that contain a double image), and requires a different mode of interpretation for the two images, as having nothing coalescent in their nature. It is the property of a proverb to *prick sharply, and hold firmly.* The first idea is included in the image of *a goad,* the latter in the *nail* — deeply, and therefore firmly, ' driven.' — *Lect. on Hebrew Poetry,* xxiv. note S. H. (Henley).

goad is felt; yet how slight and transient! We want the *fastening* impression—*the nails* driven home to the conscience — a steady Divine influence fixing our hearts in the ways and service of God. We want such truth as is commonly found in affliction—or in the exercise of deep mental conflict — such as maintains an enduring impression to the very end of life. This is truth fixed—not as a sound of words, but as an instrument of life. Christian! Do not you realize the immense moment and value of this fixing work? Every atom of truth is worth a mountain of gold. If from want of care it slips away,* how eagerly does the ever-watchful enemy fill up the vacuum with his seven-fold deadly poison! (Matt. xii. 44, 45.) Truth slightingly valued is easily lost, and unspeakably fearful is the loss! When we cease to value truth, we are already in the atmosphere of error. O my God! bind upon my heart these *words of the wise.* Let me bow to their authority with the reverence of undisputing faith, and with the grateful acknowledgment of ready and unreserved obedience. Let the Bible satisfy me in all my disputations.

12. *And further, by these, my son, be admonished; of making many books there is no end; and much study is a weariness of the flesh.*

One more last word, ere *the Preacher* sums up—addressing the reader as his own *son,* and pouring out to him the yearnings of an affectionate heart, like the aged apostle in his many loving exhortations to the Christian disciples—*My little children* †—' *By these words of the wise,* spoken by the Holy Ghost' ‡—*By these, my son, be admonished.* Take them as thy

---

* See the same idea under a different figure, Heb. ii. 1, water running out.
    † 1 John, ii. 1, *et alia.*   ‡ Diodati.

most valuable monitors—"the men of thy counsel" (Ps. cxix. 24, marg.) *given from the one Shepherd,* "that the man of God may be perfect, thoroughly furnished unto all good works." (2 Tim. iii. 17.)   To be wise without this light is to be altogether foolish.   I might have written more.   The subject is inexhaustible.— *Of making books there is no end.*— Let this suffice.

The mass of books accumulating is the best comment upon this verse.   How many of them are utterly worthless! How small a proportion even of what is valuable can be read by one man!   How many, written with much labour, are, probably, never read at all!   *"No end is there of making,"* and often *"wearisome to the flesh is the study of them."* 'Weariness to the body without any satisfaction to the soul. Therefore let these words, so few, and yet so full, be thy counsellors.   He that will not be admonished by these, shall never be satisfied with any others.   He that refuseth the wheat will be but choked by the chaff.—Well may we say to this *one Shepherd,* as Peter did—"Lord! to whom shall we go? thou hast the words of eternal life." (John, vi. 68.) Other writings are useful in their order.   These only are the rule of faith and life.'*

Very thankful ought we to be, that *the* Book—the Book of God—is a portable Book—containing all that is necessary to "make wise unto salvation" (2 Tim. iii. 15) in so small a compass.   There is wisdom in the limitation as well as in the fulness.—Each of its weighty sayings is more valuable "than thousands of gold and silver." (Ps. cxix. 72.)   Oh, that we might come to its *study* with a more vigorous appetite and a more fervent love!   The more we live in the word, the deeper will be the impression—the more glowing the warmth—the more fruitful the result.—There will be little

* Bp. Reynolds.

sense of *weariness of the flesh,* when the spirit is engaged in real communion with the Lord.

13. *Let us hear the conclusion of the whole matter.   Fear God and keep his commandments; for this is the whole (duty) of man.* *

Here is the *nail,* which the great *Master* and Prophet of his Church would *fasten* " as in a sure place." The Preacher summons us, and summons himself with us—to *hear the conclusion of the whole matter.* Two short sentences sum up the whole—*Fear God, and keep his commandments.* The sentences are in their right order. *The fear of God* is the hidden principle of obedience—not of nature's growth. It is the work of the Spirit in the heart of the regenerate. It is the covenant promise, securing the faithfulness of the children of God. (Jer. xxxii. 40.)—It is not a legal principle of terror or bondage, but the genuine spirit of confidence—the delicate expression of filial love in the heart of the child of God—the holy fruit of forgiveness.† Here we walk with our Father, humbly, acceptably, securely—looking at an offended God with terror—but at a reconciled God with reverential love. All the gracious influences on the soul—cherished under the power of the Spirit—all flow out in godly *fear* towards him.

This true evangelical principle is fruitful in all practical results. Take it away; and what remains, but unbridled license to "walk in the way of our own hearts?" The habit of godly obedience is the test of the principle. For " the man, that *feareth the Lord,* delighteth greatly in his commandments." (Ps. cxii. 1.) The inner principle produces the outward manifestation. If the religion is not expressed in the

* This verse begins with a large letter—(as Deut. vi. 4)—as Buxtorf remarks, to excite the more attention.

† See Ps. cxxx. 4.

literal terms of the gospel, it fully implies them. *The keep-ing of the commandments*—at least in the case of the disciples of the Lord—primarily regards the great commandment— " to believe in the name of his Son Jesus Christ."* The gospel, therefore, is not obscured, even when the terms of it are not expressly given ; so that—rightly understood, we fully identify the free grace and spiritual obedience of the gospel with the more legal exhortation to *fear God, and keep his commandments.* ' By faith in God the heart is purified to *fear* and love God ; and by that *fear* and love it is inclined to obey his commandment.'†

' Quitting therefore the world with all its vanities, we betake ourselves to that, which alone is free from vanity— the fear and service of God.'‡ These two points—the Preacher pronounces to contain *the whole of man*—not his *duty* only,§ but his *whole* happiness and business—the total sum of all that concerns him—all that God requires of him —all that the Saviour enjoins—all that the Holy Spirit teaches and works in him.

We cannot here do better than give Abp. Leighton's beautiful summary of *the matter*—' After Solomon had made his discoveries of all things besides under the sun, gone the whole circuit, and made an exact valuation, he found all besides this to amount to nothing but *vanity and vexation of spirit.* The account he gives of all other things was only for this purpose, to illustrate and establish this truth the more, and to make it the more acceptable ; to be a repose after so much weariness, and such a tedious journey, and so, as he speaks there (v. 10, marg.) a word of delight as well as a

---

* See 1 John, iii. 23.   † Bp. Reynolds.

‡ Bp. Sanderson on chap. vii. 1.

§ The word *duty*, interpolated by our translation, is a needless expletive, and cramps the emphatic comprehensiveness of the phrase.

word of truth; that the mind might sit down, and quiet itself in this from the turmoil and pursuit of vanity, that keeps it busy to no purpose in all other things. But whereas there was emptiness and vanity, that is just nothing in all things; there was not only something to be found, but all in this one—*the fear of God,* and that *keeping of his commandments,* which is the proper fruit of that *fear.*' *

The same track of enquiry had been traversed by the Patriarch ages before, and substantially with the same result. Successive disappointments had given their voice—" It is not in me." Where then is the precious treasure to be found, but in the ways of God? " Unto man he saith— Behold! the fear of the Lord, that is wisdom, and to depart from evil is understanding." (Job, xxviii. 12–28.) Here is our portion—our centre of rest. The more heart we give to this interesting research, the more pleasure we shall find in it.

14. *For God shall bring every work into judgment, with every secret thing, whether it be good, or whether it be evil.*†

The Book naturally ends with the winding up of our eventful history—the eternal destiny of every child of man.

* Abp. Leighton on 1 Pet. ii. 17.

† Coverdale's version of the conclusion of the Book, v. 9–14, is beautiful for its simplicity. 'The same Preacher was not wyse alone; but taught the people knowledge also. He gave good hede, sought out the grounde, and set forth many parables. His diligence was to fynde out acceptable wordes, right Scriptures, and the wordes of trueth. For the wordes of the wyse are like prickes, and nales, that go thorow, wherewith men are kept together; for they are geven of One Shepherd onely. Therefore be warre, my son, that above these things thou make thee not many and innumerable bookes, nor take dyverse doctrines in hande, to weery thy body with. Let us heare the conclusion of all things. Fear God, and kepe his commandmentes, for that toucheth all men; for God shall judge all workes, and secrete things, whether they be good or evill.'

How solemn the stamp that it will give to *the conclusion of
the matter* — the blessedness of the fear and service of God!
The day will unmask all. All things—now so inexplicable
shall be made plain. Solomon had propounded many dark
sayings in this book—many things, which he could not
comprehend*—much that *seemed* inconsistent with the holy
and just character of the Divine Government—goodness
oppressed, wickedness triumphing. All these "hidden things
of darkness will be" fully "brought to light" (1 Cor. iv. 5),
when "the Lord—the righteous Judge" *shall bring every
work to judgment,* and *good* and *evil* shall be separated for
ever.

The brighter displays of the Gospel Revelation bring the
Judge before us in all his glorious and unspeakable majesty.
God is the Judge in the person of the Divine Mediator.
(John, v. 22. Acts, x. 42; xvii. 31.) "The Great White
throne" is raised up. The Judge of the world sits thereon.
"Before his face the earth and the heaven flee away, and no
place is found for them." The dead—small and great—stand
before God. The books are opened; and another book is
opened, which is the book of life. The dead are judged out
of those things, which are written in the books according to
their works. (Rev. xx. 11, 12.)

Such is the scene of majesty unveiled, and shutting up
the Revelation of God. With this view before us—can it be
a matter of indifference—whether or not we be the true
servants of God—that is, whether or no we shall spend our
eternity in heaven or in hell? This will be no judgment,
from which any child of man can hide himself. "We must all
appear before the judgment-seat of Christ. Every one of us
shall give an account of himself unto God." (2 Cor. v. 10;
Rom. xiv. 10–12.)

---

* Such as ch. vii. 23, 24; viii. 16, 17; ix. 1–6; *et alia.*

Every work—the most minute or the most important—from the first movement of conscience to the last breath of life—all the hidden world of thought in every man's bosom—hitherto *secret*—known only to himself and to his God—all the principles and colourings of action—every *secret thing* of every sort—*whether it be good, or whether it be evil*—whether it be restrained or indulged—sins of childhood or youth, that have passed away without consciousness—every moment—every atom of our sad sorrows—of our defiled services—all will be found there—at that day—safely stored—nothing missing. If this picture be a reality—Oh! let it be realized with a deep sense of our immense interest in it! What a restraint would it bring upon our words in the recollection, "that every idle word that men shall speak, they shall give account thereof in the day of judgment!" (Matt. xii. 36.) What a stimulus to self-denying consecration is the thought of the "stewardship" with which we are invested—the "account to be given of it"—and the awful guilt of "having wasted our Lord's goods" in the indolent delusion that they were our own! (Luke, xvi. 1, 2.) Whatever refinement may be mixed with selfish indulgence, it will be found to have carried with it a mass of neglected personal responsibility. The day will declare it,—when conviction and repentance will have been too late—for truly this is the day of the revelation of God's righteous judgment. (Rom. ii. 5.) Hypocrisy shall be disclosed, sincerity shall be rewarded, because nothing is hidden from him. All other things are vain. But it is not vain to *fear the Lord.* "They that do good"—their works will follow them to heaven; "and they that have done evil"—their works will hunt and pursue them to hell. *

The acceptance in that day will be proclaimed in strict

* Bp. Reynolds with John, v. 28, 29. 1 Cor. iv. 5.

accordance with the Preacher's admonition—*fearing God, and keeping his commandments.* The line of demarcation will be seen at that day—drawn for eternity—Ah! sinner—There will be no covering—no middle—doubtful place—no difficulty in "discerning between the righteous and the wicked —between him that serveth God, and him that serveth him not." (Mal. iii. 18.) The boldness of delusion will melt away into deep, dark despair.—"The ungodly shall not stand in the judgment; nor sinners in the congregation of the righteous." (Ps. i. 5.)

And yet—while men's hearts are failing them for fear, and for looking after those things that are coming—Now— Christian—it is your time to "look up, and lift up your head." (Luke, xxi. 26–28.) The indescribable solemnity of this day has no fear for you—It is your day of unshaken and joyous confidence. Those *secret* sins which are set before your God "in the light of his countenance" (Ps. xc. 8) are screened from the claims of his justice. If the Omniscient God lays them open—"the Great High-Priest" covers them for ever, or manifests them sprinkled with atoning blood.*— And when he cometh sitting on the "Great White Throne," fear will find no place there. For he that will sit upon the throne is no other than he that hung upon the cross—and will not the sunshine of the cross sweep away the terror of the throne? Yes—Christian, the Saviour will be the Judge. —We fear not—we faint not—In the assurance of his "coming quickly"—we respond with our hearty "Amen."— So it is in thy promise—so let it be to our joy. So shall it be to thy glory!

"EVEN SO, COME, LORD JESUS." (Rev. xxii. 20.)

---

* See this balance as the stay of the Christian profession, Heb. iv. 13, 14.

INDEX.

316   INDEX.